The Ladies' Secret Society

History of the Courageous Women of Iran

From the ruling Women-Gods, 5000 B.C.E.

To being ruled by "men of God," 2020 C.E.

The Ladies' Secret Society
History of the Courageous Women of Iran

Manda Zand Ervin

Copyright © Manda Zand Ervin, 2020

All rights reserved. No part of this book may be reproduced in any form or by any means, electronic or mechanical, without permission in writing from the publisher except by reviewers who may quote brief passages in their reviews.

Published by New English Review Press
a subsidiary of World Encounter Institute
PO Box 158397
Nashville, Tennessee 37215
&
27 Old Gloucester Street
London, England, WC1N 3AX

Cover Design by Wendy M. McMillan

ISBN: 978-1-943003-33-4

First Edition

NEW ENGLISH REVIEW PRESS
newenglishreview.org

Contents

Introduction ... 7

1 - Iranian Women of Ancient Times ... 24

2 - Arab Occupation and Enforcement of Islam (651 A.D. – Present) ... 44

3 - The Origin of Shi'ism in Iran's Reoccupation (686 – 1500) ... 51

4 - Women Fall From Grace: Occupation by Safavid Turks and Arrival of Shi'ism (1501 – 1722) ... 55

5 - Women of the Zand Dynasty (1750 to 1798) ... 64

6 - Return of Harems and Clerical Power: Qajar Dynasty (1798 – 1924) ... 72

7 - Movement to Reform Shi'ism (1800s) ... 86

8 - Women for Sovereignty and Equality (1850s) ... 92

9 - Women and the Constitutional Revolution (1850s – 1909) ... 103

10 - Post-Constitutional Revolution: War Between Women and Clergy (1907) ... 112

11 - The Ladies' Secret Society (1910) ... 118

12 - America's Support and Empathy for Iranians (1911 – 1913) ... 134

13 - The Communist Revolution, World War I, and the End of the Qajar Dynasty (1914 – 1926) ... 142

14 - Reza Shah Pahlavi: Pro-Women and Patriot (1925 – 1941)   155

15 - Cold War and Iranian Women (1940 – 1946)   167

16 - Women Lawyers and the Fight for Enfranchisement (1947 – 1963)   178

17 - Red Shi'ism and Clergy Takeover (1978 – 1979)   215

18 - Women Lose the War to the Clergy (1979)   228

19 - The One Million Signature Campaign (2006 – 2008)   255

20 - Uprising: Where Is My Vote? (2009)   272

21 - The Struggle Continues for All Iranian Women (2010 – 2017)   279

Epilogue: A New Chapter (2018 – Future)   288

Appendix A: Women of Courage in Exile   295

Appendix B: One Woman's Story   303

Appendix C: Poems   310

Bibliography   317

Index   327

Introduction

S A'ADI, A GREAT IRANIAN PHILOSOPHER and poet of the thirteenth century, wrote:

> Human beings are members of a whole
> In creation of one essence and soul
> If one member is afflicted with pain
> Other members uneasy will remain
> If you feel not for other's pain
> The name of human you cannot retain

The women featured in this book are only a small sample of women-gods, only a drop of the ocean's water.

Four months after the Shi'a clerical takeover of Iran on February 11, 1979, I reluctantly fled my beloved motherland at 5:30 a.m., on June 17, 1979.

Today, forty years later, as Iran explodes in a new revolution of hope, I can dream just a little about returning to the land where I learned to walk. But, for all of these decades, since the Islamic revolution of 1979, our country has been a living hell of tyranny in the name of men in black robes. This book is written in dedication to the spirits of women-gods who have stood in defiance of tyranny.

That morning, in the summer of 1979, they turned my life upside down.

I saw my father unsuccessfully fight back tears that threatened to fog up his glasses. I held my mother, whose tears were rolling down her cheeks. My daughter would not let go of her grandparents. We unclasped, and my daughter and I slipped into a car that took us to the Tehran airport.

At the airport, for the first time in my life, I was afraid of my compatriots. As if we had been invaded, I saw strangers, not the sociable, friendly, hospitable Iranians that I had known all of my life. The lines were long. People were running away from the tyranny of the mullahs.

Airport officials searched our luggage and my bag and purse. They shook down my young daughter's backpack to make sure we were not smuggling anything valuable out of the country. I kept silent, trying to calm my nerves during the search of my body, until they began searching my daughter's body.

She started crying and screaming, "Don't touch me! Don't touch me!"

I jumped at the woman who was manhandling my child and pushed her away. I grabbed my daughter's hand and walked away, thinking they would come after us, but they did not.

When we boarded the plane, my daughter was still shaking and crying. We found our seats and sat down. My daughter would not let go of her backpack, holding it on her lap and sobbing. Unlike the buzz of chatter that usually hung in the air when Iranians gathered in one place, there was a thick hush in the air. The only voice I heard was the whispering of the attendants, offering us water and juice. The less than one-hour flight from Tehran to the border felt like an eternity to us.

Then, the pilot announced: "Ladies and gentlemen, we just left Iran's air space."

There were sighs of relief and normal chatter.

The passengers were mostly Iranians, running from the dark cloud of fear that had taken over our country. We had watched the new clerical powers unleash a reign of terror on the state, killing victims indiscriminately, young and old, rich and poor, the educated and the intellectuals. We had witnessed the destruction of our culture and all that had been built on the land with hard work and the struggles of generations of men and women who had hopes and dreams of the Constitutional Revolution come to fruition.

I was born in the city of Brudjerd, in a province called Lurestan in modern-day Iran. It sat in a region of western Iran, which anthropologists, paleontologists, and others called, "the Fertile Crescent." The Zagros Mountains framed its beauty. My ancestors were the women and men of the Neolithic era of thousands of years ago, when they became the first human farmers. Historians say that my Eurasian ancestral tribe, the Meds, also migrated to the Zagros Mountains from Eastern Europe and modern-day Ukraine, and established the Median Empire during the second millennium B.C.E.

My maternal grandfather, Grandfather Azarmi, was a self-educated historian and archeologist in his own backyard, credited with being the first person to discover tools made by ancient people with Lurestan bronze. He gave me the name, Mandana, after the princess of the Meds, who married Prince Cambyses from the neighboring tribe, called Persians. She gave birth to Cyrus the Great.

Grandfather Azarmi was born into a Muslim family in the city of Hamedan, the ancient Ecbatana, but, at the age of nineteen, he converted to Zoroastrianism, for it was a peaceful, civilized religion, as he explained to us. The love of his life, my grandmother, Badieh Khanom, had attended the American Catholic School in Tehran. In the 1960s, she fought city officials in Tehran to establish a humane society to care for stray animals. My grandmother knew the Torah, the Bible, and the Qur'an by heart. She was Baha'i.

My paternal grandfather, Zand, was of the Lur tribe, rooted in the ancient city of Nehavand. With no educational system in Iran at the time, my grandfather was tutored at home, learning to read, write, and do basic math. My paternal grandmother, Akhtar ("Sunshine") Khanom, the matriarch of the Zand family, was also home tutored. She gave birth to ten children and they all survived, a miracle for those times in Iran, because infant mortality was a part of life until the post-Constitutional Revolution when Reza Shah Pahlavi brought the establishment of a department of health, educating doctors and building hospitals. I was one of thirty-nine grandchildren who grew up, listening to her history-telling and advice, like, "Always be more ear than mouth. Wisdom comes by listening and learning." Her approval was always required, and her words were the laws of our family. Both my paternal grandparents were secular Shi'a Muslims.

My father was a government civil servant, and my mother was a progressive homemaker. They had three daughters. We were a middle-class family, and, like most Iranians, did not practice religion. My father was the first feminist in our lives and our friend and advisor.

Our elementary school and high school were housed in old mansions, donated to the Ministry of Education by the wealthy women of the *Andjomaneh Serieh Banovan*—the Ladies' Secret Society who fought clerics' Gender Apartheid for over a hundred years.

I received my education in America, partly by working at a department store, and through a Pahlavi Foundation grant for the foreign education of women.

After my graduation ceremony in 1970, I returned to Iran to be a government civil servant, like my father. By 1979, I had a great government career, loved my country and was proud to be a part of the ongoing peace, progress and prosperity in my motherland. We were finally a sovereign people and country, free from the British, Russians and the domination of the Shi'a clerics. We were a part of the international community. And, in 1978, at the international conference of the Custom Cooperation Council in Brussels, I was the only female representative, among 181 attending members.

As an educated woman, doors were open to me, and I had ambitious plans for my future, like running for political office, first as a senator in the parliament and, perhaps, someday, as the prime minister of Iran.

We were confident that the Shi'a clerics had learned their place was in the mosque. With Khomeini living in exile in the city of Najaf in Iraq, the clerics did not interfere in social, political and governmental affairs. They did not attack women from the pulpit, and, at times, they even cooperated with women's organizations at schools and health clinics in cities, towns and villages.

The number of mosque-goers had dwindled, with illiteracy diminishing in the older generation, and younger generations growing up in a system of free education from kindergarten to PhD programs at the best schools, universities and colleges. The Iranian economy was flourishing, and people were busy in their jobs and lives with better movies, theater, radio, and, especially, TV entertainment. Sports and games were promoted in society, and soccer was the national pastime that Iranians loved to play and watch. People had little time or inclination to go to the mosque.

Iranians underestimated Khomeini's determination and scheming in establishing his Shi'a caliphate, taking revenge on Iranians who had removed the clergy from power in the Constitutional Revolution of 1906. He knew that the people of Iran would never allow the clergy back in power again. He needed the United States' support to take over Iran.

For decades, from the pulpit, Khomeini had been calling the Shah "a puppet of the Great Satan," denouncing him and demonizing the United States. However, in secret channels, behind closed doors, he plotted a takeover with the United States' help, sending messages with persistence to U.S. presidents, pledging his loyalty and political accommodations to get them to remove the Shah and put him in control of Iran. Some CIA records of the negotiations and deals between Ayatollah Khomeini and President Jimmy Carter, from 1978 to 1979, were declassified in recent years and are available at the U.S. Library of Congress.

Iranians could not believe that any U.S. president would agree to give the control of a secular, peaceful and friendly sovereign state to a religious zealot, ignoring separation of state and religion. We trusted that a progressive West would stand with a progressive Iran.

In the blink of an eye, however, Ayatollah Ruhollah Khomeini, a lying, violent zealot who called himself "The Spirit of Allah," ruthlessly seized the progress that generations of Iranian women and men had built.

In the discussions between President Carter and his cabinet members, there was no talk about the Constitutional Revolution of 1906 that stood up to the rule of the king and the clerics. There was no talk about the negative reputation of the clerics among the people of Iran. The Carter administration did not think about the consequences of going backward by establishing Islamic clerical power in the most progressive society in the Middle East. Moreover, there had been no contacts with female members of the Iranian parliament or Senate by the ambassador. The only discussion on human rights for women was in support of the old mullah when Mr. Philip H. Stoddard, then a senior State Department official in its Intelligence Bureau, said, "We would do a disservice to Khomeini to consider him simply as a symbol of segregated education and an opponent to women's rights."[1]

Not only was President Carter's interference in the internal affairs of a sovereign, peaceful and secular country objectionable, but his removal of the Shah, a longtime friend and ally of the United States, created a distrust of the United States in the world and, thus, inspired clerics in Iran and other dictatorial regimes to believe they needed to possess the nuclear bomb to counter the fickle United States. Also, establishment of a religious rule in Iran set a dangerous precedent and triggered a chaos in the Middle East that continues to this day.

I remember the U.S. media talking about a million Iranians marching for Khomeini, whom U.S. reporters described as a saintly, religious man. They claimed the Iranian people wanted freedom and faith, not the Western modernity the Shah was forcing upon them. Yet, I didn't witness anywhere near a million Iranians supporting Khomeini on the streets of Tehran. We knew that many Afghanis were paid by the mosques to march in support of Khomeini.

With a booming economy in Iran, we had about two million illegal Afghans in the country in the 1970s, doing construction and landscaping jobs to send money home to their families. Many Afghans speak

---

1 "Two Weeks in January: America's secret engagement with Khomeini," BBC, http://www.bbc.com/news/world-us-canada-36431160.

Farsi, the language of Iran.

As Khomeini sent cassette tapes, instructing people to follow him by working with the mosques, marching in the streets and going on strike, a large number of government employees followed his orders by continuing to go to the office daily but refusing to work, in an effort to immobilize the government and oil industries. I joined passionate conversations with Khomeini followers, many of them first-generation college graduates and government employees. Some were communists, with support from the Soviet Embassy in Tehran. Others called themselves Hezbollah, had contacts with Lebanese and Palestinian authorities through the mosques, or they were members of a movement we called "Red Shi'ism," or "Black Marxist jihadist cults." They believed in both *sharia*, or Islamic law, *and* the doctrine of Karl Marx. Trained by Palestinians, they had been terrorizing Iran by bombing banks and police stations and conducting assassinations. MEK, now known as the National Iranian Council of Resistance, was the most dangerous of the jihadists, also assassinating at least eight Americans in Iran.

Pro-Khomeini activists told me their local mosques had them pluck illegal Afghans, standing on street corners for jobs, and pay them to march on the streets for Khomeini. The going rate was $15 in U.S. currency and a coupon for a free shish kabob meal, they told me.

The Iranian population in 1979 was 35 million, and even if the Western media were right and one million Iranians—0.028 percent of the population—were marching for Khomeini, it did not make a national revolution. That was especially true, considering 34 million Iranian men and, especially women, hated Khomeini and did not want the return of Shi'a clerics to power, and we were not marching.

When Khomeini took over and deprecated women's rights, my father worried for the safety of his professional daughters. He began urging me to leave the country. My boss, the minister of economics and finance, told me, in so many words, that I should go on a long vacation to Europe.

They were worried because I was a U.S.-educated young woman with an important post as managing director in Iran's Customs Administration, computerizing the organization to end corruption in the agency. I was a symbol of the emancipated and equal Iranian women that the Ladies' Secret Society had struggled to support. I was what a woman could not be under the gender apartheid rules of the Shi'a clerics.

I became a political refugee in Europe. At the Athens airport, immigration officials kept me standing for hours, with my daughter, before they allowed us to enter the country. In Athens, I waited on the street, outside the gates of the U.S. Embassy, barred from entering the grounds, as Greek guards laughed at me, day after day. At the Paris airport, the man behind the window did not stamp my visa to enter France.

Instead, he mocked me, asking, "Where is your hijab?"

He gave me 72 hours to leave France, after making us wait for hours and studying my permanent residency documentations for the United States. When I finally arrived in the United States, after a year's journey, I feared worse treatment, since the Khomeini regime had taken over the U.S. Embassy in Tehran, taking diplomats hostage. On June 17, 1980, I arrived at the Baltimore-Washington International Airport and followed the signs to the immigration desk, where I sheepishly placed a large manila envelope on the desk and waited.

The wait felt like hours, but it took only minutes for the woman behind the desk to check my file, study my worried face and say, with a smile: "Welcome to the land of freedom, Manda."

For the past 39 years, I have been married to Edwin William Ervin, a retired U.S. Navy and Northrop Grumman Corp. electronic engineer. We had met in Iran, where he had gotten to know Iranian people better than any of former President Carter's aides had bothered to do. Over these decades in the U.S., he has been my friend, lover, and supporter.

I wrote this book to tell America that what is happening in Iran today is not Iranian. I set about to prove this thesis by chronicling the stories of Iranian women over thousands of years of history in a land called Iran, meaning, "The Land of Gentle, Hospitable People." In this book, I explain that the women of Iran do not deserve to live as the property of men, under an antiquated foreign system of gender apartheid. I argue that the clerical regime in Iran—and its gender apartheid—are, in fact, not emblematic of the history, values, and culture of Iran.

To introduce my motherland, her people, her women-gods and men, her struggles, her humanity, her great hearts and minds, and herstory to readers; I identify how the achievements of Iranian civilization and her great land have contributed to Western civilization and are worth knowing.

We Are Iranians

While Islam is the religion of a majority of Iranians today, it is just one of many religions embraced by Iranians over history. Iranians were majority Zoroastrians with Jews, Christians, and others living in peace and harmony until the brutal occupation of Arab conquerors and the enforcement of Islam on all Iranians. It is the majority faith today because the clerics have bullied non-Muslims to either convert or leave the country. As ideological political imperialists, the ruling clergy have used religion to intimidate the world and take what they want from Iran. They have scorned Iran's history and cultural identity, especially over the past four decades, to intimidate and demoralize the people of Iran and legitimize their illicit rule in the world.

Meanwhile, a secular Iranian American community of political refugees has been quietly assimilating in the United States. Too often, they are classified as Muslims, not Iranians. The Iranian clergy not only overlook our Iranian identity, but so, too, do Euro-centric elites in the West who treat us as Muslims, while ignoring thousands of years of pre-Islamic history that included years of progressive, scientific, artistic, and humanitarian contributions to Western civilization.

Our adopted homeland in the United States has labeled us and decided that we belong in a political pot, called "Muslims," with people from 56 other "Muslim-majority" countries. Obviously, Iran's geographical location outside Europe has excluded her culture and history from being worthy of attention and respect in the West. Professor John Lee, a historian at the University of California, Santa Barbara, has written, "The denigration of the Persians by some of the Greek historians, and later the British, degraded Iranian civilization in order to legitimize their imperialist domination of Iran, which has influenced the elites of America."

I am told by two retired professors of history, that Iranian civilization courses were on the curriculum of many American universities until the 1940s, but were slowly removed during World War II. Unfortunately, the educational system has shifted away from diversity in learning historical facts about non-Western cultures, opting instead for the politically and ideologically motivated issues of Euro-centrists.

Iranian studies in U.S. universities are mostly based on political and ideological presentations of the issues related to the ruling clergy and the 1979 Khomeinist "revolution."

Hollywood has made movies idolizing Alexander the Great, but none about Cyrus the Great, who lived in the sixth century B.C.E., and his magnanimous humanity and contribution to the U.S. constitution and Western civilization, which I have developed in chapter 1. In Hollywood movies about Alexander or Greek warriors, like *300: Rise of an Empire*, Iranians are portrayed as uncivilized barbarians and savages, while Greeks are portrayed as the most civilized people of their times.

Iranian innovations and contributions, in science, math, arts, architecture, and literature, are often ignored or called "Islamic," even by the president of the United States, essentially dismissing the history of the people of Iran. A TV game show rarely has any questions about Iran in any category, but, when it does, Iran and Iranians are often presented negatively while positive achievements are contributed to some other unknown entity. When you ask about the game of chess, most people attribute its origins to Russia or India, but not Iran.

Politics

In December 2002, President George W. Bush talked to the people of Iran on Radio Liberty, Farda: and told them,

> My thoughts and prayers are with the Iranian people, particularly the families of the many Iranians who are in prison today for daring to express their hopes and dreams for a better future. We continue to stand with the people of Iran in your quest for freedom, prosperity, honest and effective government, judicial due process and the rule of law. And we continue to call on the government of Iran to respect the will of its people and be accountable to them. As I have said before, if Iran respects its international obligations and embraces freedom and tolerance, it will have no better friend than the United States of America.

The words echoed in the hearts of Iranians.

We continue to stand with the people of Iran in your quest for freedom, prosperity, honest and effective government, judicial due process and the rule of law.

Then, in 2008, in his State of the Union Address, President Bush spoke to the people of Iran and said, "We have respect for your traditions and your history. We look forward to the day when you have your freedom. Our message to the leaders of Iran is also clear. Verifiably suspend your nuclear enrichment so negotiations can begin. And rejoin the community of nations, come clean about your nuclear intentions and past actions. Stop your oppression at home. Cease your support for terror abroad."

Stop your oppression at home.

Those words motivated Iranians to rise up the next year, believing the United States would not empower the country's tyrannical clerics.

However, the only Bush statement to become talking points for the

U.S. media for years to come was the one with three words, "axis of evil," that empowered the tyrants in Tehran to crush its people. There was hardly a word of concern about the gross human rights violations of women and children, the practice of gender apartheid and the executions and torture of innocent people in Iran.

Many Americans argue that freedom and democracy are only achievable in the West. Others, including myself, believe that all beings in nature, including two-legged ones, seek freedom. No matter what our geography, culture, history, or religion, we are made of the same flesh and blood and our needs as women and men are the same.

In 2009, the people of Iran marched in the streets and called on President Obama to stand with them, chanting: "Obama, Obama, are you with them or with us?"

But U.S. policy had become one of "non-interference in the internal affairs of Iran." In reality, President Obama gave the clergy *carte blanche* to massacre the real owners of Iran, the people who asked America not to support the clergy tyranny.

Throwing Rocks to Stop Guns

From my home in Maryland, I supported the young Iranians who marched every day during their uprising. I cheered for them, laughed with the women who were picking up stones to throw at the armed paramilitary forces, encouraged them, and jumped up and down in front of my computer and television.

I cried, looking at their bloodied bodies being shoved into cars, seeing them rushed to hospitals by their friends, shouting, "Be careful! Be careful!"

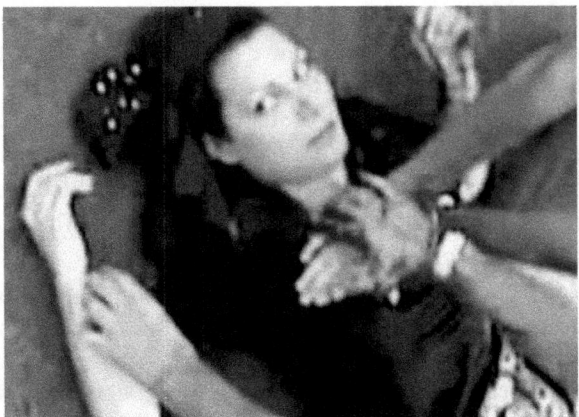

Neda Agha-Soltan

I screamed when I witnessed the beautiful, bright eyes of the young, dying activist, Neda Agha-Soltan, sprawled on the ground, staring into the camera, as if she was asking humanity, "Why is there so much discrimination against us?"

That day, I became determined to tell the story of my ancestral mothers, the Neolithic women of the Zagros Mountains, guardians of fire and the first farmers. I was committed to sharing with America, my new homeland, the stories of the women gods, the rulers, the admirals, the guardians of history, and the great archers who had survived thousands of years.

I heard some political experts say we should not try building democracies in the "Third World." However, no one has said we should not replace progressive secular friends with fanatic religious enemies nor keep empowering them against the wishes of the people who fight and give their lives for democracy.

In 2011, I witnessed the United States removing the Libyan leader Moammar Gaddafi, in support of the opposition, protesting the ruler's dictatorship, and I was envious. I witnessed the people of Tunisia given the opportunity to build a free and democratic society with the support of the United States, and I was jealous. I saw how the President of United States called for the removal of the president of Egypt because Egyptians were protesting in Tahir Square, and I wondered, "Why were the people of Iran who rose up against the clergy's dictatorial rule ignored?"

In my lifetime, I have witnessed the international community unite against communist dictatorships, nonviolently laying the groundwork for democracies in Eastern European countries that the Soviet dictatorship had crushed for so long. I have also witnessed the international community eradicate racial apartheid in South Africa, helping humanity prevail, supporting the forces of justice, without any military action.

My question has always been: "Why does the same international community that has defeated the tyranny of racial apartheid and communism ignore the inhumane policies of gender apartheid, poverty, illiteracy, and ignorance in Iran now?"

I wanted to show America that while this kind of injustice is occurring in other countries as well, the women of Iran have been fighting the clergy's rule and gender apartheid for over 150 years. I wanted to show how young generations of Iranian women have been working hard and paying heavy prices for their dignity—sometimes with their lives.

The people of Iran, especially the women, are trying to help themselves, but the international community is making it impossible for them to succeed, by continuously empowering the clerical patriarchal establishment.

It is shocking to see Western female leaders from progressive socialist countries, as they genuflect to a handful of old, tyrannical misogynist men in Iran, and wear head scarves and long loose pants to appease Khamenei for thirty pieces of silver.

In recent years, their Western sisters have not only refused to support Iranian women, but some organizations with specific political ideologies have heartlessly used them for their own agenda.

The anti-war Code Pink organization has opposed Iranian-American women activists. In one case in 2006, they took website photos of two demonstrations by Iranian women at Tehran University, protesting the forced hijab, and Photoshopped the images of the unhappy Iranian women with their own happy-go-lucky American women activists.

They replaced the messages on the original protest signs that the women held, "We want our equal rights back," and, "We are the children of Cyrus," to anti-American slogans, like, "How many lives per gallon?" and "Join us!" When we protested, Code Pink took the photos of Iranian women off their site and replaced them with doctored photos of Iraqi women.

By misrepresenting the facts of the demonstration and changing the words on the protest signs, Code Pink placed the women of Iran in danger, potentially causing them further political harm. What these American women did was a hypocritical and prejudicial act of betrayal against the women of Iran.

Because of these developments of early 21st century, I wanted to present a long history of the Iranian-American past friendship that has created a bond between Americans and Iranians. At one point in history, the only friend that Iran had in the world was the United States of America. Then, Americans were the only foreigners educating Iranian children. Their history is filled with stories of sacrifice and loyalty. The Americans John and Katelin Cochran went to Iran, built a hospital in the city of Aromia, raised five children there, including a son, David, who added a medical school to the hospital in the mid-1800s. William Morgan Shuster, who became treasurer-general of Persia, was a great friend and defender of Iran and Iranian women and vice versa. Mr. Howard Baskerville gave his life defending his Iranian students as they fought Russian invaders. So many others have joined the cause of Iranians' freedom. And, indisputably, humanitarian American governments came to Iran's aid when she needed it to sustain her sovereignty.

I have tried to prove that history had given mother Iran a chance to repair her 1,400 years of wounds and reinstate her cultural civilization of a dignified sovereignty, windswept by varieties of conquering tyrants. Iran was not copying Western civilization or modernity, as narrated by Khomeini and many Westerners.

Today, 86 percent of the people who oppose the theocratic regime in Iran would remove the clerics from power, if these clerics weren't the beneficiaries of foreign support.

The United Nations

The United Nations Commission on the Status of Women has become irrelevant to women living under gender apartheid. It is obvious that Western women, living in democracies, have no need for the UNCSW, because the constitutions of their countries have made gender discrimination illegal. American women have no need for an international body to secure their rights, but women who live under gender apartheid regimes need the support of the UNCSW and Western democracies.

When asked why the gender apartheid regime of Iran is allowed to be a member of the board of the UN Commission on the Status of Women, UN authorities effectively replied, "We did not want them on the Human Rights Commission so we gave them membership on the UNCSW, United Nations Commission on the Status of Women." It is sad when even the UN considers the status of women as a less important, inferior issue. The United Nations Development Fund for Women (UNIFEM) is the auxiliary organization of the UNCSW but they are not effective in fighting crimes against women, as UNIFEM receives big checks from the worst practitioners of gender apartheid. When asked why the UN allows this, the essential response of officials is, "UNIFEM depends on these contributions from member states to support the poor women in Africa and elsewhere."

I shake my head, trying to understand the logic of destroying the women and children of Iran, to help other women and children in another part of the world.

The United Nations represents governments or regimes, whether democratic, dictatorial or ideological tyrannies. The powerful and rich member governments, including the practitioners of gender apartheid, can always buy votes and prevent reforms for the people living under their tyranny.

I always wonder what former U.S. First Lady and feminist Eleanor Roosevelt would say about the way the United Nations has adopted a let's-make-a-deal for more money strategy to enable injustice, instead of promoting justice and human rights.

The main question for 21st-century women living under gender apartheid is: where do we go for justice?

The world of the 21st century is divided into the haves and the have-nots, nations with equality and therefore dignity, and nations whose people are deprived of basic human dignity, living under a system of gender slavery that is not part of their culture.

We have globalized the economy, established worldwide political discussions on issues from the environment to climate change. The most important issue about which we must have a global conversation is that of human rights and gender equality for all the people of our world. Promotion of humanity should also be global.

As Sa'adi of Shiraz, a thirteenth-century Iranian philosopher and poet, wrote,

"We are all limbs on one body."

Gender Apartheid

In 2003, Amir Taheri, an Iranian journalist and author based in London, wrote an article, "This is Hijab. This is Not Islam."

This headgear was invented in the early 1970s by Mussa Sadr, an Iranian mullah who had won the leadership of the Lebanese Shi'ite community. Sadr's neo-hijab made its first appearance in Iran in 1977 as a symbol of Islamist-Marxist opposition to the Shah's regime. When the mullahs seized power in Tehran in 1979, the number of women wearing the hijab exploded into tens of thousands.

The garb is designed to promote gender apartheid. It covers the woman's ears so that she does not hear things properly. Styled like a hood, it prevents the woman from having full vision of her surroundings. It also underlines the concept of woman as object, all wrapped up and marked out.

Muslim women could easily check the fraudulent nature of the neo-Islamist hijab by leafing through their family albums. They will not find a picture of a single female ancestor of theirs who wore the cursed headgear now marketed as an absolute "must" of Islam.

This fake Islamic hijab is nothing but a political prop, a weapon of visual terrorism. It is the symbol of a totalitarian ideology inspired more by Nazism and communism than by Islam. It is as symbolic of Islam as the Mao uniform was of Chinese civilization.

I hope this herstory book proves that Iranian societies have been grounded on a womanist—not misogynist—culture.

This book features the 21st-century children of the women-gods who have relentlessly fought the clergy, questioning and challenging their *sharia*. They have tried to place the issue of gender apartheid in the center of national and international debate, although, so far, unsuccessfully.

Gender apartheid in Iran is a form of slavery in the 21st century that is a stain of shame on human civilization. It is a wretched form of injustice, in many ways:

- Women and children are the property of men, meaning half of the population – men – owns the other half of the population.
- The value of a women's life is one-half the value of a man's life.
- In the justice system, the testimony of two women is equal to the testimony of one man.
- Women do not have independence in choosing their own clothing, stepping out of the home, working, getting an education, or having a say in the lives of their children.
- Men can marry at least four wives and an unlimited number of "temporary wives," with the right to divorce them, at will.
- Women do not even have equal rights to divorce their husbands.
- Children have no protection:
    o Girl children can be treated as merchandise, sold as young as nine years old, as a bride, to a man of the father's choice.
    o Older men marry girls and rape them brutally.
- The age of criminal responsibility is fifteen for boys, but nine for girls.
- Khomeini required that girls should go to their husband's home before they reach the age of puberty.
- Women are held responsible for upholding the honor of men; it is like a pre-established guilty verdict, hanging over their lives.
- Honor is not defined but left to a clergy to decide on individual cases.

Iranian women and men oppose war and violence. They want to go back and live in peace and be respected members of the international community, but they have been kept isolated from all sides. They want the international community to recognize them as the legitimate citizens of Iran, but, unfortunately, ideology and politics empower the tyrannical men. Women are the majority, the legitimate owners, the Mother-Gods of Iran, caged by a handful of old men to whom the world concedes power.

The foundation of Iranian culture is centered on the principles of the Zan-Khodayan, or Women-Gods, who ruled the Neolithic societies and shaped the transformation of humans from hunters to farmers, domesticating animals. The Women-Gods, or Mother-Gods, as they were also called, were the keepers of the fire and ruled the family, tribe, and society, as they progressed.

Iranian mythologies, literature, history, culture, and a gender-neutral Persian language are all proof that Iran has matriarchal cultural roots. Women in Iran are called the protectors of the Motherland. Little girls are named Iran, a tradition that considers women to *be* the Motherland. Despite the last 1,400 years of occupations by male-dominated foreign militaries and clergy rules, the beauty and power of Iran have survived, with the legacy of the great matriarch Women-Gods.

*Note: I have used both English language and Persian language sources. The English sources are footnoted for the convenience of American readers, but the Persian sources, translated by myself, are not. I have included those sources in the bibliography with titles translated.

CHAPTER ONE

Iranian Women of Ancient Times

THE FRENCH AUTHOR Amaury De Riencourt wrote, "Archeological evidence indicates that it is in the relatively high and well-protected valleys of southern Anatolia and western Iran that human civilization first achieved its major breakthrough. A complete mutation in the human way of life took place between the tenth and sixth millennia B.C.E., leading progressively to the first city-state of the Fertile Crescent period, during the High Neolithic (4500-3500 B.C). During this entire period, the centerpiece of mythology and worship was the Great Mother..."[1]

A statue of the Mother-God

To the early inhabitants of the Iranian plateau, God was not a male person and did not live in the skies or a mythological heaven. They worshiped the Mother-God who created them from her own body. She was

---

1 Riencourt, *Woman and Power in History*, 23.

their God who nourished, nurtured, and raised the young to become members of society. Mother-God was the authority that set societal rules for her children.

In the Persian language, *Zan-Khodayan*, Women-Gods, were called *Sein*, or *Seina*. She was the creator of the earth. "Seina had a belief in the nobility of human race, who were her thinking children. She was the symbol of free will and equality among her children. She was the nurturer and the guide," wrote Iranian publisher Shahla Lahiji and Mehrangiz Kar, in their book, *The Quest for Identity*.[2] Both are prominent women's rights advocates, arrested and imprisoned in 2002 for their participation in a conference in Berlin, "The Future of Reform in Iran."[3]

A statue of the Mother-God, or Woman-God, who lived about 4000 B.C.E., reveals her identity was firmly documented, experts say. She is clearly from the "cradle of civilization." Archeologists have discovered many of these statues in the homes of ancient city ruins, throughout the Iranian plateau, concluding that ancient Iranian tribes held the Woman-God as a divine deity and kept her statues in their homes to receive her blessing.

Mother-God Astarte

Around 4000 B.C.E., a tribe, called the Elamite, worshipped Astarte,

---

2 Lahiji and Kar. *The Quest for Identity*, 110-122.
3 Tehran Revolutionary Court I.D.H.B.B, http://www.idhbb.org/uk-page5.1.ira.htm.

the Woman-God who reigned in western Iran.

All the statues of the Woman-God show her, holding her breasts up with both hands, as a symbol of her power. The Meds, the tribe that had come to the Zagros Mountains from the steppes of Eurasia, called their Mother-God Lur. Today, the ancient Meds are called the Lur tribe, and the province is named Luristan, the land of Lurs.

Some paleoanthropologists believe that according to 5,000-year-old insignias, women in Shahr-e Sukhteh, or the Burnt City, had social and financial prominence. The archeologists discovered a 3200 B.C.E. woman's skeleton with one false eye and potteries, textiles, and personal jewelry, including a glass-and-stone bead necklace, in her possession. They also found a piece of knitting with a crochet hook.[4] The painting on the pottery illustrates a jumping deer in motion.

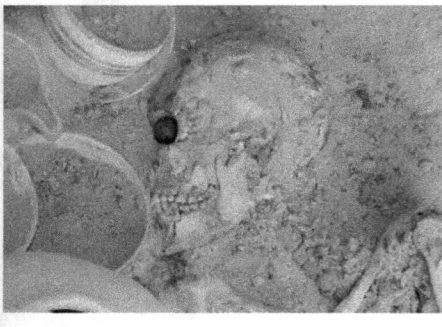

Photos by Emesik

The Neolithic women of Iran were the original farmers and shepherds. They discovered and planted beans, wheat, and barley. Archeol-

---

4 *Iran Review.* http://www.iranreview.org/.

ogists unanimously believe that farming and domestication of animals developed in the Zagros Mountains in western Iran, during the Paleolithic era of human history. They also discovered that women made clay bowls, plates, and cups.[5]

According to archeological discoveries on the sites of the Bakhtiari Luristan Mountains of Iran, among the cave dwellers of a mountain village, Tangeh-Beed, women were the guardians of the fire that was their lifeline. This tradition continued through the Zoroastrian era when women were the guardians of the temples.

The Mother-God is said to have had a cabinet of many members, assigned to different tasks. The great Sun Goddess Mehr maintained the cosmic order, without which there would be no life on earth. Mehr became the *Yazata*, or angel of enlightenment and truth, in Zoroastrianism. Under the sunlight, truths and facts are seen. The word for "sun" became *mehr* in the Persian language and *Mehr* also became the word for love and affection. She became an important part of Iranian culture.

Anahita the goddess of water the mother of Mithra

Anahita was the Goddess of the waters of earth and protector of nature. She was called the golden mother who gave birth to Mithra. Her

---

5 "Scholars rethink the beginnings of civilizations following discoveries in Burnt City of Iran," *Ancient Origins,* http://www.ancient-origins.net/news-evolution-human-origins/scholars-rethink-beginnings-civilizations-iran-020173.

full title was Aredvi Sura Anahita, meaning, "moist, mighty, and immaculate (pure)," and she traveled on her chariot pulled by four horses: Wind, Rain, Cloud and Sleet. "Closely associated with the King's investiture she is a Goddess of Sovereignty, thought by some to be the Persian Aphrodite, who also has some remarkable similarities to numerous other ancient goddesses, including Ishtar, Venus, Nana and Isis," wrote Payam Nabarz, editor of the book, *Anahita* (2013).[6]

Seemorq was the legendary, mythological, protecting Mother of the land of Iran. In ancient Iranian mythology, Seemorq is a female creature, part-bird and part-mammal, with breasts to nurture her human children. She perched on the tree of life and spread the seeds of sustenance. In the classic Iranian epic, the *Shah-Nameh*, or *The Book of Kings*, Seemorq is the god-parent and the guide of the patriots and the good kings. She lives on the highest peak of the Alborz Mountain, one of the peaks of the Zagros Mountains in Iran. *The Book of Kings* tells the story of how she saved, nurtured, and raised a prince, Zaal, the son of King Saam, born as an albino. Fearing Zaal was evil, the king had the infant abandoned in the Alborz Mountain, where Seemorq saved, nurtured, and raised him to be a great and brave man. When Zaal decided to leave the nest to join the human world, Seemorq gave him three of her golden feathers and told him to burn one whenever he needed her help.

Zaal became a brave and just king and married the beautiful Rudabeh. The only feather that Zaal burned happened when Rudabeh was having difficult, life-threatening complications while giving birth to their son. Seemorq appeared and taught Zaal how to do a cesarean section, saving Rudabeh and their son, Rostam. In *The Book of Kings*, Rostam becomes the greatest Iranian knight of all times.

Seemorq has a key role in the eternal search for God in the book, *The Conference of the Birds*,[7] by Sheikh Attar Neishaburi, 1146-1221, a legendary author, poet, and philosopher in the mystical Sufi tradition of Islam.

Amaury De Riencourt wrote in his book, *Woman and Power in History*, "The social status of woman in Persia could not have been anything but a reflection of the metaphysical outlook. Before the arrival of the Aryans, the original inhabitants of Iran were organized along matrilineal lines. It seems that in some areas women were even in command of the armed forces."

---

6 Nabarz (editor), *Anahita*. A video on Anahita: "A Goddess in Danger," World Cultural Heritage, https://www.youtube.com/watch?v=Vvie3s9j_3U.
7 Neishaburi (Attar), *The Conference of the Birds*, 84, 86.

He added, "At some point in history, a massive transfer altered the sex of most deities from female to male, the rule of kinship also changed from matrilineal to patrilineal."

The great Mother-God eventually fell from godhood. However, her values endured in Iranian culture and the in faith of Zoroastrianism, an old Mede and Persian religion that spread across Asia. Even today, despite thousands of years of wars and foreign occupation, the Zoroastrian teaching, "Good thought, good words, and good deeds," is considered a reflection of her cultural influence.

Zoroaster

In Zoroastrian Iran, every day of the month was named for a good deed. The fifth day of the month was called *Sepandarmaz-gon*, or "the festival of women." This was a day of nationwide festivities in celebration of women.

Father-God of Zoroastrianism

The Father-God of Zoroastrianism observed an equality between men and women. Many of the divine beings of Beneficent Immortals were females, charged to protect humanity and the universe against an evil spirit, Ahriman.

He adopted Mother-God's Goddesses, or *Yazata*, meaning "the good powers," as protectors for his children and creation from Ahriman.

Yazata is a word in the Avastin language for a Zoroastrian concept of a divinity. The term literally means "worthy of worship or veneration." The *yazatas* collectively are "the good powers under the lord of wisdom, Ohrmuzd."

There were several important *yazata*. Ashtad guides people to good thoughts, good words, and good deeds. Mehr is the guardian of the sun, enlightenment, and truth. Rashnu is the guardian of justice. Sepanta Aramaiti is the promoter of knowledge, credited with writing the Aramaic alphabet that she spoke. Dravaspa is the protector of children. Zam is the protector of earth. Vate becomes the protector of air. Azarvan and Nana are the guardians of greenery and nature. Diana, or Daena, becomes the guidance of Faith. Piti Ram is the promoter of peacefulness and sex. Mah is the protector of Planet Moon.

Then, there was Anahita, the immaculate one, known as the Golden Mother. She became the great *yazata* of fertility and protector of women. Anahita is said to have been the immaculate virgin mother, who gave birth to Mithra. The "seed" for the baby came from Ohrmuzd, or Ahura Mazda, the name for the creator in the Zoroastrian faith. The literal meaning of the word Ahura Mazda is the "lord of wisdom." According to Professor Kaveh Farrokh, a Canadian-Iranian author with a specialty in Iranian history, "Anahita was said to have conceived Mithra from the seed of Ohrmuzd preserved in the waters of Lake Hamun in the province of Sistan," in eastern Iran, on the border with modern day Afghanistan. Mithra was "The Great King," highly revered by the nobility and monarchs, who considered him their special protector.

The Greeks and Romans adopted Anahita and her son, Mithras, as their divinities, changing Anahita's name to Anaïtis, and added both of them to their pantheons.

Zoroastrian scriptures taught followers how to reach *Sorush*, the inner voice of wisdom within us. It teaches that we are endowed with free will, the freedom to make choices to separate good from bad and right from wrong, and the ability to reason. Reason enables us to make choices in our thoughts, words, and deeds. It teaches that when we seek knowledge and gain wisdom, goodness will follow because it is grounded in wisdom. With free will and free choice also come responsibility and accountability.

Unfortunately, not much is known about when Zoroaster, the founder of the faith named for him, lived. Dates vary from 1500 to 2000 B.C.E., according to some Greek historians. Archeological evidence proves that Zoroastrianism was practiced throughout central Asia and

China since 3000 B.C.E. Many believe Zoroastrianism is the foundation of Buddhism and Confucianism. The oldest surviving manuscript of the book of Avesta, the Zoroastrian scriptures, is said to be from 1000 B.C.E., and it was found in northern China. It is presently in the British Library in London.

Mithra's Enduring Legacy
(Left) Mithra at Taghe Bostan, western Iran,
(Middle) Deo Sol Invictus, Italy,
(Right) Statue of Liberty, Staten Island, New York
Source: Kaveh Farrokh

The Persian Empire was established in 575 B.C.E., by the Persian prince, Cyrus, the Achaemenid. Cyrus was a Zoroastrian who believed in the philosophy, "Good thought, good words, and good deeds." Iranian women and men were equal and treated equally, according to the natural and social laws of the land. Women continued to share in all aspects of society, including the military.

Cyrus was the son of Cambyses, the prince of the Persian tribe, and Mandane, the princess of the Medes, the neighboring tribe in the north. He rose to unite the tribes in the plateau, first by taking Media, his maternal grandfather's empire, then established a new united empire that was called Iran, the first nationhood in 559 B.C.E. He went on to create the first federation of independent states and one of the greatest empires of human history. While expansionist, Cyrus the Great was an exceptional humanitarian leader, not a barbarian tyrant.

Although Greeks called the country Persia, because Cyrus was from the Persian tribe, Iranians have always called their country Iran, to encompass the Indo-European tribes that had gradually migrated, over hundreds of years, to the plateau from the Eurasian Plains in today's Eastern Europe and Ukraine.

During World War II, the British accused the patriot of Iran, Reza

Shah Pahlavi, of Fascism, and exiled him. One of the excuses were that in 1933, he had insisted that the name of his country was Iran, and not Persia. The word Iran was misrepresented to invoke the "Aryan" fantasies of German fascism. In truth, the country has always been called Iran by her people, even by the Persian Cyrus the Great. The word "Iran" is derived from the 900 B.C.E. Zoroastrian Scriptures, the Avesta, and the Hindu scriptures such as the Vedas. In Pahlavi or Middle Persian language, Aryan means "Land" and Arya, derived from Sanskrit, means "hospitable." Another meaning for Aryan is said to be "noble" for the people of Hospitable Land.

 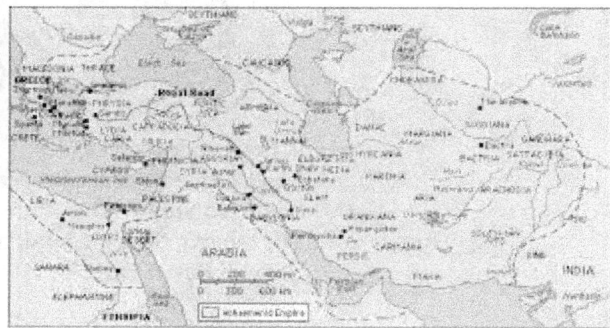

Cyrus the great, the map of the Persian Empire

In a book, *Cyropedia*, chronicling the life of Cyrus, Xenophon, a prolific Greek historian from the fourth century B.C.E, wrote, "The father of Cyrus, so runs the story, was Cambyses, a king of the Persians. His mother, it is agreed, was Mandane, the daughter of Astyages, king of the Medes. Of Cyrus himself, even now in the songs and stories of the East, the record lives that nature made him most fair to look upon and set in his heart the threefold love of man, of knowledge, and of honor. He would endure all labors, he would undergo all dangers, for the sake of glory. Blessed by nature with such gifts of soul and body, his memory lives to this day in the mindful heart of ages."

He continued, "In their cities they have an open place or square dedicated to Freedom ("Free Square," they call it), where stand the palace and other public buildings. Every Persian is entitled to send his children to the public schools of righteousness and justice."

The Greek philosophers called Cyrus the Great by many names: the law-giver, a man of freedom, and a man of tolerance. The Romans called him the "father of men," and the Lord YHWH (the Jewish word for "God") called him *moshiach*, or messiah, in Hebrew, meaning "annointed." Cyrus is the only non-Jew who was called the annointed friend and the shepherd of YHWH in the Torah. The people of Iran simply called him "the Father," a term which in ancient times meant a teacher, a legislator of laws, and an authority with compassion.

Cyrus the Great carried out the heritage of the Woman-God with his respect for human dignity, as reflected in Zoroastrian belief. He gave clear advice to his leaders: "Your people are your most precious treasures."

And, according to the book *Cyropedia*, he said: "Only those who serve the people deserve to rule the people."

To Cyrus the Great, respecting diversity was important, and so, the laws of the land were written in the six languages spoken across the empire, as a symbol of respect for all citizens. He believed in freedom of worship and religion, but argued for a separation of religion and state. Cyrus the Great was against slavery and freed all of the slaves in the empire, including 50,000 slaves who were Jewish, when he took control of Babylonia. He then repatriated the displaced people back to their homelands and declared a Proclamation of Human Rights in 538 B.C.E.

Cyrus cylinder of Proclamation of Human Rights in British Museum. A replica is in the United Nations.

Thus, throughout Iran's long history, we have never practiced slavery. The cities, palaces, and temples of other ancient civilizations of the world were built by slave labor, but Iranians have always used paid labor, as evidenced by payroll ledgers, discovered in the archives of a basement library under the main hall of the Persepolis and presently on loan to the University of Chicago. These documents prove that paid laborers built Persepolis, not slaves. The payroll ledgers also show that women and men had equal opportunity in holding any job or position, receiving equal pay for equal work. What's more, women received childcare support and paid maternity leave.

In his essay, "The Jews of Persia," Ismail Butera wrote: "Cyrus is credited with issuing the world's first human bill of rights, as he granted religious freedom to all the peoples of his empire. The Jews were liberated from their bondage, as Cyrus gave them permission to return to their ancestral land. He ordered the rebuilding of the 2nd temple. They were free to travel anywhere in the empire they wished, and worship as they desired. Their sages were free to interpret and debate texts as they saw fit."

Butera continues, "The Jews of Persia are saved, and they lived in peace and tolerance. It is believed that Jews made up some 20 percent of the population when ancient Persia was in its heyday. By the time of the rise of the Roman Empire, many Jews living in Judea fled to Babylon, itself under Persian rule. Roman rule was harsh and unfriendly to the Jews, and after the Bar Kochba revolt [132–136 C.E.] and the destruction of Jerusalem by Roman forces, one of ancient history's most infamous massacres, many Jews found refuge under the tolerant Persians. Some joined the Persian army and fought against the Roman legions that were unsuccessful in conquering Persian lands. Shapur I is known and highly regarded in Jewish history by his Aramaic name Shvor Malka. Shapur II had a mother who was indeed Jewish, and he was a close friend and protector of the Babylonian rabbi named Raba. It can be said that in ancient times the Jews as a people flourished and did well in Iran."

Cyrus wrote his Proclamation of Human Rights in 538 B.C.E., one century before the birth of Plato in 437 B.C.E. and long before the concept of Athenian democracy. Today, many leading historians and researchers trace the foundation of Western democracy to the Proclamation of Human Rights by Cyrus the Great. In a paper, "Reflecting on the Ambiguous Universality of Human Rights: Cyrus the Great's Proclamation as a Challenge to the Athenian Democracy's Perceived Monopoly on Human Rights," Iranian-Dutch attorney Hirad Abtahi documents a bias by Euro-centralists who overlooked the influence of Iranian cultural civilization on the West.[8]

Abtahi argues, "Athenian democracy did not abolish slavery, nor did it grant slaves citizenship. Such privileges were applicable to the adult men only, excluding women and slaves. Even two hundred years later, the distinguished Greek thinker Aristotle (384–322 B.C.E.) considered slaves as pieces of living property, which existed only in the service of their masters."[9]

---

8 Cave, *Persianology: The Road to Persiana*. http://www.arsehsevom.net/site/wp-content/uploads/2013/06/Hirad-Abtahi_English_with-ISBN-small.pdf.
9 Aristotle, *Politics*, I. 2.

The Greek philosopher Plato wrote: "The Persians under Cyrus maintained the due balance between slavery and freedom, they became, first of all, free themselves and, after that, masters of many others. For, when the rulers gave a share of freedom to their subjects and advanced them to a position of equality, the soldiers were friendlier towards their officers. Therefore, if there was any wise man amongst them able to give counsel, he imparted his wisdom to the public since the king was not jealous, and allowed free speech and respected those who could help at all by their counsel. Such a man had the opportunity of contributing to the common stock, the fruit of his wisdom. Consequently, at that time all their affairs made progress, owing to their freedom, friendliness and mutual interchange of reason."[10]

Democracy as a physical structure of governance under a system of parliamentary representation has been used and abused by the fascists, communists, Islamists, and secular dictators throughout history, continuing in the present day. The heart and foundation of a democracy must first and foremost be the acceptance of human rights and dignity of the citizen constituencies.

Thomas Jefferson's copy of Xenophon's *Cyropaedia*

The Greek historian Xenophon (431-355 BC) wrote the book of *Cyropaedia*, an anthology of Cyrus the Great's style of righteous statesmanship. Today, the Library of Congress has two copies of this book that Thomas Jefferson had in his personal library. I was told that the U.S. Army War College includes another book, Xenophon's *Cyrus the Great: Arts of Leadership and War*[11] in its list of required reading.

In 2013, the British Museum agreed to put the Cyrus cylinder on

---

10 Plato, *Laws*, III, 694a, 694b.
11 Xenophon, *Xenophon's Cyrus the Great: The Arts of Leadership and War*. (https://www.amazon.com/Xenophons-Cyrus-Great-Arts-Leadership/dp/0312364695).

tour in the United States. The cylinder was on display at the Smithsonian Museum's Arthur M. Sackler Gallery that March, beside Thomas Jefferson's copy of Xenophon's *Cyropaedia* and a letter from Jefferson to his grandson, encouraging him to read the book.

British Museum Director Neil MacGregor noted that Jefferson's *Cyropedia* is the Glasgow edition obtained by Thomas Jefferson and that Jefferson was in communication with Scottish intellectuals, who referred to the accounts of Cyrus the Great, in their efforts to sort out the "pressing question of church and state."[12][13]

Julian Raby, director of the Freer Gallery of Art and Arthur M. Sackler Gallery, believes that Thomas Jefferson studied the *Cyropaedia* closely and the bold black line over one of the passages, seen in the copy on exhibition, shows the degree of attention Jefferson paid to this book.

British Museum exhibition curator John Curtis said, "The tolerance shown by Cyrus toward diverse religions and cultures was a historical first. The Cyrus Cylinder and associated objects represent a new beginning for the Ancient Near East. The idea of freedom of religion appealed to the founders of the United States, which was originally colonized, in part, by Europeans escaping religious persecution."

One revelation of the Cyrus Cylinder exhibition, according to Neil MacGregor, Director of the British Museum, is, "the importance of Cyrus to those who wrote the Constitution of the United States." He added, "The story of Persia—Iran—is part of the story of modern United States. Although eighteenth-century Europeans read and commented on the tenets of religious freedom and tolerance set down by Cyrus, only the United States' founders enshrined them in law."[14]

"Worshiping woman god was looked down upon and became an act of paganism," said De Riencourt, "from all this, it should not be gathered that women were without protection or influence, again, as in Persia, they were well protected by law and tradition."[15]

Eventually, the Father-God defeated the Mother-God, but not before she had left a lasting heritage of courage, responsibility, and humanity on the Iranian culture. This heritage may have been abandoned and

---

[12] "The Cyrus Cylinder," *Smithsonian Magazine*. https://www.youtube.com/watch?v=NTAgTCXja4Q.

[13] "The Cyrus Cylinder," Getty Museum. https://www.youtube.com/watch?v=nRMzrzu0wRw.

[14] Frye, "Jefferson and Cyrus." http://richardfrye.org/files/Thomas_Jefferson_and_Cyrus_the_Great.pdf.

[15] Riencourt, *Women and Power*, 86.

discarded over a few thousand years of history—especially over the past four decades of the present regime—but it has lived deep in the heart and the soul of Iranian culture.

The languages spoken in a country are windows into its socio-cultural foundation. The language of Iran is rooted in Old Persian, the language of the Zoroastrian scripture, the Avesta. The Persian language is perhaps the only gender-neutral language, proof that the gender of people was never an issue among Iranians. In the Persian language, there is no feminine or masculine version of words to differentiate women from men—there is no "he" or "she." One pronoun, *ao*, is used to refer to women and men. There have also never been separate words for married and unmarried women. In this language, instead of saying "men and women," Iranians say, "women and men," using the word for women, *zanan*, before the word for men, *mardan*. Archeological discoveries prove that, in pre-Islamic Iranian societies, lineage and heredity were passed through mothers first, and then, fathers.

Unlike in many Western languages, in which "king" is the word for a male ruler and "queen" is the word for a female ruler, the gender-neutral Persian language refers to male and female rulers by the same title, *padshah* or *shah*, for short.

In marriage, Iranians were equal partners. In the gender-neutral Persian language, the word used for husbands and wives is *hamsar*, literary translated as "of one mind" or partner. Iranian women have always kept their last names, after getting married, and they do not legally adopt their husband's name.

Women Warriors

Throughout history, Iranian women have been great warriors, including as archers. In 2004, Alireza Hojabri-Nobari, an archaeologist working in the northwestern city of Tabriz, reported that his team had discovered a 2,000-year-old skeleton of an entombed woman warrior with a sword, proven to be hers through a DNA test.[16]

The stories of renowned women warriors fill Iranian history. Artemisia was a naval strategist, commander, and the sister, wife, and successor of Mausolus, ruler of Caria. She lived between 353 B.C.E. and 351 B.C.E. and was the commander of the Iranian naval forces, but Hollywood has grossly misrepresented her in films, such as *300: Rise of an*

---

16 "Ancient Iranian Tomb Was for Woman Warrior," *Los Angeles Times*. http://articles.latimes.com/2004/dec/11/science/sci-briefs11.2.

Empire, where she is portrayed by actress Eva Green as an evil, crazed military advisor. Artoonis was a general to Darius the Great. Stateira was Princess Warrior in the 320s B.C.E. Aspas was commander of the police force in 530 B.C.E. Negan, a freedom fighter, was partisan commander of the resistance in battles against the Arab invasion. Pantea was commander of the Immortal Guards. Youtab was commander general to Darius the Great. Pari Satis was a queen and field marshall. Roxanna was the warrior who surrendered to Alexander and became his first Persian wife. Princess Rhodogune led a successful revolt against her dictator husband-king, Demetrius II, in 138 B.C.E. Sura was a genius military strategist to 226 C.E.. Banu and her husband, Babak Khorramdin, led a heroic 23-year rebellion against Arab occupiers of Iran.

Scythian woman warrior

Women in Business

Archaeological evidence from the Burnt City, of 2000 B.C.E. to 3000 B.C.E., shows that 90 percent of the graves, in which seals of power were discovered, belonged to women. According to the Persepolis archives, Iranian women were government officials and independent business owners. Some women had titles with recognized authority at the court and in the management of private businesses. Sasanian women were influential administrators and participated in the economic and political affairs of the estate. In 1901, archaeologists discovered a tomb of a woman, living between 350 and 322 B.C.E., that was adorned with masses of gold jewelry and surrounded by burial goods and two gold coins, reflecting her power and standing in the society.[17]

From the eighth century B.C.E. Elamite era, a businesswoman spins thread on a spindle. A maid fans her, with a dinner of fish, waiting on the table.

The accounting ledgers from the archives of the city of Persepolis include the names of independently wealthy women. Among the women chronicled in the ledgers: a nanny for a princess, Artim, received rent for property she owned. Another woman, Madamis, paid property taxes. Irdabama, a successful business woman, was a landowner, running a winery and grain business at the time of Xerxes II, in 424 B.C.E. The fortification tablets at Persepolis contain information about her wealth, workshops, and hundreds of male and female workers she employed. She had her own seal, which meant she had great prestige and power.[18]

Women in Power

Queen Irandokht ("Daughter of Iran") was co-ruler with her husband, King Xerxes I, in 486 B.C.E. Queen Anzaze was joint local ruler with her husband, Kamnaskares III, during the Parthian era, 100 B.C.E. Pad-shah, Monarch Napir Asu, 1350 to 1300 B.C.E., was politically influential, with her statue in the Louvre Museum.[19]

---

17 Time-Life Books, *Persians: Masters of Empire*, 107.
18 Massoume Price, "Women's Lives in Ancient Persia." http://www.cultureofiran.com/women_in_ancient_persia.html.
19 Time-Life Books, *Persians: Masters of Empire*, 106.

40 ∞ *The Ladies' Secret Society*

Royal couple at Hatra Parthian dynasty, 247-224 B.C.E. (Picture source: Farrokh, page 150, *Shadows in the Desert: Ancient Persia at War*.)

Pourandokht's image on a Sasanian coin

Pourandokht, 590 C.E. to 628 C.E., was the first of two consecutive female monarchs to rule over the Sasanian dynasty. The major foreign policy of her reign was the dispatch of an ambassador to Emperor Heraclius, led by the Christian dignitaries of the Iranian church.[20] The purpose of the mission was to establish peace by resolving several matters between the two powers, including the restoration of the True Cross to

---
20 *Anonymous Syriac Chronicle, Chronicle of Seert* II/2, p. 237.

Heraclius.

Azarmidokht succeeded her sister and is remembered as a reformist who re-structured and lowered taxes. Queen Zand was a senator and the wife of Khosrow Anoshirvan of the Sassanid dynasty (224 to 651 C.E.). She was Jewish. Queen Shirin was a senator and the wife of King Khosrow Parviz of the Sassanid dynasty, from 590 to 628 C.E. She was a Christian. Apranik was the general of the Iranian military during the reign of Yazdgerd III. Azad was a guerrilla commander and freedom fighter during the Arab occupation. Booran was the prime minister during the Arab occupation of Iran. Queen Susan was the Jewish wife of Yazdgerd, the Iranian emporer during the Sasanian dynasty. She built the city of Jee, today a part of the city of Hamadan, in the Zagros Mountains.

Seyyedeh Malek Khatun was a ruler, after the death of her husband. She became regent to her son when he was four years old. However, she was the true ruler, until her death in 1029.

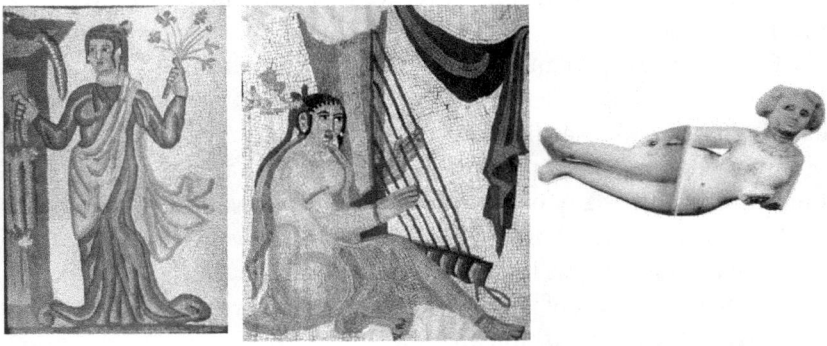

(L-R) **Sassanid era, sixth century-woman dancer and harp player in music. Marble statue of an Iranian woman, from Parthian era, in the second century.** *Persians, Masters of Empire*, **section four.**

At home and in workshops, the women of Iran, in both nomadic tribes and villages and towns, have always been a part of the textile industry and Persian carpet weaving.[21] Ancient Iranian women wore lace, and it was later worn by Italian nuns in the sixteenth century. Three Iranian textile creations were velvet, seersucker, and taffeta.

---

21 *Art.com*. Art.com Inc.

Using looms, women wove images onto fabrics that suggest a sophisticated textile industry during the ancient and medieval eras. The first image put on a silk fabric is said to have been of the mayor of the city of Rey on her horse in the tenth century. The portrait of an unknown Parthian woman was woven onto a wool fabric, between 247 B.C.E. and 224 C.E.

For centuries, Iranians exported textiles, garments, and hand-knotted Persian carpets to markets in Europe. Some 100 fragments of fabric exist today, providing a glimpse into a once-flourishing industry with an output that traveled far and wide over the Silk Road, linking Asia and Europe by trade. Many of the European pieces owe their preservation to their inclusion in church treasures. Scholars even say the rich and intricate Iranian designs influenced medieval European art.

Along with the art of textile, Iranian women have proven their talent and taste in the art of fashion and jewelry.

The image of an Elamite woman, 2000 to 2500 B.C.E., etched on a silver cup.

The marble statue of a woman, in the fashion of second century B.C.E., Parthian era.

Women's hand ornament, 2000 to 1500 B.C.E.

Second century B.C.E., a jewelry forehead band and necklaces made of gold. National Museum of Iran

CHAPTER TWO

Arab Occupation and Enforcement of Islam (651 C.E. – Present)

Before the dawn of Islam in the seventh century in modern day Saudi Arabia in the Arab Peninsula, there existed great civilizations, such as the Persian empire, Egyptian empire, Syrian empire, Mesopotamia, and Carthaginian empire. Unfortunately, the history and achievements of all the ancient civilizations have been recorded in the history books of the West as Islamic civilization.

Iranian historians have recorded that the invading Islamic Arab military attacked Iranian Sassanid Empire in 633 AD with the speed of a brushfire. They massacred indiscriminately—men, women, children and even the animals—and took the young men and women to sell as slaves in their markets. They looted the cities, burnt down the libraries, universities, schools and the great Iranian observatories, leaving nothing behind that they could not take. In all, they destroyed everything that had been created and built by the Iranian empire over the preceding 1200 years.

The military campaigns of the Nadjd Arabs established the supremacy of Islam and the Arab race and culture. First, they had to wipe out the existing cultures and national identities of the occupied people and then replace them with the Arab Islamic culture.

The Arab occupation of Iran put down insurgencies in every corner of the country for over fifty years. Women were a great part of the resistance. The tribes' people, including the women, defeated the Arabs in the mountain passes of northern Iran, Azad Daylamee, a guerrilla commander and partisan leader whose name, Azad, means "freedom," fought for many years with her band of freedom fighters against the Arab oppressors during their occupation.

The Arab invaders destroyed and burned the schools, libraries, observatories, and records of Iranian history and culture to ashes. With occupation came the Arabization of Iran, which forced the Arabic language and Islamic religion and laws on the people of Iran. On threat of death, they forced Iranians to convert to Islam from Zoroastrianism, Judaism, and Christianity. Women became the first casualty of the Arab invasion, but not before fighting gallantly for their freedom and sovereignty.

In the late seventh century, Purandokht, the daughter of Puran who was the Shahanshah (the King of Kings), bravely fought the Arab invaders before she was killed on the battlefield. Apranik was general of the Iranian military during the reign of Yazdgerd III. During the invasion, she fought gallantly against the Arab oppressors.

(left-right) Queen Pourandokht leads the cavalry. A reconstruction of the late Elite Sassanid Cavalry.

In a significant foreign policy decision during her reign, Purandokht dispatched an ambassador to Heraclius, Emperor of the Byzantine Empire in the seventh century. The mission was led by the Christian dignitaries of the Iranian church[1] in an attempt to resolve several matters between the two powers. In particular, they aimed to restore to Heraclius the "True Cross" on which Christians believed that Jesus had died.

Eventually, the women of Iran were forced to assume roles as women in an Islamic society, their social standing dissolved, and their names removed from Iranian history. However, the women of Iran became legends. They had become politicians, masters of Islamic law, activists, soldiers, scientists, poets, musicians, painters, and astronomers. They

---

1 *Anonymous Syriac Chronicle*, loc. cit., *Chronicle of Seert* II/2, p. 237.

impacted government policies and reigned over the land for their underage sons, leading the military in battle while clad in headscarves as required as a part of the Islamic rule.

Iranian Revival: Women in Ninth-Century Post-Arab Occupation

Without the continuous resistance of the patriotic men and women of Iran against the occupying Arab Islamic forces, Iran would have become an Arab country, like the others in the region. One man—and a book that took him 30 years to write—saved Iran.

A statue of Ferdowsi

His name was Abolqasem Ferdowsi, and he lived between 940 and 1020 C.E. He is, perhaps, the most venerated hero of post-Islamic Iran. His statues were in just about every town square and park, before the Islamic clerics tore them down after their takeover in 1979. Across Iran, there are streets, public buildings, schools, and cultural, national, and historical events named after Ferdowsi. There may not have been a Qur'an in every Iranian home, but there has always been at least one copy of his book, *The Shah-Nameh, The Epic of Kings*.

Ferdowsi spent 30 years traveling throughout the country in search of Iran's lost history, culture, and language. He found in the memories of the Iranian people his one and only poetic opus and grand national epic, the *Shah-Nameh*, capturing an oral history that Iranian tribes had transmitted over thousands of years.

In 60,000 lines of poetry, the *Shah-Nameh* captures Iran's national identity in over 1,200 years of pre-Islamic history, chronicling the adventures of the superheroes and superheroines of the country's history, the stories of patriots and traitors, and the tales of noble kings and corrupt kings. It tells of the tragedies and joys, the wars and peace of a ancient, great nation.

For over one thousand years, with the homeland invaded and occupied time and again, Iranians have been reading the *Shah-Nameh* to their children. The stories of the *Shah-Nameh* have been also enacted and recited in public arenas by actors, called *naqqal*, who specialize in the *Shah-Nameh*. In just about every city, town, and village in Iran, the traveling *naqquals* are the featured performing arts attractions in teahouses and all the *caravan-saras*, enacting the stories of the *Shah-Nemeh*. In the Persian language, *sara* means "house." The *caravan-saras* were hotels for the caravan travelers. A center platform was built for performances for religious events, but they were mostly used as a stage for the actors of the *Shah-Nameh*. *Naqquals* as performers of *Shah-Nameh's* stories have been the Iranian version of English Shakespearians.

Caravan-sara

The *Shah-Nameh* is important not only for the literary significance of the stories that Ferdowsi told, but because the writing of the *Shah-Nameh* in the Persian language, banned by the occupying Arab Muslims, represents a significant patriotic accomplishment in the revival of Iran's lost pride.

Ferdowsi begins his book saying, "In this year of 30, I tried hard to revive Iran with her Persian language." And, indeed, he accomplished his historic mission, and Iran did keep her identity and language. Ferdowsi also begins the *Shah-Nameh* with a Zoroastrian tradition, in the name of the God of knowledge and wisdom, followed by the statement, "If there is no Iran, there is no I." Throughout the book, Ferdowsi refers to his country as "Iran."

A miniature painting book cover of Ferdowsi and his kings, heroes, and heroines.

Dick Davis, a professor of Iranian history at the University of Ohio, who translated the *Shah-Nameh* to English, wrote, "Among the greatest works of world literature, and perhaps the least familiar to English readers, is the *Shah-Nameh*, *The Persian Book of Kings*..." in his introduction. He continues, "The sweep and psychological depth of the *Shah-Nameh* is nothing less than magnificent. In its pages are unforgettable moments of national triumph and failure, human courage and cruelty, blissful love and bitter grief."

Professor Davis goes on to say, "As a window to the world, it belongs in the company of such literary masters as the *Mahabharata* of India, Dante's *Divine Comedy*, the plays of Shakespeare, and the epics of Homer—classics whose reach and range bring whole cultures into view."

Edward Byles Cowell, a renowned professor of Persian poetry in the late nineteenth century at Cambridge University, wrote, "Augustus said that he found Rome of brick, and left it marble. Ferdowsi found his country almost without a literature, and has left her a poem, that all succeeding poets could only imitate and never surpass, and which, indeed, can rival them all even in their peculiar styles, and perhaps stands as alone in Asia as Homer's epics in Europe..."

A former scholar of Persian literature at the University of Tehran, Zabihollah Safa, wrote, "Ferdowsi's *Epic of Kings* is a collection of writings giving a fairly continuous picture of all the cultural history and traditions of the Iranian Empire from before the creation of the known world to Iran's sub-ordinance under the Muslims."[2]

Patriotism had become a sin under the Arab Muslim rulers who took many freedoms away in the name of *sharia*. Even today The *Shah-Nameh* speaks of patriotism and loyalty to the king and country, traits that the clergy view as endangering their power. Today, more people have been in the teahouses listening and watching performances of the *Shah-Nameh* than in the mosques, listening to the clergy. Therefore, Ferdowsi has been a thorn in the side of the ruling clergy.

Miniature painting of the Iranian woman warrior Gordafarid, as depicted in the *Shah-Nameh*, *The Epic of Kings*

Among the notable women of the era, one is Rabehe who was a musician and poet. Rabehe was the daughter of Kaab (914-943). She was one of the first women poets of post-Islamic Iran. Shokooh Bakhtiar, an expert on the poetry, writes "Rabehe was a great poet and had a sad, short life being the Iranian daughter of an Arab conqueror Governor, who fell in love with an Iranian named Yektash, who was her brother's slave servant. When her brother learned about their love affair, he had

---

2 "Taziyeh: History, Form and Contemporary Relevance," Alemohammed, http://wrap.warwick.ac.uk/36312/1/WRAP_THESIS_Alemohammed_1995.pdf.

both Yektash and her sister Rabehe killed. Rabehe became known as the mother of the Persian Satire."[3]

---

[3] "The Pursuit of Freedom, Democracy and Secularism in Iran," https://www.fozo-olemahaleh.com.

CHAPTER THREE

The Origin of Shi'ism in Iran's Reoccupation (686 – 1500)

After the death of the Prophet Muhammad in 632 AD, his friends and original followers, called the *Bani Umayya*, chose an elder statesman and friend and father-in-law of the prophet, Abu Bakr, as his successor and the first *caliph*, or leader in Islam. They overlooked the prophet's young son-in-law and cousin, Ali Ibn Abdullah. Under the new leadership, Muslim conquerors expanded the Islamic empire, from Mecca to the western borders of India and the western shores of North Africa, supplanting every ancient civilization in between. Conquerors established the Islamic empire with bloody wars, massacres, and destructions, and they ruled with absolute brutality, according to historians.

At the dawn of Islam, the only Arabs were the nomads of the peninsula, living in modern-day Saudi Arabia (which was created in 1932, in negotiations between Saudi tribesmen and officers of the British MI6 intelligence agency).

The Arab Islamic Empire created a subclass of the forcefully converted non-Arabs, which the rulers called, *Mawali*, meaning the non-Arab people of slave origin in Arabic, even though most of these slaves were people who had had a much greater civilization than their occupiers. The conquered people were not only Islamized, they were Arabized. The Arab rulers discriminated against the *Mawali* and segregated them, in their own countries. They heavily taxed them, excluding them from government and denying them participation in the social, economic, and political affairs of their own homelands. They received much lower wages than Arabs did, and they were forbidden from marrying Arabs and from buying land in their own countries. The Arab rulers destroyed their temples, replaced their languages with Arabic, denounced their religions and replaced them with Islam, and erased their histories and cultures to replace them with an Arab Islamic history and culture.[1]

Among many scattered Iranian uprisings against the Arab occupation, one Iranian, Mokhtar Saqafie, stood up for the human rights of his fellow Iranians against the tyranny of the Umayyad caliphate in 686 C.E. After the passing of Prophet Muhammad, Mokhtar led a civil war against the new Arab leadership's occupation and mistreatment of his fellow countrymen.

With the passing of the Prophet Muhammad, the Islamic empire became a fundamental subject of division among its followers. The prophet's son in-law, Ali Ibn Abdullah, claimed the leadership in the name of *Bani Abbasids*. However, the leadership of the Hashemite tribe and the first followers and advisors of the prophet disagreed and claimed the empire for the *Bani Umayyads*. In the war for power between the Umayyads and the Abbasids, Mokhtar aligned with the Abbasids, who promised justice and the elimination of the slavery laws against the *Mawali*.

By the ninth century, the original movement of Mokhtar for human dignity of the occupied peoples was no longer relevant. A series of internal conflicts within the movement had changed its original intent into a political belief that recognized the inheritance of the prophet's progeny in ruling the Islamic empire.

The civil rights movement of Mokhtar evolved into a sect of Islam called Shi'ism. In some Arab countries, it became a sect of fundamentalist religious ideology.

By the time the Islamic empire lost control of occupied countries, they had succeeded in changing the face of the nations from the Far East to South Asia and North Africa, from multicultural, multi-racial, multi-religion, and multilingual countries to one Muslim Arab empire.

In Iran, the military had been weakened, lacking strong leadership while recovering from Arab domination, leaving the country vulnerable to attacks from the brutal Turkic, Tartar, and Mongol tribes from the west, east, and north. Between 950 and 1501, three Turkic militaries of Ghaznavids attacked and occupied Iran, adopting Iranian culture.

The great Iranian writer and poet Ferdowsī completed his national

---

1 "Mawali," *Encyclopedia of the Middle East*, http://mideastweb.org/Middle-East-Encyclopedia/mawali.htm.

epic, *Shah-Nameh, the Epic of Kings*. Between 1010 and 1037, the Saljugs, a Turkic tribe, defeated the Ghaznavies and occupied Iran, adopting the Iranian culture and Persian language. The Kharazmians, northern tribes which had been driven from their lands by the founder of the Mongol Empire, Genghis Khan, invaded Iran from between 1200 to 1220. Then Genghis Khan's army followed them into Iran, sweeping through the heart of the country, leaving little but destruction behind. The Mongols set cities on fire and massacred men, women, and children.

After the Arab invasion, Iranians had gone through a period of recovery to reestablish their cultural, scientific, and social foundations, rebuilding schools, libraries, and universities. But the Mongol warrior Genghis Khan destroyed all that again. It is said that when the Mongols set the University of Nishapour on fire, it burned for months before all of its books and treasures were consumed.

As a result of the devastation of decades of Genghis Khan's brutal massacres, by the end of the thirteenth century, the survivors faced a famine of untold proportion. Their lands, farms, and irrigation systems of underground rivers, or *qanat*, that Iranians had developed over thousands of years, were obliterated, and there was no manpower left to rebuild the country.

Between 1220 and 1258, the population of Iran dropped drastically.

Eventually, the Mongol Khan separated the territory of Iran from the rest of his empire and appointed a provincial ruler over Iran. Slowly, the provincial rulers became independent and learned that they needed Iranian administrators to govern the empire, adopting the civilization they had conquered. They made Persian the official language of the court, and, in time, many of the descendants of Genghis Khan married Iranians, remaining Buddhist or Shamanist and not converting to Islam.

By 1381, the Mongolian warrior Tamerlane conquered Transoxiana. His conquests were slower and less savage than those of Genghis Khan or the Hulagu Khan. Nevertheless, he virtually leveled the cities of Shiraz and Esfahan. Tamerlane also adopted the Iranian language and culture and he allowed Iranians to continue their administrative roles in the affairs of the country. After his death in 1405, Mongol tribes, Uzbeks, and Turkmens ruled Iran until the rise of the Safavid Turkish tribe of Anatolia. Sociological studies and history show that, in time, Mongol occupiers assimilated with Iranians, adopted Iranian culture, and respected the rights of women in some respects.

During Mongol rule, they appointed women to offices, such as regents, governors, and mayors. From 1257 to 1282, Sultan Turkan Khatun ruled as a regent of the province of Kerman. She became a sovereign by having the *khutba*, or prayer for the sovereign, read for her in the mosque in a proclamation of her legitimate reign. Her daughter, Padisha, later reigned over the Kingdom of Kerman. After the death of her husband, Regent Princess Turkan Khatun was confirmed as the ruler of the province of Fars, from 1261 to 1263. She married a kinsman, who killed her in a drunken frenzy. Later in the thirteenth century, another woman, Abesh Khatoon was governor of the province of Fars.

The wax reproduction of Jahan Malek Khatun, in the city of Shiraz Wax Museum. (Photo by Amir Hosein Zolfaghari for ISNA.)

Jahan Malek Khatun was a great poet of the fourteenth century and exchanged poems with the other great Iranian poet philosopher, Hafez. She headed a literary society, which met at her residence. A copy of her poetic works exists in the National Library in France. Dick Davis, a scholar of Persian literature, wrote, "Jahan Malek Khatun was a previlaged princess who could evoke passion, longing and heartbreak with uncanny power."

Jahan wrote:

I am like the moth that flutters round a light,
Risking my soul for love and love's delight:
In love with you I'm like the candle too, Dissolving,
burning, weeping, through the night.

Mahasti Ganjavi was a great poet and musician. Bibi Monajameh was a skilled astronomer of the thirteenth century. The king gave her the title of *monajameh*, or astronomer.

CHAPTER FOUR

Women Fall From Grace: Occupation by Safavid Turks and Arrival of Shi'ism (1501 – 1722)

Throughout the Arab Islamic occupation and domination, Iranians faced a physical and emotional assault on their culture and heritage. Still, no national religion was established in Iran, since freedom of worship and respect for diversity had been specifically decreed in the culture of Iranians. The Muslim population were mostly Sunni. Some were Shi'a. However, during the thirteenth century, a school of Islamic jurisprudence called Hanafi and a mystical school of Islam called Sufism had become popular under the influence a great Iranian philosopher and poet, Mowlana Jalaluddin Rumi. Older religions, such as Zoroastrianism, Judaism and Christianity, still flourished among their followers, and they were respected in society as well.

Ismail Safavie was the leader of the Safavid Turkish tribe, rooted in a mostly Shi'a part of central Anatolia. He attacked and defeated the Mongol rulers and occupied Iran in 1498.

The Safavids believed that Allah sanctified their rule, and therefore, they believed they should establish their sect of Islam, Shi'ism, in Iran, as a national religion. However, there were only a few Shi'a clerics in Iran, and so they imported clerics from Western Anatolia, today's Lebanon. Hence, a tie developed that explains the historical connection of the Iranian Shi'a establishment to the Hezbollah in Lebanon.

Once established, the imported Shi'a clerics demanded that, in the absence of the "hidden Imam," or the twelfth descendant of the Prophet (for which they still await today), power over the faithful belonged to them. They believed that Allah gave them superior legal power to rule and they insisted that the king should share power with clerics. Shah Ismail Safavie, however, disagreed, but conceded to declaring the state a theocracy. Hence, after over 2,000 years of secularism and freedom of worship, Iran had forcefully become a theocratic state.

In 1979, the Ayatollah Khomeini reclaimed the same power of jurisprudence of Allah for himself against the monarch, Mohammad Reza Shah Pahlavi. He reiterated the same argument that had been laid by the top imported cleric, Mohammad Baghir Madjlesi, in 1694. However, in 1979, he succeeded in overthrowing the shah and establishing the rule of Allah for the first time in history, by lying to the world, as I will discuss later.

Painting of Shah Ismail Safavie, the conqueror of Iran in 1501

In 1694, the new king, Shah Sultan Hossein Safavie, elevated the position of the clergy by creating a new office of the *mullah bashi*, or head clergy, and appointed Mohammad Baqhir Madjlesi, the outspoken extremist member of the established Shi'a religious institution, to lead it.

Madjlesi had written a book in Arabic, *The Seas of Light*, which he claimed contained the words and deeds of the Prophet Mohammad. He practiced the law of Mawali, which considered Iranians to be people of slave origin, and so, he established the law of the *Velayat E Fagheeh*, the absolute right of jurisprudence of Allah through the clergy. It gave them power over everything and everyone. Mullah Madjlesi was determined to enforce a new legalistic form of Shi'ism by adopting and enhancing *sharia* written at the end of the seventh century for the purpose of ruling the Arab Islamic imperial caliphate.

Under his *sharia*, human rights and freedoms were taken away, and Iranians became the slaves of Allah. With the law, however, came the full force of the shah and his government police, giving the clergy complete authority to abuse, intimidate, and punish anyone who disobeyed them.

The institution of Shi'ism as the national religion gave Mullah Madjlesi the power to denounce all other religions, even other sects of Islam such as the majority Sunni sect of Islam, the Hanafi school of jurisprudence, and the mystical Sufi school of thought. He used his laws of apostasy and blasphemy to persecute non-Muslims, such as the Iranian Zoroastrians, Jews, and Christians. The law against blasphemy was one of the last to enter the books of the religious orders, and it brought the nation of Iran under total submission to the Mullah's regime.

Madjlesi and his fellow *ulama*, or clerics, succeeded in establishing a Shi'ism that became increasingly uncompromising, fascist, and powerfully influential in the social, political, and economic affairs of Iran. To enforce their laws, they hired and unleashed hoodlums and thugs, as an army for the clerics. After his 1979 takeover, Khomeini founded the Islamic Revolutionary Guard Corp to protect their regime in Iran. The IRGC was the same enforcement system, though on a much grander scale, that the Shi'a clergy have used to enforce their rule since the sixteenth century.

Ismail Butera wrote in his essay, "The Jews of Persia:" "The growing power of a Shi'a clergy began to make its presence known. All throughout the Islamic world the caliphs and emirs began to incorporate the Muslim clergy, known as the *Ulama*, into their government, making rules, and interpreting religion and scripture for the masses. The doors of Islamic critical thinking, a tradition that included the works of Jewish and Christian scholars alongside Muslim sages, began to close and so did tolerance and intellectual pursuit."

When Shi'a Islam became the state religion of Iran under Shah Ismail Safavie, the clergy insisted on following rules of purity, known as *tahara*. This meant that non-Muslims were considered unclean, and therefore, the outlook for Jews became increasingly grim, as the power of the Shi'a clergy grew. The mullahs began to influence the affairs of state, and their influence was anything but tolerant. As their power increased, granted by the shah who sought to consolidate his Shi'a kingdom and unify it against the Sunni Ottomans and the Uzbeks, the rights of individuals began to disappear.

Until then, people were not distinguished by their faiths. However, under the new rules of the clergy, Iranians were separated by religion and non-Shi'as became minorities. "The Jews became a despised subject people. Public humiliation of Jews became a common practice. Only among a few mullahs who were courageous dissenters in religion and among the Sufis would the Jews of Persia find friends who would support them."[1]

Mullah Madjlesi declared war on Iranian women, subjecting them to the most draconian laws. He announced that women were not to be considered a sovereign human beings , but rather the property of men. Their human rights and dignity were taken away, replaced by barbaric property laws that held women to be merely objects of sexual pleasure for men and incubators of "their" children. The children became the property of their fathers the minute they were born. In every way, women became only half-persons. The testimony of two women became equal to that of one man. Daughters got only half the inheritance of sons.

Under *sharia*, women became responsible for the honor of the men and, therefore, punishable for any action deemed to dishonor men. However, that "honor" issue has never been defined nor explained, even today. It all remains at the discretion of a clerical judge. Women were removed from all aspects of society and listed under the category of people who should be supervised, such as those with mental illness, convicted criminals, and underage children. The clerics then targeted girls, making nine the age of marriage eligibility and criminal responsibility for them, while it was set at fifteen for boys.

---

1 Butera, "The Jews of Persia."

In addition to such denigration, the clerics decreed that women were not allowed to travel, work, learn to read or write, or leave the house without the permission of their fathers, brothers, or husbands. They also had to live where their husbands decided to live. Mullah Madjlesi ensured that the status of Iranian women would be as slaves, not citizens. They were put under the absolute control of the men, who were in turn under the control of the mosque. Khomeini reestablished the same laws in Iran in 1979. In his book on Islamic governance, Ayatollah Khomeini states that young girls should be residing in their husband's home before they reach puberty.

Not only did they import and enforce Shi'ism, the Safavids also imported the culture of the *harem*, practiced in the royal court. There are reports that women of the royal court in the early Safavid era were educated, intelligent, and powerful advisors of the kings on the affairs of the country. This influence affected the political and economic policies of the kingdom and was deeply resented by the clergy establishment. As the Shi'a clerical establishment became more powerful, the conditions in the harems became akin to slavery, especially for the young, temporary wives.

Harems had a hierarchal system, the highest woman being the all-powerful first and permanent wife of the king and the mother of the crown prince or the mother of the king. She typically ruled the harem and, in many cases, even ruled the country.

The next level of the royal harem hierarchy was composed of the other permanent wives, who were either members of the same tribe or from prominent wealth-and-status families. They were also the mothers of the princes and the princesses, with mid-level power, carrying out their own agendas. They typically were at the heart of any palace intrigue, gossip, conspiracy, and plot.

Lastly, just as there were courtesans in the courts of Western high society and concubines in the royal courts of China, the royal harems of the Safavid kings had limitless temporary wives, called *siqeh*, under *sharia*. The king or any prince could marry any young woman for a limited time. The duration of these marriages and the women's residency in the palace could be decided by the king, or perhaps, last as long as the queen mother allowed. Their tenure often depended on how clever the young women were in their ability to manipulate the king, queen mother, or the eunuchs, the harem's "sex police."

In the eighteenth century, the French author, Charles de Secondat, Baron de Montesquieu, wrote the tales of the Safavid kings' harems and the women of the Royal Court of Persia in his book, *The Persian Letters*. He wrote about the kings who had countless temporary wives, authorized by the clerical establishment. Even the stories of the eunuchs, the harems' "sex guards," are presented as amusing in the book. *The Persian Letters* tells how the eunuchs oversaw the activities of the wives, mostly the younger ones, to make sure there was no immoral sexual behavior or corruption within the harem's domain.

The Safavid dynasty is credited with the development of arts, architecture, and the construction of palaces, mosques, bazaars, and the *caravan-saras* (hotels for the caravan travelers), roads, bridges and the revival of Iranian gardens and landscaping. The Safavid era architecture is a magnificent combination of varieties of arts coming together in the creation of masterpieces.

(left) Masjid Jummah (Friday Mosque), (center) the Shah's mosque, and (far right) the forty pillars Palace. The Safavids used the square center as a polo field, and the royal family watched polo games from the palace balcony.

As a result of the established social laws that women should neither be seen nor heard, their economic and social impacts during the Safavid era have never been addressed. No credit has been given to the women who were behind much of what was built. The rich, powerful women of the harem served as patrons of the arts and played a notable role in the construction of the great architectural legacies of the Safavid era, now some of the most important tourist attractions in Iran.

Under the patronage of these women of the harem, literature flourished. Some of these women were also writers of love stories, memoirs, and poetry that were never published. *Khanum* and *begum* mean "lady" in Turkish and were adopted into the Persian language.

A painting of the harem's Sowgoly, the favorite wife of the Shah.

Women in the Arts and Architecture

Under the patronage of rich women—royal and non-royal—many roads, bridges, *caravan-saras*, and schools were built throughout the land. Building many landmarks, their work guaranteed a positive historical image for the Safavid dynasty with future generations. Yet, because of the influence of clergy, the Shi'a establishment received many more grants for building mosques and shrines than for the institutions benefiting people and society.

- Golbadeh Beigom was born in 1523. There exists an incomplete copy of her memoirs, *Homayoun Nameh, The Important Letters*, in the British Museum.
- One of the artists supported by the Queen Mother was Riza Abbasi. His paintings were mostly of the kings playing polo and hunting or of a favorite new young wife, chubby harem women with round faces, deer-like eyes, rosebud lips, and small waistlines.
- Tadjlu Khanum (Lady Tadjlu) lived in the early 1500s. The favorite wife of Shah Ismail, she was a wealthy woman who donated handsomely to the mosques and shrines.
- Princess Mahin Banu was the daughter of Tadjlu Khanum. She not only patronized shrines with the wealth she inherited, but she established an endowment to protect poor women.
- Zaynab Begum was another wealthy woman of the royal court who made investments in building roads, bridges, and caravan houses (hotels).

- Dilaram Khanum, the mother of Shah Abbas II, commissioned the construction of many caravan houses, shopping bazaars, and schools. She also left a trust, *waqf*, for the schools that she had built.
- Princess Shahr Banu was the sister of the Shah Sultan Hossein Safavie. She built a mosque, a school and a bathhouse from 1694 to 1722.
- Zinat Begum, the wife of the physician Hakim ol-Molk, built schools from 1705 to 1716.
- Ezzat ol-Nesa Khanum was the daughter of a rich merchant and she was married to another rich merchant. She built a number of schools from 1687 to 1698.

- Maryam Beigum built schools. A mansion that she had commissioned for herself and built in the early seventeenth century is now a museum of art (above).

- Sahib Sultan Beigum was the daughter of the royal physician. She sponsored the building of a mosque in the 1680s that is one of the wonders of Iranian architecture (above).

Self-Educated Women Scientists

- Bidjeh Monajameh was an astronomer, scientist, and poet of the seventeenth century. She successfully derived the dates of the calendar.
- The wife of Mirza Khalil wrote the first woman's travelogue in 1692, describing her travels from Isfahan to Mecca and Damascus, in 1,300 lines of poetry. Her name is unknown,
- Jahan Beigom was a scientist and astronomer during the first half of the 17th century. She wrote a book of clarification of the Qur'an that opposed the interpretation of the king's grand clergy, Mullah Madjlesi. She never married although she was a beautiful woman. The story is that King Jahangir of Georgia was one of her persistent suitors whom she refused. To answer his advances she decided to cut her long hair and send it to him. She died in 1659.

CHAPTER FIVE

Women of the Zand Dynasty (1750 to 1798)

FOR THOUSANDS OF YEARS, the tribal women of Iran have kept alive their heritage of the Woman-God and a culture of independence and patriotism. They have always been ready to defend their homes and families. They are historically known as the best horse riders among women and the most accurate archers and sharpshooters of the land. To some extent, one of the reasons that tribal women have remained independent has been the mountainous regions where they live, making them inaccessible to foreign occupiers.

Karim Khan Zand (1705 to 1779)

The founder of the Zand dynasty was Karim Khan Zand, lord of the Zagros Mountain region's Lur tribes, who are descendants of the ancient Meds. After 1,000 years of foreign occupation, following the attack by Muslim Arabs in the seventh century, he was the only Iranian to take over the government of Iran.

In 1874, British historian Clements R. Markham wrote about the etymology of the name Zand: "This tribe received the name of Zand from being charged by Zoroaster with the care of the Zand-i-Avesta, or scripture of that Prophet." On Karim Khan Zand, Markham wrote: "Under the Zands the Islamic clergy had little or no role in government, and their influence had been reduced by having to work for a living, like the rest of society. The separation of religion and state was the law of the land again and upheld by the government."[1]

Mary Boyce (1920-2006), a professor of Iranian studies at the School of Oriental Studies in London, wrote: "The Zand tribe is a branch of the numerous Lak tribes. During the various invasions of Iran over the centuries, the tribes have managed, as a group, to maintain their Iranian culture and identity. They inhabited the most inaccessible mountains and were able to maintain their traditions and values. As the consequence they were away from the cities and received little by way of written education. However, they retained their own Iranian culture and traditions through the development of a strong oral history tradition over the ages. The continuity and strength of the oral tradition over the ages is demonstrated by the close correspondence of extant accounts, which happened to be recorded, widely."[2]

Alessandro Bausani, a historian of Iran at the University of Rome, wrote, "As the Zands were Iran's only rulers of Iranian origin in many centuries embodying native values and culture, their government was tantamount to what a democracy would produce. It best represents what a democracy would be, whether for Iranians or the outside world dealing with Iran. Karim Khan Zand called himself *Vakil*, meaning, Attorney of the People, Representative of the People and or the Advocate of the People but never a king."[3]

In his introduction to *The History of Zand-ieh*, professor Saeed Nafisi (1895-1966), the symbolic dean of Iranian history and sociology, wrote, "Among the dynasties that have ruled Iran, there have been none

---

1 Frye, "The Zands in Iran" http://richardfrye.org/files/The_Zands_in_Iran.pdf.
2 Ibid.
3 Ibid.

like the Zands who possessed chivalry, virtue, justice, ethics, kindness and were fond of their country, resentful of invading tribes and those appeasing them. Karim Khan Zand is one of the most beloved men of history and, besides kingship, he would be fit to serve as a model of ethics for mankind."[4]

As Iranian historian Amine Pakravon (1893–1958) wrote on Karim Khan Zand: "Although his bones may have withered, his lasting legacy today is more than mere memory, the Vakil [Advocate of the People] continues to live, among the people." "Iran under the Zands was a multi-ethnic, multi-cultural society comprised of Muslim, Christian, Jewish, Zoroastrians, and other religious communities since ancient times. Iranian society as in other respects resembled pre-Islamic Iran."

Pakravon continued:

> In the age of Karim Khan there were no signs of religious fundamentalism, or mournful and sad faces. His grace extended to everyone, including foreigners, Jews and Christians.
>
> The Zands fostered and encouraged gatherings and had social patrols whom they charged with going about the neighborhoods at night time and on the weekends to enquire and report where there were no parties and where the sound of people and children making merry could not be heard.
>
> Until that age, it had been unheard of that a king or regent would turn into an act of government the very enjoyment of life. Karim Khan's wish was to see happy, prosperous people around, as the pre-Islamic religion of Iran: 'Zoroastrianism is a religion which enjoins upon its follower the pleasant duty of being happy.'[5]

Historian Abbas Parviz, a native of Iran, wrote, "Since Safavids brought the Arab Shi'a clergy to Iran and established them with endowments from the state, they had not worked to earn a living, except during the period of the Zand rule."

Professor Parviz continued, "Karim Khan Zand, is characterized by historians, to have regarded the clergies as, 'parasites' on society. He thus discontinued their stipend from the public treasury, set up by the Safavid kings. The attitudes and policy of the Zands in this regard, being the temporal representative of the people, is reflective of how the majority of the Iranian people view the clergy."[6]

---

4 Ibid.
5 Ibid.
6 Ibid.

Mohammad Reza Shah Pahlavi also took the same action of cutting off the Shi'a clergy's stipend that the Qajars had reinstituted, a decision that angered the Shi'a clergymen like Khomeini and others.

Abbas Parviz wrote, "As in pre-Islamic times, recounted in Esther and several other books of the Bible, under the Zands, Jews were present at the court. Some rose to prominent positions, such as Ibrahim the governor of Shiraz, appointed by Jafar Khan Zand. As with Esther the Jewish queen of ancient Persia, the Jewish wife of Karim Khan bore him sons, in line of succession to the throne."

A painting, "The Lovers," shows a short period of happiness and good life, promoted during the Zand era. The wine they are drinking would be forbidden during the past Safavids and the future Qajars.

Iranian historian Parviz Radjavy wrote, "After Karim Khan, historians without exception have extolled the traits of character of this king, the king who held no throne and wore no crown."

Professor Richard N. Frye, at Harvard University, wrote, "In my opinion, the persistence of motifs about the founder of such a dynasty in Iran can be attributed to several factors:

- First, the resilience of the Persians under pressure of foreign rules and mass invasions has been demonstrated time and again throughout history.
- Second, the tenacity of the Persians in maintaining old traditions is a feature of their history . . .

• Third, Iran is one of the few countries at present, which has an epic tradition."⁷

The Zands governed the country with a separation of religion and state, without clergy interference in the social, economic, and political affairs of the country. Once again, women were free and equal under the laws of the land, carried forward from Women-Gods, by the tribal traditions.

"Karim Khan Zand had a gender neutral policy, even the military was made of both men and women soldiers and commanders. Warriors were often accompanied by their wives into the battle. The Lur female archers and sharpshooters were instrumental in the defeat of the invading Afghan warlords," as noted by Iranian historian, Dr. Foad Izady. "The Afghan officers ridiculed the Zands for having women warriors, accusing them of hiding behind their women's skirts."

Young Lur women pose with their pistols and rifles, circa early 1960s. Source: Shahyar Mahabadi and the Moradi clan⁸

---

8 "The Official Website of Kaveh Farrokh," Kaveh Farrokh, https://kavehfarrokh.com/.

Tuti Beik was one of the most prominent women soldiers of the Karim Khan Zand period. She was the wife of Fathali Khan Zand, governor of Azerbaijan.

Even today the tribeswomen of Iran are avid shooters

Salmeh-beigom Shirazi lived during this era of freedom of religion, and she believed in Gnosticism. In 1751, she wrote a book, *Jame ol-Koliat* (*Opus of Principals*), with fourteen chapters on Gnosticism.

In one of his travelogues, *West of the Indus*, Justice William O. Douglas (1898-1980) of the United States Supreme Court referred to Iran as "a country I had visited so often it was a second home to me." He wrote, "The Qajar dynasty reached as far into the hinterland as it could, but the fastness of the mountains held treasures it could not reach. These treasures were the main tribes: the Kurds, the Lurs, the Bakhtiaris, and the Ghashghais. They remained independent and largely untouched by the oppressive hand of the central governments."

In the 2012 Olympics, women athletes from Iran participated in target shooting, archery, karate, and wrestling.

In the lower echelons of the society, the women of Iran have historically been economically independent. They have had a great share of the cottage industries. They designed and created the famous, sought-after Persian carpets. They created fabrics such as velvet, taffeta, lace, needlepoint, and seersucker, or *sheer* and *shekar* in the Persian language, meaning the texture of milk and sugar. The history of Iranian velvet and taffeta garments with gold-and-silver threaded brocade dates back to the second century C.E. Iran exported textiles to Europe and Rome, as garments for the kings and popes during the Medieval through the Renaissance eras.

A horse blanket from the Sassanid era, around fifth or sixth century.

For thousands of years, Iranian women have planted the cotton, spinned the wool and cotton threads, and made the most beautiful Persian carpets and fabrics.

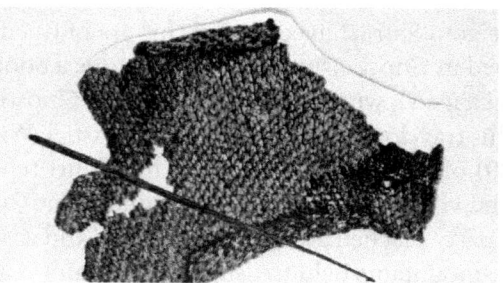

This piece of torn knitting and the crochet needle were discovered in an archeological dig in the Burnt City, third millenium B.C.E.

They created lavish gardens for the floors of every room and brought the beauty of nature inside their homes. Persian carpets have been a constant source of financial stability for their families and the Iranian economy.

The rice, tea, cotton, and silk farmers of Iran have almost all been women. They harvested crops and tended sheep, next to their men. These were the women that Princess Taj Saltaneh of the Qajar dynasty envied.[9]

I lived with these women in my tribal ancestral land of Luristan in the Zagros Mountains. As a young girl, I spent summer vacations at my grandparents' estates and rode horses into the mountains where these great women lived. I saw pride in their eyes and a graceful independence in their body movement.

---

9 Frye, "The Zands in Iran," http://richardfrye.org/files/The_Zands_in_Iran.pdf.

CHAPTER SIX

Return of Harems and Clerical Power: Qajar Dynasty (1798 – 1924)

THE QAJARS WERE another Turkic-Tartar tribe that Safavid Shah Abbas protected from the Mongols, giving them land in northern Iran. In return, the Qajars converted to Shi'ism and became the military power of the Safavids.

In 1795, their leader, Agha Mohamad Khan Qajar, launched a long, extremely brutal war against the Zands and took over Iran. He slaughtered or blinded every adult male in the city of Kerman and took 20,000 young women and children as slaves for his soldiers. When he died in 1801, his nephew, Fath-Ali Khan, inherited the throne and reestablished the absolute rule of the shah and clergy, in full force.

The Shi'a clergy came back to power with a vengeance and resumed receiving their monthly stipends from the treasury. Once again, the gender apartheid laws were reinstated and enforced through fear and intimidation. The culture of the royal harem also resumed with the blessings of the clergy establishment.

The Qajar put discriminatory tribal policies in place against women and the Iranian people. They gave the title of "prince" only to the sons of fathers who were Qajar, not the sons of Qajar mothers, because their connection to the Qajars was through a woman.

European imperialist powers found their way to Iran and began taking what they wanted through threats and bribes to the shahs and clergy. The Russian Tsars had a geopolitical interest in gaining access to the warm waters of the Persian Gulf for navigation and their military could march into Iran at any time, threatening occupation unless they got what they wanted. In 1813, Fath-Ali Shah Qajar signed the Treaty of Gulistan with the Russian Tsar. In 1828, he signed another treaty called the Treaty of Turkmenchay that gave another large part of the Central Asian territories of Iran to Russia. Iran was forced to pledge payments of 10 million rubles in gold to the Russian aggressors. The treaty stipulated the forced settlement of Iranian-Armenians to the Caucasus. Iran was also forced to capitulate to terms and concessions that compromised her sovereignty and economy, keeping the people poor and illiterate.

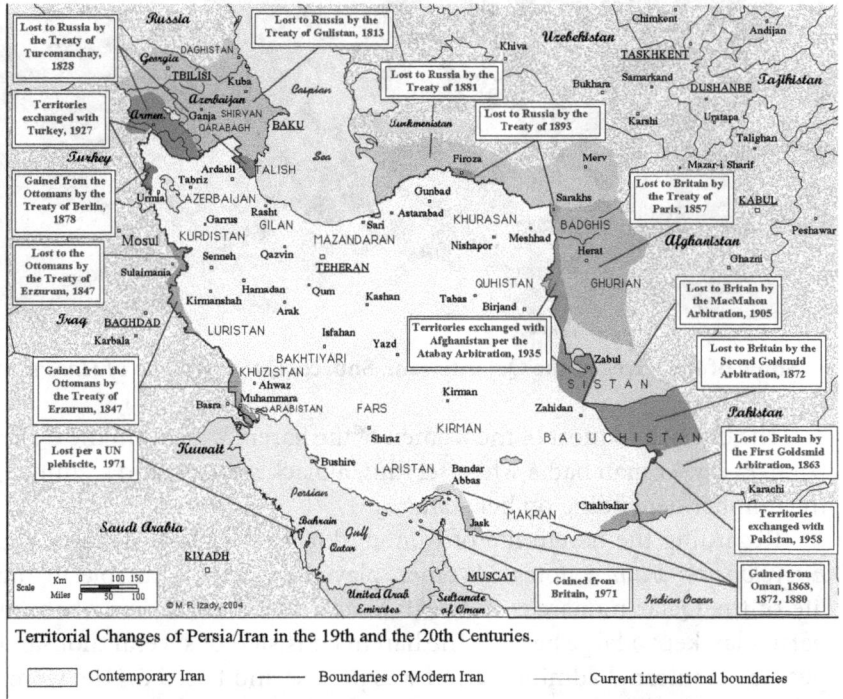

Territorial Changes of Persia/Iran in the 19th and the 20th Centuries.

☐ Contemporary Iran   ── Boundaries of Modern Iran   ── Current international boundaries

Herat, in northeastern Iran, was known as the "Key to India." With the Russians taking the northern territories of Iran, Britain took the province of Herat in 1884 and the rest of the Iranian territories after World War I.[1]

Unsuccessful in defending the territorial integrity of the country, Fath-Ali Shah Qajar asserted his power over his harem.[2] During his reign, he had over one thousand wives and fathered over two hundred children with over one hundred of his wives. He relied upon his large family of heirs to support the throne. More children meant the survival of the Qajar dynasty, which grew to one thousand Qajar family mem-

---

1 http://www.answers.com/topic/fath-ali-shah-qajar#ixzz1v9to1oIr/.

bers who became the controlling feudal lords of Iran.

Some of the wives of the Qajar harem. Source: *Qajar Women of Harem*

The queen and most of the women of the harem were from the Qajar tribe. Every woman had a white servant, a black servant, and a eunuch, the number depending on her status.

Regarding the harem life of women during the Qajar dynasty, the *Encyclopedia Iranica* notes, "Women played an important role in the life of the Qajar monarchs. Fath-Ali Shah and Naser-Al-Din Shah, in particular, kept a large harem. The harem consisted of several thousand people, its internal administration was precise and based on the women's rank. At the top of the hierarchy was the shah's mother, who was referred to as Mahd'eh Olya ("Sublime Cradle") and had, amongst other duties and prerogatives, the responsibility of safeguarding the harem's wealth, especially the jewels, which she administered with the help of female secretaries."

Encyclopedia Iranica continues: "The distribution of assignments and roles was often a matter of squabbling and dissension among women who sought material benefits for themselves, higher ranks for members of their own families, or precedence for their own children. Tension in the harem was increased by the fact that, until Naser-al-Din Shah's reign (1264-1313/1848-96), the Qajars did not have an effective rule of succession to the throne. As a consequence, the potential candidates' mothers would fight with all means within their power for their sons' eligibility."

Women carried out a wide range of activities, some ran the royal coffeehouse *(qahwa-kāna,* q.v.) inside the harem. Other women commanded the body of female sentinels who protected the king's nightly rest.

While women were responsible for activities in the harem quarters *(andarun,* q.v.), the links with the other parts of the palace *(biruni)* were kept by the eunuchs, for instance, women were usually in charge of the royal kitchens, but carrying and serving the food was the duty of eunuchs. Thus eunuchs, as well as tailors, physicians and both female and male relatives who regularly visited royal women, constituted an important channel of communication between the harem and the outside world. The frequent social entertainments, engagement and wedding parties, as well as picnics in the summer estates, were other occasions when women and men had chances to meet.³

(L) A painting named, "Islamic art," depicting the stoning of a woman, ordered by the clerics. (R) One of the young women of the Naser Al Din Shah Qajar's harem named Lady Sun

During the Qajar rule, a new architectural style of home building

---

3 Soltān-Ahmad Mirzā, 30.

was created to accommodate the lifestyle under the laws of the king and clergy in Iran. The residences of the rich aristocracy, the royal palaces, and mansions, were built in two sections: the *biruni*, or outside-house, was where men lived, socialized, and did business. *Andaruni*, the inside house, in contrast to the *biruni*, was a part of the house in which the women and children were free to move about without being seen by an outsider. Only the lord of the house, his sons and boys under puberty, were allowed in the *andaruni*. Women were never allowed to see the inside of the *biruni* and their communications with men were only through the eunuchs who were allowed in both sections.

Naser-al-Din Shah continued his predecessor's tradition of making alliances through marriages; consequently, he brought the daughters and cousins of notables and princes into his harem. He also married girls of humble background, some of whom enjoyed the favor of the Shah more than the Qajar princesses did. Though Naser-al-Din Shah could not boast a harem as large as that of Fath-Ali Shah, he married some hundreds of wives during his lifetime.[4]

Naser-Al-Din Shah Qajar

---

4 For a partial list of Nāser-al-Din Shah's women and children, see Al-Mamālek, 16-17.

According to *Encyclopedia Iranica*, "The Qajar women could not leave the harem precinct on their own, inside the harem they had daily entertainments such as music, dance, theatrical performances, and games. Qajar ladies, or at least some of them, also kept an interest in literary and artistic achievements. In fact, in addition to the religious instructions that they received from both male and female teachers, they were also taught calligraphy and poetry."

Nilofar Kasra, author of the Persian book, *Politics and Harem*, wrote about the prevalent caste system within the Qajar royal court. Some of the wives from upper-class families were superior to those from less lofty backgrounds, because they were the more formal spouses of the harem, while the wives from lower class families just "provided lustful nights and temporary leisure."

Kasra reveals: "Respectable wives used to parade in front of the Fath-Ali Shah, each morning, queuing behind each other proportionate with their father's wealth. If they had any request, they would just whisper in his majesty's ears."

She adds: "Most women in those harems were young, thus the king would have had them attend special training courses and study books in royal libraries." Kasra adds that "the parade was made customary during the reign of Agha Mohammad Khan, the founder of the dynasty."

One of the Qajar princesses, Zia-Ol-Saltaneh, was Fath-Ali Shah's daughter from his thirty-ninth wife, Miriam. Miriam, who was given the title of Shah-Beygom Khanom, was born Jewish, though she converted to Islam in order to marry the Shah.

Young royal Qajar princesses were tools of power for their royal father, brother, or whoever happened to be occupying the throne. Some of them were married off, only to be torn away from that marriage a few years later, then married off again, for the second husband to be killed, and for a third husband to take over, and so on.

Qajar women had a vital duty to keep their tribe in power and the bloodline of their ruling men pure, through their intermarriage within the Qajar clan. They were charged to ensure that the Qajar dynasty had the total loyalty and security of power through kings who had 100 percent Qajar Tartar blood from both parents' lineage. Therefore, the king—and no one else—decided their marriages.

The matriarchs of the harem managed the king's relationships with the women in his harem. In Naser al-Din Shah's harem, his mother, Malek-Jahan Mahd'eh Olya, was in charge and, after her death, his influential wife, Anis ol-Dowleh, took over. Historians write that harem matriarchs were influential not only in the harem, but in political decisions of the Shah and other high-ranking government officials. However, this was a strictly-kept secret.

Naser al-Din Shah was said to be bisexual. It is said that he spent his hours of leisure with his favorite young male companion, Malidjak, who was also influential and present at every event. On May 1, 1896, Mirza Reza Kermani assassinated the Shah while visiting the Shah Abdol Azim shrine on the eve of his royal jubilee.

The influential Maleka Jahan Khanum Qajar (1805-1873) was one of the most powerful Qajar women, with the official title, Malek-Jahan Mahd'eh Olya, meaning, "The World Queen Sublime Cradle." She had received the best education, just like all of the Qajar princesses. She was an artist and master in the art of calligraphy, as well as being well versed in literature. It was rumored that she had a love affair with Agha Khan Nouri, the prime minister of Iran after her son, Naser-al-Din Shah, assassinated Amir Kabir.

Mahd'eh Olya was one of the many granddaughters of Fath-Ali Shah, and became the first wife of her cousin, Mohammad Shah Qajar. She gave birth to Naser-al-Din Qajar and became the queen mother when her son grew up to become the Shah. She was one of the strongest women of the Qajar Dynasty. In 1848, given that there was no system of dynastic inheritance within the ranks of the Qajar kings, she wielded her power with the family council from within the harem to ensure the ascent of her son, Naser-al-Din Qajar, to the throne. Upon the death of her husband, Mohammad Shah, in 1848, Mahd'eh Olya moved to secure the throne for her son, who was traveling from the city of Tabriz to Tehran. She took the reins of the government and ruled Iran for 50 days. It is said that she was a better ruler than her father, husband, and son. She fired the regent, who was disliked by the people, lowered the people's taxes and gave them economic freedom.

She refused to see the Russian and British ambassadors, who had been using the Qajar kings. She told them, "My husband has passed away and my son is in the city of Tabriz. Therefore, until his arrival, I rule over Iran." When they suggested naming someone as the new regent, she told them that "she will personally choose a suitable regent whom the people will approve of, not the imperialists."

Mahd'eh Olya

Even when her son ascended to the throne of Iran, her interference in the affairs of the country continued. She believed that her duty was to preserve and ensure the strength and survival of the Qajar dynasty. She has been characterized as a cunning and accomplished woman of great political power and bearing a strong personality.

Women have ruled Iran and, from time to time, they have taken the position of regent for their underage sons. However, they were hardly recognized for their power and rarely, if ever, mentioned by Muslim historians. Some were even demonized as enemies of Islam.

Fath-Ali Shah's daughter, Malekzadeh Khanum, was married off to Mirzā Taqi Khan Amir Kabir, a fatherly figure, prime minister to Nasir al-Din Shah. Amir Kabir was one of the few principled men in the Qajar court who fought against corruption. He was a reformist who wanted to create a Western-style administration with a strong military. He proposed educating the people and creating industries. But Qajar nobility, including the queen mother, Mahd'eh Olya, and the clerical establishment, considered his reforms treason against the king and the Qajar family.

The queen mother influenced her son to dismiss his premier, Mirzā Taqi Khan Amir Kabir, and subsequently to have him assassinated in 1857.[5] Although he was her son-in-law, Mahd'eh Olya cared more about the survival of the Qajars on the throne of Iran than her own daughter and grandchildren. Various historians have candidly stated that, in fact, her son, the king, disliked her.

As queen mother, Mahd'eh Olya was not the only powerful woman in the harem. Later, Naser-al-Din Shah's favorite young wife, Anis-al-Dawla, also exerted her power to establish certain policies and even brought about the dismissal of her husband's regent, Mirzā Hosayn Khan Mošhir-al-Dawla, in 1873. The political successes of the leading women of the harem proved the power of the institution, resulting in policymakers and foreign diplomats seeking support from within the royal harem.

The Qajar harems also cultivated the courtly epistolary art and letters left by Naser-al-Din Shah's mother,[6] and three of his daughters[7] testified to their artisanship. All these women were also accomplished poets, and one of them, Taj al-Saltaneh, wrote her own memoirs (*khaterat*) about her father's harem.

Taj Saltaneh, meaning, "the crown of the throne," was one of Naser al-Din Shah's many daughters. She grew up in her father's harem until the age of thirteen, when her father chose Shoja'-ul Saltaneh, an adolescent, bisexual cousin, as her husband and married her off to him. She was sent to her father-in-law's home. Her marriage did not last long, as she was able to convince her father to grant her permission to divorce her husband. After her divorce, in 1873, she went to Europe for a few years for a Western education.

As a Qajar princess, she had experienced the injustices of her father's royal court and his rule against the people, especially women. She had questioned the unjust conventions that divided Iranian society and separated women, treating them as second-class citizens and depriving them of education.

---

5 q.v., Amanat, *Pivot of the Universe: Nasir al-Din Shah Qajar and the Iranian Monarchy*, 134-36, and passim, Ādamiyat, 666 ff.

6 Ibid., chap. 4, passim.

7 Mahdavi, 198, n. 169.

Influenced by the European women's movement of the mid-nineteenth century, she decided that Iranian women must also begin fighting against the gender discrimination of Qajar tradition. Upon returning from Europe, Princess Taj Saltaneh Qajar joined Iranian women activists and became an outspoken campaigner for gender equality, fighting her powerful brother and the Shi'a clergy. Taj also joined the underground Iranian women's movement.

In a critique of the unjust treatment of women and the tradition of the harem, Taj wrote her famous book of memoirs, *Khaterateh Taj Saltaneh*, or *The Memoirs of Taj Saltaneh* (1884 to 1914), about her childhood and youth when she lived in her father's harem and later in her husband's *andaruni* or the "inside house."[8]

In a 100-page introduction to Taj's memoirs, the contemporary Qajar historian, Abbass Amanat, wrote, "She admires the relationships between women and men in the villages who work side by side on the farm. She appreciates unveiled farm women and their productive lives...."

She wrote about her cold and calculating mother, who never showed any affection toward her, and a decadent, dictatorial father who loved her. She also wrote about her cohabitants in the harem as prison inmates. She gives an account of her own personal life as a depressed, discontented young woman, living with the hundreds of other young women who were her father's wives. Taj also wrote about how the Qajar kings administered the country's affairs, about the corruption within the royal court and the government, ruled directly and absolutely by her father and the *mullah bashi*, the rank-and-file of the clerical establishment. She describes her father's mishandling of Iran's foreign policy, the constant border attacks and the occupation and annexation of Iranian lands and territories by the Russian government and the constant interference of the Tsars in Iranian internal affairs. The British had dominated the southern borders of Iran in the Persian Gulf, sabotaging Iranian sovereignty in the south, where they created divisions among the local leaders and the central government by empowering separatists. The French did not hesitate to take every piece of Iranian archeological heritage without permission. Taj criticizes her father's incompetence and the inability of the Qajar kings to defend the sovereignty and the integrity of Iran.

She also describes the socioeconomic changes that she witnessed in Europe during her travels throughout the continent. She urges her father and the ruling men of Iran to adopt European-style modernity.

---

8 Taj Al-Saltana, *Crowning Anguish*, 59, 74, 83-84, 98-99, 209, 309-10, 328-32, 339-40.

She believed Iran was being left behind because of the domination of the clergy and her father's resistance to change that the people of Iran so desperately needed.

Princess Taj Saltaneh, at the age of ten, when she was forced to marry her cousin, and, at thirty-one, after her return from Europe.

Her book of memoirs is an exposé of Iranian society under the rule of the Qajar dynasty and the clerical establishment's domination. She wrote, "Iranian women are only permitted to have contact with animals; they are forbidden interaction with other humans. Their freedom is only in crying, wearing the black mourning dress or wrapping their body in the white coffin cloth. This is an example of the clergy who have had the permission of the kings, not morality leaders."

After the assassination of the Shah in 1896, formal protests of Iranians, especially women, who opposed the dictatorship of the kings and the Shi'a clerics, intensified. Taj's position, as a Qajar princess and the king's sister, gave her the power to speak out much louder and more effectively than the average "activists." Many women of the royal court were also educated writers and poets, but in the early days, none were brave enough to go public with their thoughts and demands.

Princess Taj became a prominent member of the *Anjoman Horriyyat Nsevan,* the Society of Women's Liberation, and a defender of the

Constitutional Revolution for modernity, sovereignty, and prosperity. Taj's memoirs cover thirty years of her life, extending to 1914 in the aftermath of the Constitutional Revolution of 1906.

Amanat wrote: "Had she not been a princess and the daughter of a strong king she would have been punished by the clerical power."

She was no different from the rest of the intellectuals who opposed the destructive power of the clerics. She wrote: "As I progressed in my studies day by day, my irreligiosity grew, until I was a complete naturalist myself."[9]

> Taj's perceived religious affiliation may reflect something of this popular image. As she tells us, her mother accused her of being a *Babi*, meaning of Baha'i belief, when she heard Taj's atheistic pronouncements. Whatever her religious sentiments, by the time she was writing her memoirs, Taj seems to have been experiencing a crisis of faith. With some trepidation, she had parted with the folk religion of her mother and nanny and opted for her mentor's irreligiosity. But her new convictions did not bring her spiritual satisfaction.
>
> "I suffered a loss for having knowledge," she declares with nostalgia for her old beliefs. "Lacking fear of anything and freed from any particular beliefs," she was transported to a hedonistic plane of living where "there was nothing in life I considered bad."[10]

In his introduction, Amanat explained: "Taj's memories are a sad story of a woman who reached a certain degree of political and sexual awareness yet lived and died inside the walls of prisons built by patriarchal values and practices. Her love affairs were not signs of liberation but anger and rebellion against those walls which finally crushed her without being slightly scratched."

During the reign of the Qajars, clerics denounced all forms of performing arts, such as music, singing, dancing, and acting, as *haraam*, or religiously prohibited and taboo according to *sharia*. This law was strictly enforced on women. Therefore, many people, especially women in the performing arts, were stigmatized and judged prostitutes or of low moral and social standing.

---

9 Taj Al-Saltana, *Crowning Anguish*, 309-10.
10 Taj Al-Saltana, *Crowning Anguish*, 98-99 (from editor's introduction.)

Music bands engaged in several types of entertainment, such as singing, dancing and comedy acts. Most of the time, boys dressed as women to depict female dancers in the group.

Iranian women, as seen by Americans (1830 - 1870). Images of women from Holland (far left), United States (second from left), Persia (second from right), and Spain (far right) on the label of a patent medicine (women's hair tonic) which "restores gray hair ... cures dandruff and prevents baldness." Source: The Library of Congress

Return of Harems and Clerical Power   85

Iranian woman of the Qajar era

CHAPTER SEVEN

Movement to Reform Shi'ism (1800s)

AFTER FIFTY YEARS of freedom of worship, separation of religion and state, and respect for the rights of all citizens in the Zand era, the people of Iran were not ready to go back to the dictatorial rule of the king and clerics.

Challenging the clerical establishment was not easy, but the ever-increasing power of the mosque and the dictatorial, dogmatic laws of the patriarchy had become intolerable, causing younger Iranian clerics to begin questioning their predecessors' traditional interpretations of the Qur'anic canons and *sharia* as enforced by the establishment.

In 1790, at the end of Zand era, a cleric by the name of Sheikh Ahmad Ehsaie preached a new interpretation of the Qur'an and the Prophet Muhammad's *hadith* (his statements and actions), spawning a movement called the Sheikhieh Order for the reformation of Shi'ism. By the early 1800s, Iranians began examining the issue of separation of religion from the state, spawning a movement for modernity and the burgeoning of the Constitutional Revolution of the late 1800s.

However, in a feudal society of illiterate peasants, the movement advanced slowly under the watchful eyes of the dictator Qajar Shah and his clerics. But many seminary students and young clerics wanted change from within the ranks and a cleric by the name of Báb (1819—1850) emerged from the Sheikhieh Order and claimed he was the Hidden Imam, a messiah awaited by the Shi'a. He launched a revolutionary movement, called Bábism. His followers were mostly young clerics, challenging the entrenched authority of the establishment. In Shi'ism, imam means "saint," not "cleric," as in Sunni Islam.

In the next decades, Bábist teachings, promoting a separation of religion from political and state affairs, the equality of men and women, and civil liberties, spread rapidly in Iran. In the late 1840s and early 1850s, however, the military forces of the Qajar monarchy massacred more than 20,000 Báb followers, known as Bábies, in bloody confrontations. Thousands perished across the country before the Qajar police arrested Báb and publicly executed him in the city of Tabriz, on July 9, 1850.

The execution did not quash the spread of the idea that religion should not comingle with politics and government, and that the existing interpretation of the Qur'an was fictional. Among the young followers of Báb was a cleric who called himself Baha'u'llah, meaning "Glory of God." In its earliest days, he had embraced the Bábi concept of faith and he had become the leader of the Bábi movement by announcing that he was the long-awaited Messenger of Allah. In this way, the original movement (1863-1892) developed into a new religion, known as the Bahá'í faith, and ended the movement of reformation of Shi'ism from within the establishment in Iran. The issue of reforming the establishment had failed. Ever since, the Shi'a clerical establishment has carried a grudge against the Bahá'í, and, since its rise to power in 1979, it has imprisoned, abused, harassed, and executed the Bahá'í minority in Iran.

The Bábi movement was genuine, dynamic, and progressive in calling for the emancipation of women. This attracted many Iranian women, who became some of the country's most prominent activists. The movement remained sectarian, and women's liberation became secondary to the religious movement and, therefore, lost the public support of many women. However, women in religion did not give up, continuing to challenge the powerful authorities of the king and the clerics. Among them was a woman who gave up everything—including her life.

Fatimah Zarin-Tadj or Tahereh Ghorrat Ol Ein (1814 -1852)

Professor Edward G. Browne, a British Orientalist (1862–1926), wrote: "In every cycle of history a woman like Tahereh appears in some country that will create an exceptional evolution. But such an exceptional event happening in Iran is more of a miracle."[1]

Her name was Fatimah Zarin-Tadj. She was born in 1809 in a devout Shi'a family in the city of Qazvin, one of the clerical centers of influence in Iran. Her father was a well-known Shi'a *alim*, or scholar, who

---

[1] Edward G. Browne, *A Traveller's Narrative*, vol. 2, p. 309.

had authored many books on religious laws and canons. At an early age, Fatimah learned to read and write from her father and began to study religion. In a few years, Fatimah became such a religious scholar that even her father and uncle were astonished by her scholarly opinions on the Qur'an and *sharia*. Her father is said to have been disappointed that all that talent and knowledge was wasted on a woman, and he wished she was a boy who would have illuminated his home and taken his place.

Fatimah Zarin-Tadj or Tahereh Ghorrat Ol Ein

Fatimah became a gifted poet, writer, and speaker, and in time, she became fluent in Persian and Arabic. Fatimah memorized the Qur'an and *sharia*. She achieved such mastery in theology that she was positioned as protector of the Qur'an, a title never before given to a woman. She received the title, *tahereh*, or "pure" in Arabic and became known as Tahereh. She did not limit her study of Islamic laws and theology to her father's and uncle's teachings. She sought out other interpretations of what she had read and learned. In fact, Fatimah was questioning the dogmatic interpretations of the ruling establishment. In her studies, Fatimah came across a new, more hopeful message that a few progressive, younger clerics were discussing about traditional interpretations from the pulpit and the emergence of a new divine revelation that promised progressive changes to Islam. At thirteen, Fatimah was forced to marry her cousin, a cleric, and she continued her teachings and studies after her marriage. She traveled with her husband to the city of Najaf, in modern-day Iraq, to further his education in Islamic laws. Fatimah used the opportunity to further her own research of the divinities in the city of Karbala, one of the holy cities of Islam in modern-day Iraq, but then in Iran. She finally decided to join the Sheikhiyeh movement, which presented a hope for change and a less dogmatic and more acceptable interpretation of Islam than previous preachings.

Thirteen years later, the family returned home, and she joined the Sheikhiyeh movement in Iran against her husband's wishes. Her marriage began to deteriorate and finally ended, due to her husband's opposition to the Sheikhiyeh movement and her refusal to give up her commitment to it. After their divorce, Fatimah had no choice but to return to her father's home and, per *sharia* enforced in Iranian society by the ruling clerical elite, gave custody of her children to their father. Fatimah became involved in the Sheikhiyeh school of thought and returned to the city of Karbala to join the new movement. Soon, she was a renowned teacher and missionary, who taught some of the best-known religious scholars of the time, who also became her followers. She had become one of the renowned *ulama*, or religious scholars and her words reached across the land, making her eminent throughout the Shi'a world. Nevertheless, Tahereh was not allowed to be seen by her followers, nor allowed preach from the pulpit, because of her gender. She had to speak from behind curtains.

When Báb declared he was the herald of a new Islamic doctrine, Fatimah was there to follow him, and she spoke out on the new doctrine, which not only removed her doubts but answered the questions she had always asked. She became a master in the teachings of the new faith and, armed with both the traditional and the new doctrines, she became a missionary for the new and progressive religion that had been promised and never delivered.

She began writing and publishing her opinions and speeches in poetry that circulated throughout the land. Her poetry resonated with people and became known as the people's words. She had arrived at a destiny that would make her spend the rest of her short life traveling to spread the word of the new tolerant faith that, above all, accepted women as equal partners to men.

Dr. Jacob Eduard Polak, an Austrian physician who lived in Iran between 1844 and 1865, wrote about Fatimah in the first volume of his book: "Among the followers of the Báb there was a woman, in the city of Qazvin, called Tahereh who was a poet and an intellectual of high caliber. This lady who was a religious scholar became Báb's follower, especially because Báb insisted in the equal rights of the women in his teachings. She even took her veil off in the Badasht conference of the followers of Báb."[2]

Fatimah opposed discrimination against women in the traditional interpretations of the Qur'an. She was against depriving women of education, knowledge, and sciences. Dr. Polak was right. In July 1848, Tahereh was the first Iranian Muslim woman who dared to take off her mandatory hijab, when she rose to speak in public at an all-male Bábi conference in the village of Badasht.

Some credit Fatimah with moving an old traditional religion to a new faith. Others believe that she was a god-woman who rose in defiance of intolerant clergymen. Many view her action as a first feminist statement toward the future Iranian women's movement in the constitutional passage for modernity. But Bahá'í adherents believe Fatimah was only a faithful believer of the new faith. Her presence without hijab, as she stood to deliver a speech, shocked the audience and her speech divided the followers of Báb. In her speech, Fatimah advocated for separating the new faith from Islam and its traditional laws, but conservative followers argued that it should remain a movement within Shi'ism, with the goal of slowly reforming traditional interpretations to modernize Islam. The effort to reform Shi'ism continues today, with many arguing that history reveals that an entrenched establishment of power will never be reformed and should simply be removed.

To defend the separation of the new faith from Islam, Fatimah said she would debate the leader of the opposition, Mohammed Ali Barfroush. He agreed to the debate, which Fatimah won, arguing that the laws and canons of the establishment were outdated and highly discriminatory. Fatimah was one of the original eighteen followers, chosen by the Báb. He gave her the title, Qorrat al-Ayn, meaning, "the light of the eyes."

Tahereh's fame, popularity, and strength made the institutional powers insecure. Her influence among the people, especially women, stoked fear in the hearts of the clergy, who had the Qajar kings fully under their control. They feared this woman of superior intellect and understanding of the Islamic canons and *sharia*. They feared the challenges put forward by this young woman, who had surpassed the scholars of Islamic theology. The establishment was afraid she could expose their fallacious teachings and challenge the power they had so surreptitiously devised. They expressed their concerns to the king and put fear of Tahereh in his heart, urging him to silence her or risk losing his throne. The decision

---

2 Polak, *Persien: Das Land und seine Bewohner* (1865), 294-5.

was made. Tahereh was arrested in Tehran at the age of 36, accused of being a Bábi. The clerics were not satisfied with just her imprisonment and demanded the king execute her. One year later, she was secretly killed, a silk scarf stuffed into her throat. Her body was thrown in a well, for fear of a rebellion by her followers.

During the time of her imprisonment, the king, Naser al-Din Shah Qajar, wrote her a letter, offering her amnesty if she married him and stopped her writings. She responded with a two-line poem that she wrote on the back of the king's letter, refusing his offer.

Professor Yousef Salim Chashti (1895–1984) a Pakistani scholar and writer stated: "Tahereh never fell in love with any man because she was in love with the faith that she preached until the last moment of her short life."[3]

The Qajar government pursued the followers of the Bábi faith relentlessly, in every village and town. The powerful Shi'a establishment issued a *fatwa*, or clerical ruling, against the Bábi people, and they faced mass persecution by government forces.

Like many Iranian women who had found refuge in the struggle for freedom and equal rights, Zeinab Rostamali had also converted to the Bábi faith. As a girl, Zeinab lived in a village near the city of Zandjan when government forces attacked. She joined her comrades in resistance and fought for her beliefs disguised as a boy for eight months, with only a sword and a brave heart. Her secret was revealed when she was killed in battle and her clothes were removed in the morgue.

As Taj Saltaneh grew out of the powerful king's house to repudiate her father, Fatima grew out of a powerful clerical house, to renounce her father. Two women, staunch defenders of human dignity, rebelled against the authoritarian powers of both religion and state and declared their opposition to their fathers' crimes against humanity.

---

3 Quoted by Sabir Afaqi in his book, *Tahirih in History*, p. 33.

CHAPTER EIGHT

Women for Sovereignty and Equality (1850s)

B Y THE 1850S, more than eighty percent of Iranian people lived as peasants, in a feudal system defined by the twin dictatorship of the crown and the mosque. The powerful institutions of the royal family—the Hezaar Famil, or the "One Thousand Families," and high-ranking ayatollahs—owned most of the lands as feudal lords. The majority of the population were mostly illiterate, poor laborers, earning very little, and taxed heavily by the clerical establishment.

The Qajar kings were weak, and the imperialists not only occupied Iranian territories as they wished, but they robbed Iran of her wealth, even taxing the citizens and collecting customs fees. Iran had no financial and economic system in place. The central government was comprised mainly of an inefficient, weak king, while foreign powers—mostly the British, Russians, and French—had manipulated various opportunists and governors of provinces to claim autonomy. In many cases, territories and provinces of Iran had been subdivided.

Between 1863 and 1914, imperialist powers seized control of the Royal Bank of Iran, the Mortgage Bank, the Indo-European Telegraph Co., the Karoon River navigation rights, the Iranian police department, Caspian Sea fishing rights, and the tobacco industries. They grabbed rights to build national railroad, irrigation, and telegraph systems, to navigate in all Iranian rivers, exploit Iranian mines and harvest her forests for seventy years.

The British foreign minister, Lord Curzon, had said: "These concessions were the deed of the ownership of Iran and the total submission of all its resources to the foreigners."

By paying the Qajar kings, the British businessman Lord Reuter obtained many of the new concessions, including the first oil contract in 1901.

The women of Iran during the Qajars lived without any human rights as the property of men under *sharia* law enforced by the powerful clerics. However, despite the threats of the clergy, they had become concerned about the future of their country and the complete colonialization of their homeland by foreign powers. They organized as activists, using every opportunity to protest, speak, and write about their concerns.

A magazine cover published by women activists in 1869, at the beginning of the constitutional movement. The magazine logo was the Lady Sun of enlightenment shining on the lion of Iran.

Women and the Tobacco Boycott

In 1889, the British ambassador, Sir Henry Drummond Wolf, invited Naser al-Din Shah Qajar to London. The British government spoke to him about another concession, allowing the British the right to cultivate and market Iranian tobacco. The Shah, who wanted his European travel expenses covered, agreed to the terms and conditions of the concession, in a deal with British Major Gerald Talbot.

On his return to Iran, Naser al-Din Shah signed the concession with Talbot's company, RJY, on March 20, 1890. The concession was for 50 years, and the Shah would receive £15,000 sterling a year, as well as one-fourth of the company's annual net profit. The people of Iran would get nothing.

Tobacco was one of the few products that Iran exported, and its trade was important for the Iranian economy. Tobacco farmers and traders were not happy that the British were taking over the last part of their economic sovereignty. They asked some clerics to talk the Shah out of this concession, but failed in their effort. The Shah refused to rescind his promise to the British.

Meanwhile, the Russian government protested and demanded another concession from the Shah—or else.

The Talbot RJY Company imported 200,000 foreign workers to Iran, taking jobs from Iranian farmers, laborers, and merchants. However, the most important impact was a building resentment by the clerical brass, who saw their power diminished by the influence that non-Muslim foreign laborers had in their sphere of religious influence. When the clerics couldn't force the Shah's hand, they campaigned against the non-Muslim foreigners, whom they called *najis*, or "unclean." They had the support of the farmers, merchants, and intermediaries, who handled the Iranian tobacco industry. From the pulpits, they preached to the poor who had lost their jobs and to the women whose husbands and fathers had lost their livelihoods. The tobacco movement grew into a national uprising and boycott.

In white scarves and black chadors, women of all classes marched to tobacco shops and destroyed British-produced tobacco. In a march against the RJY Company, women were in front of the crowds, demonstrating against the foreign intervention in their country.

In December 1891, during a Friday prayer, a prayer leader denounced the boycott of tobacco. A woman interrupted the cleric and yelled: "If, today, our men must sit at home, like women, we women will wear their pants and risk our lives by going into the town square for the restitution of our lost rights."[1]

Congregation members pulled the cleric off the pulpit and left to join the public protests.

The women of the royal harem also participated in the tobacco boycott, even though the Shah and his wives smoked *kalian*, or water pipes. Anis ol-Dowleh, the Shah's new young wife, collected the *kalian* and stored them away.

When the Shah asked for his *kalian*, his young wife replied, "The man who presided over our marriage, has prohibited the use of tobac-

---

1 Mostafa Elm, *Oil, Power, and Principal*, page 2.

co." [2]

A few days later, the Shah cancelled the tobacco concession with the British RJY company.

Princess Malik Taj

One of the more important Qajar princesses was Malik Taj, Najm al-Saltanah Qajar (1852 -1931). Like other women of her status, the private tutors her father's harem probably oversaw her childhood and education. And, like other Qajar women, she was married off at sixteen to a man her father, Naser al-Din Shah Qajar, chose.

After her father, first husband, and then her second husband died, Najm al-Saltanah Qajar inherited their wealth, becoming a key figure in the post-Qajar social history of modern Iran. She was a well-known philanthropist, endowing important projects, including the first modern hospital in Iran, Najmieh Hospital, inaugurated in December 1929 and named after her.

One of her sons, Dr. Muhammad Mossadegh Ol'Saltaneh Qajar, studied law in Switzerland and became a lawyer. He was later appointed by Mohammad Reza Shah Pahlavi to the position of prime minister of Iran in 1951, in a post he held for two years. He won notoriety for challenging the British-owned Anglo-Iranian Oil Company and the British government in order to nationalize the Iranian oil industry. The United States supported him for eighteen months, although British Prime Minister Churchill opposed his efforts.

(left) Princess Malik Taj Najm al-Saltanah Qajar and her last husband. (right) Her children after the modernity movement of the Pahlavi era. Prime Minister Mohammed Mossadegh Ol' Saltaneh Qajar on the left.

---

2 Ibid.

Ashraf Ol'Moluk, or Fakhr-Al'Dowleh (1883-1955), was another wealthy and influential Qajar princess. Her strength of character earned her the respect of Reza Shah Pahlavi, who is said to have commented: "The Qajar family only have one 'man' amongst them, and that is Lady Fakhr-Al'Dowleh." There are rumors that she was involved in a love affair with Reza Shah Pahlavi. They both denied the allegations. She was also the first Iranian woman to be recognized as a photographer in the Qajar era.

Lady Fakhr-Al Dowleh

In March 1848, an American Presbyterian missionary, Rev. John Cochran and his wife, Kathleen, opened the first girl's school in the city of Orumiyeh in western Iran. American Catholic missionaries opened similar schools in Tehran, Tabriz, Mashhad, Rasht, Hamadan, and other cities, and the children of religious minorities attended those schools. However, Shi'a clerics barred Muslim girls from attending the schools. In the 1870s, Muslim girls began attending the American school in Tehran, despite the clerics' orders.

In 1873, Nasser al-Din Shah Qajar traveled to Europe and on his return, his daughter, Taj Saltaneh, encouraged him to allow the American and French missionary schools to educate a limited number of Muslim girls. In 1881, despite the opposition of Russians, another group of Americans established the American Memorial School in Tabriz.

In 1906, during the Constitutional Revolution, scholar and writer

Malakeh Jahan, another one of Nasser-Al'Din Shah's daughters, wrote a book, *The Threatened Faith*, criticizing the clerics' constant control and meddling in governmental affairs.

Malakeh Jahan during the Qajar era (left) and the Constitutional Revolution (right)

At a time when the wealth of the country was under the control and ownership of the Shi'a clergy and the Qajar clan members, known as Hezar Famil, it was the women of the "One Thousand Families" who were educated, wealthy, and powerful enough to challenge and escape the wrath of the clerical establishment. These women were the intellectual pioneers who became the feminist activists and philanthropists in Iran's twentieth-century post-Constitutional Revolution.

The clergy was mostly influential in urban areas. The villagers were hard-working peasants who had nothing to offer the clergy. Peasant women followed customs that allowed them to work freely beside their men, as partners and not objects of control. They lived as they wished, while they lived in the rural areas, but in the cities and towns, they had to follow the strict rules of the clerical establishment and government. Both institutions of power understood that the lifestyle of people from Iranian tribes in the mountains made them autonomous from central governments. They had fought to maintain ancient traditions observed for millennia, regardless of who was in power in the country.

Maryam Amid was the daughter of Naser al-Din Shah Qajar's personal physician. Although she was prohibited from getting an education, her father secretly taught her to read and write. She learned French and read many of the French philosophers and writers. She learned the art of photography. One of Iran's first female journalists, she published an eight-page magazine for women in 1897, but soon after, clerics protested its publication and it was shut down. Later, she established a covert girls' school in her home.

Maryam Amid, Iran's first female journalist and photographer

As the underground Baha'i movement continued to grow, secular movements for modernity slowly flourished with the help of a small group of men and women intellectuals.

Mollafezeh was a literary scholar and calligrapher who earned her living, writing manuscript copies of books. She wrote a book, *Kashf al-Qeta*, with her interpretations of *sharia*. In February 1834, her book became popular with women.

Kolsum Borqani was born in 1809, in the city of Qazvin, and was a religious scholar by age twelve. In addition to studying *sharia*, Kolsum did extensive research in civil laws, earning the title of jurist consult, giving her the authority to argue against the establishment and develop her own interpretation of the Qur'an and *sharia*. Kolsum was a writer, a licensed advocate attorney in civil law, and eventually, a traveling teacher and legal advisor to women. In 1851, she founded a women's center for religious studies to which she donated her works, including her books and essays on civil rights.

In the 1840s and 1850s, Khadijeh Khanoum, known as Molla Badji, a title for women tutors of the harem, was a tutor to the princesses of Naser al-Din Shah Qajar's harem and companion to Shokooh Saltaneh, one of the Shah's many wives. She was a well-educated and enlightened woman. Critical of how women were treated in the harem, she taught women to stand up for their rights.

Khadijeh Khanoum was an independent woman, married to one of the Shah's friends, Bagher Khan Shirkesh. A few years later, when her husband married five more wives, she took both of her children and left for Mecca. Upon her return, Khadijeh Khanoum left her husband and continued to teach at the harem, single-handedly raising her two children. Khadijeh Khanoum raised her daughter, Bibi Khanoum Esterabady, to become one of the members of the Ladies' Secret Society, a champion of women's rights and an integral part of the Constitutional Revolution for democracy. (This will be discussed at length in another chapter.) Bibi Khanoum was one of the earliest women's rights activists, establishing the first official girls' school in Iran.

As academics and educators, Bibi Khanoum Esterabady and her mother taught more than just reading and writing to the women of the harem. In fact, their educational efforts were instrumental in making activists out of many Qajar women, motivating them to join the Constitutional Revolution and the Ladies' Secret Society and to continue the fight against clerics after the Constitutional Revolution.

As the women of Iran began to speak up against the social laws that discriminated against them, the patriarchal powers stood against them. In 1888, one such public opposition came in the form of a small booklet, *Makr'eh Zanaan* (*Women's Trickery*), written by an anonymous writer, said to be one of the Qajar princes. The book argues women are like children and must be taught to obey the rules set for them by society. For example, it said, "...the only reason for marriage is men's sexual gratification. Women must be quiet and obedient at all times, except in bed. Women must be silent unless they are permitted to speak. The duty of a woman is to serve her husband and ensure his comfort. A woman must never make any requests from her husband. It is the absolute obedience to her husband that secures the salvation of a woman. Women must move as slowly as old people do..."³

But women were not going to stay silent.

Certainly, Bibi Khanoum was not going to leave the book unanswered.

Bibi Khanoum

Bibi published her own book, *Ma'ayib al-Rijal* (*Men's Shortcomings*). She wrote: "The genius of the world and unique writer of our times, seems strangely bereft of his senses. He should have first corrected his own vices and then given us advice. One who has no share of existence, how can he inspire life? ...He regards himself as 'Westernized and civilized,' but in fact he is not even 'quasi-civilized.' Does he not know that Europeans treat their women like flowers, and women freely associate with men?"

Bibi Khanoum concludes, "...the writer's understanding of keeping women in their place implies the continuation of total subjugation of women..."⁴

The reference to the author's Westernization meant that he must have been from the so-called Qajar intellectuals influenced by Europeans. Strangely, European women had very few rights at the time, and they had only been able to claim a few rights in some parts of the Western world.

As a member of the Ladies' Secret Society, Bibi Khanoum continued

---

3 Mathers. *Eastern Love*, 1904.

4 These two works were later published by Hasan Javadi, an Iranian author and historian, as "Two Qajar Essays on Men and Women: Ta'dib al-Nisvan and Ma'ayib al-Rijal," in Washington, D.C., in 1992.

her fight after the Constitutional Revolution of 1888 to 1906. She was supported by the Association of the Patriotic Women, or *Anjomaneh Nesvan Vatan-khah*, which made it their task to collect the booklets written against women and burned them in a bonfire in the city square.

The main objective of the activists was to educate girls and women. Bibi Khanum opened one of the first girl's schools in Tehran, called *Doshizegan*, "The Young Girls." Both her daughters, Afzal and Moluk, also became teachers, like their grandmother and mother. Bibi never stopped writing articles in defense of women's rights.

Alamtaj 'Jaleh' Qa'em-Maghami (1883-1947) was a revolutionary poet during the crucial period of the constitutional movement. She changed the style of women's poetry from general advice to revolutionary protest. Some say that Jaleh's poetry captured the transition from the era of the harem to the period of modernity.

First girls' school in 1890

Fluent in Arabic and French, Tooba Azmoodeh (1881-1939) was one of the few highly-educated women of Iran during the Constitutional Revolution of 1906. She established one of the first girls' schools in her own home in Tehran. Although mobs targeted the school and threatened and abused her, she fought to expand it. In her school, she educated many of the most prominent women of the Ladies' Secret Society, after the Constitutional Revolution.

During the constitutional movement of the 1890s, Mahrokh Goharshenas (1871-1938) created the Association for the Recognition of Women's Rights. She also established a secret girl's school, even without the knowledge of her husband. She said, "When my husband learned about the school, he was very upset and kept telling me that in the next world, when your father asks me why I let his daughter participate in activities contrary to religion and virtue, what shall I tell him?"

A few years later, in 1903, Tuba Roshdieh set up a school for girls with four classrooms, in a detached section of her family home. The clerical establishment predictably threatened her and closed the school four days later.

CHAPTER NINE

Women and the Constitutional Revolution (1850s – 1909)

BY THE END OF THE 1800s, the corruption of the Qajar king and his royal court had spun out of control.

Iran faced a financial crisis. Its citizens, mostly peasants, lived in abject poverty amidst the corruption of feudal lords who were part of a power-circle of the King and the clerical establishment. Women were second-class citizens, forbidden to learn to read and write. Neither was there an education system for men, who were also generally illiterate. Some men were only allowed to learn to read the Qur'an and, even then, only in Arabic, since the translation of Qur'an to Persian was forbidden until the 1950s.

The Shah gave long-term economic concessions, such as tobacco farming, industries, and mineral development rights, to foreigners. European companies and governments had taken control of Iran's customs administration, taxes, and nascent banking system. Iran gave its wealth away to Europeans, was plundered by the French, the Dutch, and Belgians, but mostly the British and Russians, who took all they could as reimbursement for payments made to the personal coffers of the Shah.

The Qajar dynasty began to crumble from within, beginning in the 1840s and continuing through the end of the century.

Education was only accessible to the children of the One Thousand Family feudal lords, the Qajar princes and princesses. The younger members of the privileged One Thousand Families hailed from Qajar nobilities. Iranian teachers taught them, inside and outside of the harem, and they were educated in Europe, where ideals of European constitutionalism inspired them. One second-generation heir to Qajar power, Princess Taj Saltaneh, identified as Iranian, but not as a member of the Qajar tribe.

However, the main goal of the new generation of Qajar families was to safeguard their rule over Iran. To stay in power, they were willing to adopt a Western-style constitutional monarchy, and reduce the power of the Shah, but the clerics refused to cooperate.

Meanwhile, taxation without representation had taken its toll on the bazaar, which had always been the backbone of the Iranian economy. In a way, the bazaar had been the Wall Street of the Iranian economy, influencing trade, jobs, and financial transactions for hundreds of years. The merchants of the bazaar had been supporters of the clerical establishment, but eventually, they began to organize and support the opposition to the twin power of the crown and the mosque. The king was raising taxes, not for the people, but for the expenses of his harem and his royal court's trips to Europe.

During that period, the Shi'a clergy also faced opposition from within, against the established interpretation of the Qur'an and *sharia*. A new generation of religious scholars had different interpretations and questioned the validity of *sharia* as well as its divinity. They opposed the rule of the clerics in Islam, and they looked at Islam narrowly as a personal moral compass, not a way of life for the country. They opposed religious and clerical meddling in politics and governance.

Thus, when Seyyed Ali-Mohammad Shirazi (1819-1850), the high-ranking cleric known as Báb (the gate to the Hidden Prophet), claimed to be the vessel that had come to begin the messianic movement, the younger generation of clerics followed him. Bábism marked the beginning of a movement to reform Shi'ism for the modern world. However, they faced the wrath of an establishment that would not tolerate change. There was only one way the nation would establish a constitutional monarchy: *revolution*.

A tight group of intellectuals, including women, began the country's constitutional revolution.

It's not clear exactly what year a brave group of women founded the Constitutionalist Women's Association, but it was sometime in the late 1880s that this group of women writers, journalists, and French-educated holders of nobility launched their new organization. They were patriotic women, opposed to British and Russian domination of their homeland, and they wanted a French system of government that removed the clergy's influence on government and their private lives. All that spelled a constitutional system.

They faced many challenges. The old clerical institution was losing power, but it was still influential and persistent. An unknown historian wrote: "While the revolution helped weaken the old order of twin pillars—the Qajar monarchy and the Shi'a clerical establishment—it did not remove the nobility."

One of Nasser Al-Din Shah Qajar's daughters, Malake-ye Iran, emerged as a leader of the new movement. Her husband was a member of the Society of Brotherhood, a group of pro-modernity intellectual Sufis, practicing a mystical interpretation of Islam. Despite its name, the Society of Brotherhood included men and women. Malake, a musician, writer, poet, and speaker, often addressed the meetings. She composed a song with her own music for the organization. She took photos with her two daughters, also members of the order, without hijab. When Russians bombed the first constitutional parliament in 1910, her house was also attacked by the order of her cousin, Mohammad Qajar, the Shah.

The constitutional movement had three goals: modernity, sovereignty, and prosperity. The constitutionalists aspired to remove foreign intervention in Iran, limit the power of the Shah, separate the mosque from the government, and establish a parliamentary secular system to give the people a voice in the affairs of the state. Originally, intellectuals kicked off the movement, but later, bazaar merchants and clerics tried to reverse the original intention of the movement from a constitutional monarchy to the absolute rule of religious laws, as Ayatollah Khomeini eventually established in 1979.

Slowly, the war of words and intellectual opposition turned into a physical war, because the men in charge refused to relinquish any of their power.

In the mid-1800s, a constitutional revolution began, finally succeeding in 1906. Iranian women played a large part in its success, but their roles were largely erased from the narrative. They circulated information, participated in demonstrations, wrote articles, and published magazines to enlighten not only women but also men. The women of the Shah's harem challenged him, as did activists, such as Fatimeh, who were brave enough to challenge the clerical establishment. It was not only Iranian men who brought the Constitutional Revolution of 1906 to fruition but also militant women from all social echelons—poor peasant women and rich princesses—and ethnic and religious minorities and majorities, who participated and fought alongside their armed men. They provided food, arms, boots, and blankets. When needed, they attacked government establishments and the estates of feudal clergy.

In an August 1890 issue, *Qanoon*, a monthly Iranian journal published in London included the following passage: "Women make up half of any nation. No plan of national significance will move forward unless women are consulted. The potential of a woman aware of her human essence, to serve in the progress of her country is equivalent to that of 100 men."

In Tabriz, militant women joined armed men, attacking government warehouses to get food for revolutionary soldiers.

In its August 6, 1904, evening issue on the women's demonstration in front of the government buildings, a Tehran newspaper reported, "One of the women participating in today's protest rally who was apparently pregnant, gave birth to a baby girl with the help of the crowd who carried her in to a house and helped her deliver her daughter that they named Mashruteh (meaning Constitution)."

Around the country, bands of women, including the wives of high-ranking men, armed with bats, protected pro-constitution speakers from thugs sent by the clerics. Women from all faiths—Muslim, Christian, Jewish, Baha'i, and Zoroastrian—organized and joined the strikers for the constitutional movement.

Prince Kamran Mirza, the vice regent, was a vocal opponent of the constitutional movement. A group of women confronted him in the street and told him that he and his cronies had run out of time, and they had better join the movement. According to *Sur-Israfil Magazine* (*The Horn of Israfil*), "Mrs. Jahangeer, the aunt of the martyred journalist Mirza Jahangeer Shirazi, stopped Muzafir al-Din Shah Qajar's carriage on the street and advised him to endorse the constitution or else."

Progressive daily and weekly publications, such as *Sur-Israfil, Habl ol'Matin, Qanoon, Soraya*, and *Neda'yeh Vatan*, published articles by men and women writers, calling for a constitutional governmental system and gender rights. In its July 1906 issue, the *Habl ol'Matin* daily evening edition published an article by an outspoken woman, Mohtaram Eskandari, about women's rights to health and medical care, education, employment, and technical training. Mrs. Eskandari later established the first Communist Party in Iran.

The movement included women from all ranks, such as Zeinab, born into a poor peasant family, in a village in the northwestern province of Azerbaijan. Her birth date is not known, but her life has been celebrated as a heroine of justice. People had given her the title of *Dehbashi Zeinab* (Village Leader Zeinab). In Tabriz, she joined her sisters-in-arms in a revolt for bread. Many women were reportedly killed. Later, she traveled to Tehran in the tobacco uprising against the British. When the Tabriz bazaar was closed during the tobacco concession, and the government agents forced merchants to open their shops, Dehbashi Zeinab and a group of women rushed to close down the bazaar.

In an article in *Baya* magazine, women's rights activist Nooshin Ahmadi Khorasani wrote: "When a group of men in one of the city's tea houses were complaining about the poor living conditions and the government's role in their misery, Zeinab stood up and told them: 'If you men do not have the courage to make the abusers pay for their crimes, if you are afraid to cut off the hands of the thieves and robbers from what rightfully belongs to us, and the homeland, wear our Chadors, and hijabs, and stay at home and never brag about your manliness and masculinity. We will do the fighting against the aggressors.'"

The active involvement of the women of Iran during the Constitutional Revolution of 1906 and beyond did not go unnoticed by men. Many writers and poets wrote articles, acknowledging and praising the tireless efforts of the women activists. In an article in *Qanoon* newspaper, Mirza Malkom Khan, a political activist in the constitutional movement, wrote: "The rush of women to participate in the movement of humanity is surprising. The state of affairs is such that many of our noble women have exceeded men in defending and promoting humanity. Women have understood the meaning and advantages of humanity much better than men or rather non-men."

As the constitutional movement was beginning, Mah-Soltan Amirsahi was born in 1873. As a young woman, she established a school, *Talimeh Zanon* (Teaching of Women) that became the target of the religious cabal. The clerics threatened her students, and the sign above the school's door was repeatedly vandalized. Mah-Soltan joined the Constitutionalist Women's Association and, in a demonstration organized by the National Women's Association, she raised a banner that read, "INDEPENDENCE or DEATH."

Dor'rat ol-Mo'ali was one of the organizers of the women's groups protesting the British Tobacco Treaty. She encouraged the women of Iran to boycott foreign products. Dor'rat opened her first girls' elementary school and later the first secondary girls' school in 1904, before the constitutional revolution came to fruition. Her birth date is unknown but she is known to have died in 1923.

When the revolutionary militias fought hunger or needed clothes, boots and shoes, women activists stepped forward to help. They raised funds by baking cookies and soliciting money from their friends, family, and husbands, to support the ragtag revolutionary militias. Many went to merchants and big feudal farms to get food and supplies for the soldiers.

One of these women's groups was the Seven Sisters Brigade, led by Bibi Shah Zainab and seven devoted comrades who carried rifles under their chadors and supported the cause of the constitutional revolutionary militia.

Bibi Shah Zeinab with her Colt, and a statue made in her honor

When Naser-Al-Din Shah signed another concession with the Russians, the people protested. They went to the merchants who ran the bazaar and asked them to close their shops in protest. The merchants refused. In Tabriz, Bibi Shah Zeinab and her armed Sisters Brigade persuaded the merchants at rifle point that closing their shops would be beneficial to them and the country. Merchants closed their shops and went home.

The Seven Sisters Brigade raided the warehouses of the rich feudal estate owners, mostly high-ranking ayatollah clerics. They stole flour, chickens, vegetables, goats, and sheep from the estates of those who refused to support the revolutionaries. They were master markswomen and were armed with Winchesters under their chadors.

These women also provided shoes, blankets, and rifle ammunition. Their network provided stables for the soldiers to rest. They staffed the trenches, guarding them while the soldiers rested, and put gunpowder in the guns.

During the constitutional revolution, Wladimir Ivanow was a Russian orientalist in Iran. In his book, *Fifty Years in the East*, he wrote, "I have the photo of a group of about 60 veiled Iranian women, armed with rifles. They guarded one of the trenches."[1] According to various accounts, eight years before the constitutionalist victory, the Seven Sisters Brigade, led by Bibi, attacked the estate of one wealthy cleric. Although men were guarding the silo, full of freshly-harvested grain, the Seven Sisters succeeded in confiscating the wheat and delivering it to a baker, to provide bread to the militia.

Bibi Maryam Bakhtiari

Bibi Maryam Bakhtiari (1873-1948) hailed from the Bakhtiary Lur tribe in the city of Isfahan, and was a skilled rider and master markswoman. She is said to have bravely fought against foreign invasion. During the constitutional movement, she rode overnight and snuck into Tehran, hiding on a rooftop, across the street from the headquarters of the Russian Cossacks, a group of East Slovic people. All night, she surveilled the movements of Russian soldiers, until her comrades joined her in the morning. They fought opponents of the constitution and took

---

1 Daftary and Taurus, *Fifty Years in the East: The Memoirs of Wladimir Ivanow*.

the capital city back from them. After this battle, her tribesmen gave her the title, *Sardar,* or Commander.

Two years after the success of the Constitutional Revolution of 1906, Sardar Bibi Maryam Bakhtiari and her sister, Bibi Leyla, commanded a column of the Bakhtiari cavalry, taking back Isfahan from the anti-constitution forces of Mohammad Shah Qajar.

During World War I, forces of the Western Allies occupied Iran, and political activists and intellectuals hid in Sardar Bibi Maryam's house in Isfahan. In her diaries, she wrote: "The only reason that the women have been left behind is because we are illiterate and have no knowledge of our rights. If we knew why we were created, we would have fought for our rights. We now think that we are here to satisfy men's sexual urges or to be their slaves…"

During the Constitutional Revolution, Iranian women cut their long hair to join the militia's soldiers of freedom, disguised as boys. There is no report of how many women were soldiers, but notable Iranian historian and reformer Ahmad Kasravi wrote in his book, *The History of the Constitutional Revolution,* "The newspaper *Heil ol'Matin* reported that among those killed by order of the Shah, during the last week's clashes with the constitutional forces, were 21 women in men's clothing. The bodies were therefore transferred to the women's morgue."

He also wrote, "One day in the Mirza Mousa Mosque, a woman listening to the cleric on the pulpit, stood up and said 'why is the government borrowing money from the foreigners? Are we dead? I am a maid and I am willing to pay one Tuman, Iranian curency. All the women are willing to pay.' These kinds of outbursts by women were common during the revolution."

On January 10, 1906, the Shah's carriage was on its way to the home of a wealthy aristocrat, when it was blocked by a multitude of women marching in the streets. One of the women read a statement addressed to the king that said: "Beware of the day when the people take away your crown and your mantle of governance."

Another woman, Farangeez, bravely fought Russian soldiers who had occupied her village in Azerbaijan, forcing villagers to flee from their homes and hide in the valley.

Later she said, "We fled to the valley but after a whole day, the children of village were hungry, thirsty and had nothing to eat. With my father and brother, we returned to the village and upon seeing the Russian soldiers, I was enraged and attacked them with the ax in my hand. I killed one and injured another, arresting him for the authorities to pick up. I could not let the children go hungry."

Farangeez became the hero of her village, adorned today with her statue in the center of the village square.

Farangeez

These women were peasants, tribeswomen, and the wives of butchers, bakers, carpenters, and yes, some of the elites. They were of all faiths and ethnic groups. They made up the Ladies' Secret Society named the "Patriotic Women of the Homeland." They worked underground and in secret for fear of the cleric's retaliation.

By 1909, the Qajar dynasty had lost power, but the Qajar nobility, members of the One Thousand Families, were the only educated, well-traveled elite and they had the means, connections, and knowledge to become politicians in the new, modern Iran. The revolution was not as satisfying for the women of Iran, but it did bring Iran to the threshold of modernity. It opened the doors for ordinary people to participate in the socio-economic and political affairs of their country.

CHAPTER TEN

Post-Constitutional Revolution: War Between Women and Clergy (1907)

THE REVOLUTION SUCCEEDED. Mozaffar ad-Din Shah Qajar signed the country's first constitution on July 15, 1906. New laws were written for the establishment of a constitutional monarchy and a parliamentary secular government of the people.

When the time came to relinquish clerical power, a small group of clergy who had joined the revolution turned against implementation of a constitutional government. They misrepresented the goals of the revolution, in large part to oppose the separation of the government and the mosque.

When arguments, intimidation, threats, and fights did not help, the clergy resorted to violence by issuing *fatwas* for the killing of the constitutionalist leaders. A *fatwa* is a religious ruling. The Islamic clerics issued *fatwas* declaring their enemies apostates in order to put a virtual death sentence on their adversaries, because renouncing Islam is punishable by death. It was a hit order against the person named in the *fatwa*. Years later, Ayatollah Khomeini issued a *fatwa* against the author Salman Rushdie for the book, *Satanic Verses*.

Sheikh Fazlollah Noori (1843-1909) was an ayatollah notorious for his fierce opposition to the Constitutional Revolution, and he believed that the new Majlis, or the Parliament, should have been Islamic and the government based on sharia and the teachings of the Prophet Muhammad. Today's Islamic regime in Iran relies on a vision Ayatollah Noori forged for Islamic rule, based on the teachings of Ayatollah Mohammad Baqer Madjlesi, imported to Iran from Lebanon by the Safavid Turks in the sixteenth century. He protested establishing an educational system, especially for girls. He opposed women being allowed to dress like men and insisted that the Majlis should be a place for promoting the prescribed or that which is acceptable (*amr e beh marouf*) and prohibiting the forbidden (*nah ye ze monker*). This type of system encouraged vigilantism against any citizen deemed to violate the rules of clerics.

Following methods of intimidation used by the clerical establishment, Noori incited mobs and dispatched his hired hoodlums to assassinate constitutionalist leaders. He accused the members of the Majlis and the cabinet of apostasy and atheism and issued a *fatwa*, calling for their murders. In a published pamphlet he wrote, "They are secret Bobies, of Baha'i faith, and *koffar al-harbi* (warlike pagans) whose blood must be shed by the faithful."

Ayatollah Noori allied himself with the new king, Mohammad Ali Shah Qajar, who had opposed his father's signing of the new constitutional document and wanted to return to the old dictatorial rule. Under the Qajars, the Russian military had been stationed in Iran to protect the ruling class and its own interests. Together, Mohammad Ali Shah Qajar and the clergy establishment had the Russians stage a military coup against the newly-established Iranian Parliament in 1907, bombing the parliament and killing the legislators.

Constitutionalist forces had no choice but to march back into Tehran, arresting Sheikh Fazlollah Noori. They tried him under the new laws of the constitution and he was found guilty of treason and sentenced to death. In July 1909, he was hanged. Today, the Islamic regime of Iran considers Sheilk Fazlollah Noori a martyr for his opposition to the establishment of parliamentary democracy in Iran.

In an effort to accommodate the clerical establishment and prevent more bloodshed, constitutionalist leaders agreed to allow them to join the new government as members of the Majlis, giving them control of family law. The civil code became secular but family law, including the rights of women and children, remained within the domain of *sharia*, under clerical control.

The revolution, meant to usher in modernity, sovereignty, and prosperity for all, failed half of the population. It betrayed the women who had been an integral part of its success in the combat trenches and in the intellectual war of ideas; their equal rights were omitted from the new constitution. Although they had eagerly participated in the revolution, little changed in the lives of women. They remained second-class citizens under the laws that placed women in the same category as convicted criminals, those with mental illness, and minors. The Foundation for Iranian Studies wrote, "Women were told their education and training should be restricted to raising children, home economics and preserving the honor of the family." The new constitution denied women the right to education and participation in the new political process, including the right to vote or to run for political office.

It was easier for the revolutionary leaders to get Mozafar Al-Din Shah Qajar to sign the document relinquishing his absolute powers to the people than getting the clerical establishment to stop interfering in the affairs of the government and grant women equal rights.

The clergy establishment had succeeded in manipulating the constitutional laws in favor of their participation in the parliamentary process. With their power at the pulpit, they guaranteed themselves a large number of the seats in the Majlis, and therefore, were able to bar women from participating in the political process for years to come.

The clergy blocked the efforts of women to win new rights in the Majlis. As history proves, every effort to change the status of women was received with hostility and consequently refused by the people's house, the Majlis. Iranian women were left with no recourse. The Shi'a clerical establishment had hijacked the constitutional system that the people—and women—of Iran had envisioned for Iran. They maintained their power and prevented the separation of government and mosque. Men abandoned the cause of women and ultimately sold them out to the clerics.

This betrayal made the women of Iran even more determined to defeat the clergy. A war between the women of Iran and the clergy establishment had begun.

* * *

On December 14, 1905, a group of women protested at the holy mosque of Abdol-Azim in southern Tehran to demand their rights, when they suddenly came under attack by armed men sent by the government. The women ran to the rooftops and showered the attackers with rocks. The government arrested Sheikh Mohammad Vaez, a moderate pro-constitution cleric, but a few days later, on January 9, 1906, a group of women stormed the cell where he was being held and freed the cleric. The following day, the regent of the king, Einoddoleh, announced that Iranian women were all under house arrest and any woman seen outside on the streets would be arrested, per the ordinance.

***

The first women's organization that actively joined the constitutional movement did not appear until 1890, but it was after the Constitutional Revolution of 1906 that it formally began its new activism. Disappointed by the feebleness of the new constitutional leadership and non-clergy members of the Majlis in confronting the clergy establishment, women decided to organize for their rights. However, since they would be the target of the clerical wrath, they organized underground as secret societies.

In a protest rally, a woman rose and sang a song. No one knows her name, but Iranian women today continue to sing this song.

> Sad Daughters of Cyrus, lament for how long?
> Under men's thumbs, prisoners for how long?
> My dear,
> Under men's thumbs, prisoners for how long?
>
> Daughters of Sassan, in such a society?
> Silence till when, oh women of Iran
> My dear,
> Silence till when, oh women of Iran
>
> No one speaks, nor thinks of the good and evil
> Oh intelligentsia of Iran, are women not human?
> Oh compatriots
> Are women not human?
>
> You who are veiled, how long will you remain dormant?
> By the Sheikh, such havoc is wreaked, Country is ruined and its nation is asleep
> O women of the nation,
> It is high time for a revolution[1]

The song referred to the "daughters of Sasan," for the Sasanian dynasty in Iran between 224 B.C.E. and 651 C.E, before the occupation of Arab Muslims.

It was on January 20, 1907, that a group of activist women launched

---

[1] Aasoo, https://www.youtube.com/watch?v=ksWRXIi_3rY (text is in another language).

the organization of *Anjomaneh Serrieh Banovon* (The Ladies' Secret Society), to formally declare war against the clergy establishment. Underground branches of the Ladies' Secret Society grew throughout the country, as the women of every class and status joined the struggle. The village and city women, young and old, powerful and powerless all joined under the banner of the Ladies' Secret Society to liberate themselves from the clerics' rule over their lives.

On March 2, 1907, *Edalat* (Justice) daily newspaper reported that the matriarch of Tabriz, Haji Alaviyeh Khanum, a patriotic woman, had delivered a strong speech regarding the boycotting of foreign products. She had urged women, "Patriotism means that you rather do without, than buying imperialist products..." To organize their protests, women in Tabriz usually met at Alaviyeh Khanum's home.

On July 27, 1907, The Protesters, an anti-constitution group, published their demands on the rights of women, stating, "The inauguration of women's education and girls' primary schools is along the same lines as the consumption of alcohol (forbidden in Islam) and the promotion of whore-houses."

On October 1, 1907, The Ladies' Secret Society sent an open letter to the Majlis, later published in the *Vatan* (Homeland) daily. In the letter, they demanded an immediate amendment to the constitution, saying that if delegates proved incapable of doing their duties, they should resign and hand over their jobs to women.

Meanwhile, that year, Bibi Vazirof opened *Madresseh'yeh Doushizegan* (The Young Ladies School). She was forced to close the school, but she bravely re-opened it in her own home. Learning from Bibi's experience, Tooba Azmoodeh opened the *Nawmoos* (Chastity) School for Girls in her home. In no time, children who had been deprived of knowledge were getting an education. Schools for girls opened in private homes all over the country.

The Secret Alliance of Women was the next women's organization to join the war against the clergy establishment, which refused to release its grip on Iranian society.

In 1907, the Society for the Freedom of Women (SFW) was established to give women the self-confidence to participate in society, to comfortably discuss issues and to speak publicly, especially in the presence of men. This organization included women and men, but the organization was meant to empower women, so men were the listeners, while women were the speakers. The Society for the Freedom of Women became the most active of the secret societies, attracting prominent activists, such as Sadigeh Dawlatabadi, Muhtaram Eskandari, and many others. The importance of SFW was that it also attracted women of different religions. Many Qajar princesses, including Taj Saltaneh, were among the active members of the SFW. Other members included harem teacher Baji Khanoom and Mrs. Jordan, the wife of the American missionary school principal.

They held their meetings in secret, at a flower nursery on the outskirts of Tehran, and new members attended only with the endorsement and recommendation of a female member. One time, a man who asked to attend could not come because he did not have a woman member to sponsor him. The man mentioned this to a local cleric, who immediately shut the organization down. A Christian boy who overheard that discussion at a bakery rode his bicycle to the nursery, to warn the members of imminent danger. After the members fled the nursery, the SFW meetings stopped.

In its April 16, 1907, issue, the *Habl ol'Matin* newspaper reported, "Five hundred women rallied in Baharestan Square today. 'Long live the constitution, Long live the law, Down with dictatorship and dictators' were some of the slogans they were chanting."

CHAPTER ELEVEN

The Ladies' Secret Society (1910)

THE LAW OF THE WOMEN-GODS kept the fire of enlightenment alive. The first and foremost goal of the Ladies' Secret Society was education, especially for women.

In 1910, Iranian women hosted a national conference in Tehran, where they adopted ten resolutions related to education. First, they launched schools for girls. Then, they abolished *jahazi*, dowries that women had to give their husbands at the time of marriage. The idea was that a woman's dowry could be better spent to educate women, leading to the establishment of a trust to fund the education of women.

The clerics, who had succeeded in forcing the constitutionalists to capitulate on the issue of gender rights, had not anticipated any resistance. Facing the resolve of women in their struggle, they concluded that the women would not give up their quest for equality, and decided to stop them at any cost.

After the Tehran conference, the women began to establish girls' schools, despite the threats of clerics. The clerics fought back by preventing the women of the Ladies' Secret Society from renting classroom space by threatening the landlords, harassing the children on their way to school, and setting the schools on fire.

The resolve of the women was to never surrender, even if it meant transforming their homes into schools for girls. Robabeh Mar'ashi had been the first to begin teaching girls at her home, establishing the first home school for girls in 1891, almost two decades earlier. Now, women armed themselves with Winchesters, guarding their children at school and home. They took turns guarding their homes while students were in class, and they steadfastly continued to educate girls in Iran.

Safieh Yazdi, the wife of a pro-constitution cleric, Mohammed Yazdi, opened the *Effatiyeh* School for girls in 1910. Her action was a lesson for the clergy and encouraged others to open more schools. Despite threats and abuse from the religious authorities and their mobs, the education of girls continued.

That year, Dr. Kahel, a trained medical doctor at the American missionary medical school in Tehran and the wife of Dr. Hossein Khan, published the first post-revolution women's magazine. She published thirty issues of the magazine before the clerics, delivering fire-and-brimstone sermons from the pulpit, encouraged a mob to attack her house.

Progress

In 1911, Mahrokh Gowhar-Shenas opened *Taraghi* (Progress) Girl's School in Tehran, despite her husband's opposition. That year, Mah Sultan Amir-Sehei opened *Tarbiyat* (Educating) School for the Girls. On August 4, 1911, Vakil ol'Rowaya, a male member of the Majlis, sparked a conversation on the issue of women's enfranchisement. The clergy responded with rage.

At their conference the year before, Ladies' Secret Society members had laid plans to raise funds to develop their education projects. On July 2, 1911, for the first time in many centuries, Iranian women brought a show, *Disaster*, to the stage in the Masoodieh Park in Tehran. They built the stage and provided chairs. The actors were all women, but the audience was mixed. During that event, they raised a large amount of money.

In 1910, women established the Association of the Ladies of the Homeland Society (*Anjoman'eh Mokhadarat'eh Vatan*) to fight foreign interference in Iran's internal affairs and to oppose the Qajar Shahs from getting loans from foreign powers in exchange for Iranian lands and economic concessions.

During the nineteenth century, the Russians had taken seventeen northern provinces of Iran in Central Asia and the British had taken a large swath of the northeastern provinces of Iran.

In a protest against a second ultimatum by the Russians to occupy the capital, the Association of the Ladies of the Homeland held a demonstration on January 31, 1911, in front of parliament. Thousands of women participated and announced a boycott of Russian and English products.

By 1913, there were nine women's societies and sixty-three girls' schools in Tehran with close to 2,500 students. These schools produced the first generation of prominent, well-educated twentieth-century Iranian women, who were not a part of the One Thousand Families of insiders.

Foroogh Azarakhshi, a member of one of the prominent families of the holy city of Mash'had, was one of the women of the Ladies' Secret Society, and she established a girls' school in her home. Mobs targeted the school, again encouraged by a cleric from the pulpit who urged worshipers to set her home on fire after they left the mosque. Her home survived, but she and her friends turned to arming themselves with rifles to protect their school and students.

W. Morgan Shuster, an American accountant in Iran during the 1910s, wrote, "What shall we say of the veiled women who overnight became teachers, newspaper writers, founders of women's clubs and speakers on political subjects?"

Later, in 1928, Reza Shah Pahlavi established an education system for all Iranian children, including girls. The country's treasury was empty, and there was no funding to build the needed schools, but the same mansions that educated the girls were donated to the new education system.

My local elementary school was one of those mansions, belonging to Mrs. Keikavoosi, a member of the second generation of suffragettes. She had donated her family home to the Ministry of Education to be converted into a girls' school. The women of the Ladies' Secret Society donated many more homes to be used as schools because they were determined to educate women who were illiterate, as well as girls. Unable to stop the Ladies, the clerical establishment began a campaign against literate young women. They stood on the pulpit, preaching to the young men that it is un-Islamic for a man to marry a literate woman. By using the power of the pulpit to intimidate families to choose between literacy and husband and family, they continued their call for the closing of the girls' schools.

They stepped up their threats by issuing *fatwas* and encouraged thugs to harass women activists, throwing rocks at girls who attended schools. The *fatwas* also called for attacking and burning down homes that schooled girls.

Women on Bicycles

The Iranian women's movement had begun slowly in the late decades of the nineteenth century among women of nobility connected to the royal family. They were the women who could be educated through private tutors in all subjects, including foreign languages (mainly French), bringing them an awareness of modernity and progressive movements in European societies.

The British had been in Iran since the beginning of the 1800s and the Russians had historically been the aggressor next door with outright leverage in Iran. They stood by the clerical establishment and the Qajar kings, keeping the Iranian people poor and illiterate, leading to additional resentment of the British and Russians by Iranians. As a result, Iranian elites chose French culture, literature, and socio-political methodology. They learned English only when Americans came to Iran and opened schools and colleges.

For three centuries, the women of Iran had been kept away from participation in the sociopolitical affairs of their country. Not only were they kept illiterate, they were denied respect and social interaction skills.

Therefore, the most dedicated soldiers of the Constitutional Revolution were the women who had been living under the most egregiously inhumane *sharia*, dictated by clerics for almost three centuries. The women of Iran, who had been able to hang onto some of their human rights after the initial Islamic attack in the seventh century, became the first casualties of the Safavids, who imported Shi'a Islam into Iran, changing the character of Iranian society and the course of its history.

Women of all social strata came together and kicked off their efforts somewhere in the mid-nineteenth century. As we have seen, these included the Qajar Princes, the harem tutors, the tribal women, peasants, and the wives of the bazaar merchants and laborers. They all had a part in the revolution.

Women were not allowed to ride bicycles but they did pose on bicycles for photos at photo studios. Today the Islamic regime has forbidden bike riding for women because they consider it sexually pleasurable for women!

Foreign occupiers left their footprints on Iranian civilization and society, but they could not eliminate the heritage of the Women-Gods that had survived in the anima of Iranian society.

Under the feudal system of the king and clergy, there was no education system for anyone but the nobility of the One Thousand Families and the clerical class. The only way to achieve literacy was in the *maktab*, or religious schools. Girls were not allowed to attend the religious schools to learn reading and writing. Boys were only allowed to attend religious schools to learn Arabic, not Persian, so that they could learn the Qur'an and *sharia*. They were not allowed to learn to write. Clerics had forbidden the translation of the Qur'an to the Persian language until the mid-twentieth century, during the Pahlavi dynasty.

The only schools open to educate girls were the American Presbyterian and American Catholic Missionary schools, and a French Catholic school called École Franco-Persane for boys that later added a school for girls called Jeanne d'Arc. Empress Farah Diba Pahlavi is one of the graduates of the Jeanne d'Arc girls' school.

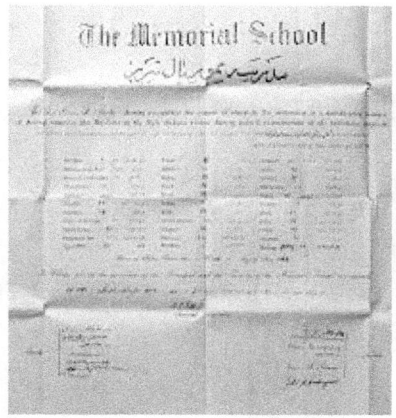 

(left) A graduation certificate
(right) The first day of the forty-second academic year at Memorial School on August 30, 1923. Note: the two girls attending the school are not wearing the chador.

In her publications on Iranian history,[1] Mansoureh Ettehadieh, an Iranian cultural activist, describes how Iranian women wanted to remove their hijab and dress like French women. They were willing to wear hats instead of the hijab, and in defiance of the powers that be, they created their own fashion by wearing Western-style dresses with French hats under their chadors.

My maternal grandmother, Badieh Davari, was one of the few Iranian girls who attended the American Catholic School in Tehran. Although she was a faithful Baha'i, she not only knew the Qur'an, but she had memorized the Torah and Bible.

Later in the mid-1930s, my grandmother sent her daughters—my mother and aunt—to the closest branch of the American Catholic boarding school in the city of Hamadan. At the same time, Iranian religious minorities, including Christians, Jews, and Zoroastrians, began to establish schools to educate their children.

Ms. Shams Kasmaii was born in 1883 to a family of nobility. During the post-revolution women's movement, her home became a literary

---

[1] Acquisition Notes: This collection consists of materials found in the Farmanfarma family papers in Tehran and made available to *Women's Worlds in Qajar Iran* by Mansoureh Ettehadieh (Nezam-Mafi in 2010).

salon. Shams was a defender of women's rights and emancipation and wrote for a publication, *Azadestan* (The Land of the Free).

Girls in uniform at the Catholic school. Photo by Antoin Sevruguin.

On December 6, 1911, the National Women's Society dispatched a telegraph to the new Majlis, urging legislators not to give way again to Russia's ultimatum.

Ms. Maryam Amid (1880-1945) was born in the city of Semnun in northern Iran, during the constitutionalist movement era. She founded the Women's Society of *Shokoofeh* (Blossom), on July 2, 1909, drawing 5,000 members within five weeks. She also began publishing the *Girls'* magazine, an official publication of their organization, in 1913. During the next two years, Maryam built two girls' schools in the city of Semnun in northern Iran. When confronted by the clergy about educating girls, she responded with a simple message, "I publish a magazine for ladies, if the girls are illiterate I cannot make money to pay taxes. The only way I can increase my readership is educating girls."

By 1913, there were nine women's organizations, sixty-three girls' schools in Tehran with close to 2,500 students, and fifty-one girls' schools in the other cities.

To prove their resolve, women regularly marched and held sit-ins, in front of the Department of Justice Building and the Majlis, their children and babies in their arms and on their laps.

In 1915, non-Muslim women joined the struggle, with the Society of Christian Women Graduates of Iran and the Zoroastrian and the Jewish

Women's Associations formed to educate and organize women in their own communities.

Mohtaram Eskandary

Mohtaram Eskandary (1894-1923) was another princess in the Qajar family, educated in Europe. In 1907, upon her return from France, she was one of the first women to appear without her hair covered. She studied Persian and French literature and became one of the activists of the Ladies' Secret Society, fighting the powerful clerical establishment. Like her sister activists, she was disappointed with the results of the revolution on the issue of gender equality. Following the 1910 women's conference, Mohtaram established educational classes for adult women and began to organize conferences and debates. In 1911, she also founded the left-leaning *Jam'iyat'eh Nesvawn'eh Taraghi-khah* (Association of Progressive Women), with an official branch, *Jam'iyat'eh Nesvawn'eh Vatan-khah* (Association of Patriotic Women), opposing foreign domination of the homeland. Mohtaram Eskandary died at the age of twenty-nine.

Mohtaram's successor, Mastureh Afsar, continued to lead the Society of Progressive Women until 1933. In 1932, it organized the Congress of Eastern Women, including delegates from Arab countries, Turkey, and Australia. In 1935, it established the Lady's Center (*Kanouneh Banowan*), with many of the society's members joining the new organization to help educate women.

It was the Association of the Patriotic Women of Iran that had assisted the harem tutor, Bibi Khanoum, in her battle against the Qajar prince who had written the pamphlet, *Women's Trickery* (*Makr'eh Zanaan*). Members of the association bought and collected as many of the pamphlets as they could and called on women to participate in building a bonfire in the middle of the town square, to burn the pamphlets.

Seal of the Association of the Patriotic Women of Iran

Fakhrafagh Parsa (1897-1985) was a symbol of perseverance. Her name, meaning "Pride of the Universe," was given to her by her second husband. Her strict Muslim father wouldn't allow her to be educated, but her mother, an artist, educated her secretly, without her husband's knowledge. At fourteen, she was forced to marry a man her father had chosen. Soon after, she divorced her husband and moved to the home of her maternal grandparents, who helped her get her high school diploma. At sixteen, she married a man of her choice, Farrokhdin Parsa, a journalist and pro-modernity intellectual who supported his wife's thirst for education and freedom.

Not only did Fakhrafagh master Persian literature, but she also learned French and Arabic. When her husband was assigned to the holy city of Mashhad in northeast Iran near the Afghan border, she began teaching at the private school of a Qajar princess. On February 4, 1914, Fakhrafagh published the first issue of a women's magazine in Mashhad, *Jahaneh Zanan* (*Women's World*), for women and by women.

In the magazine's fourth issue, she published a letter from a woman in the city of Kerman who noted, "The clerics are determined to keep women ignorant."

She had only published four issues when the governor asked her husband to leave the city—and take his wife with him. The clergy had not directly threatened their lives, but they had indirectly delivered an ultimatum via the governor of the province of Khorassan in eastern Iran.

Publisher Fakhr Afagh Parsa, young and older

Covers of the second and fifth issues of the *Women's World* magazine

In Tehran, Fakhrafagh published just four more issues of *Women's World* magazine when the office of the regent called in her husband and told him, "Get your wife, and go as far away as you can, break her pen and keep her mouth shut." Her husband replied, "I will never tell my wife to leave her home and family but you can tell her yourself, in writing."

In one night, Fakhrafagh Parsa broke four rules of the clerics:
1. She rode in a carriage.
2. She sat next to a man (her husband) in the carriage.

3. She dressed in Western-styled clothes and did not wear a headscarf.
   4. She attended the theater.

Later, she wrote, "In the fourth issue I wrote two articles, one about the plight of women and the need for changing the marriage laws, as well as the call for the education of women. When these two articles came out some people began to attack me, shouting, why doesn't anyone stop this woman?" She continues, "I became fearful for my children's lives and so we went into hiding."

The regent gave in to the clerical hierarchy and exiled Fakhrafagh to the holy city of Qom, the Vatican of Shi'ism in Iran, in an effort to frighten her into silence. But Fakhrafagh decided to continue the publication of her magazine in Qom, mailing it to her loyal readers. There, too, her husband stood by her. And there Fakrafagh gave birth to a daughter, Farokhrou, who would grow up to become the first woman minister in Iran and a member of the cabinet in 1976. It is said that, while Fakhrafagh gave birth to her daughter, she dictated an editorial for her next issue, in between her pushing and breathing. She published only two more issues before the clergy denounced her as a blaspheming woman and an enemy of Allah and the Prophet of Islam. The clerics warned her husband that if his wife did not stop publishing her "un-Islamic rags," they would put a *fatwa* on their children.

Fakhrafagh had no choice but to stop the publication of *Women's World*. She wrote, "We spent the two-year period of exile in the city of Qom and the government kept telling us to be patient. The members of the media were all very supportive of me until we were finally let go. When I arrived back in Tehran I was gloriously welcomed by the people who were lined up on both sides of the streets."

The government barred Fakhrafagh from writing, but she continued her activism. She immediately joined Ms. Mohtaram Eskandary and the Association of Patriotic Women of Iran. In an interview, Fakhrafagh said, "I immediately joined the women of APWI and began to write letters about the inhumane status of the women of Iran. We delivered the letters to Minister Teimoortash of the royal court of Ahmad Shah Qajar. I even went to meet with his wife but we never heard from them afterwards."

When the parliament removed the Qajar dynasty from the throne in 1925 and Prime Minister Reza Khan Pahlavi became the Shah of Iran, the women found a supporter who would stand by them.

Fakhrafagh wrote: "In 1935, one day we stood on the street on Reza Shah's route for hours until we saw his car approaching, raising our hands with the envelope, we stood in front of his car. He stopped the car and I stepped forward to the open car window and said, 'your majesty, I have a letter from the Association of Patriotic Women of Iran.' He said thank you and took the letter. A few days later we received his response where he had written only one line: 'You will also get your wishes, give me a little more time.' Two months later his Majesty Reza Shah Pahlavi not only ordered the implementation of the law passed by the Madjles (parliament) in 1928, he enforced the removal of the hijab from the lives of the women of Iran. That really was the day we got one of our wishes."

In 1920, Fakhrafagh Parsa began to publish her new magazine, *Awlam'eh Zanan* (*Women's Universe*), with support of the graduates of the American girls' school. *Women's Universe* was the first real magazine published by the women activists in standard magazine size, with forty pages and elaborate editorials, advocating for women's progress.

The Ladies' Secret Society emerged in every city of Iran and added new organizations to its rosters. The Association of the Ladies of the Homeland was followed by the Society for the Welfare of Iranian Women, Women of Iran, the Union of Women, Women Suffragettes, and the Central Women's Council.

In 1910, women in the city of Shiraz in southern Iran founded the first political organization, the Women's Movement. Ms. Zand-Dokht (1890-1932), a poet and writer, published a magazine for the organization. At a very young age, she had published *Iranian Girls* magazine. She had published only seven issues of *Iranian Girls* before the clergy banned it. At eighteen, she founded the Revolutionary Women's Association and published the organization's monthly magazine, *Zanan'eh Irani* (*Iranian Women*), the first journal written, edited, and published by women in Iran, the second and third journals following in 1912 and 1913.

Sadigeh Dawlatabadi (1882-1961) was one of the early leaders of the women's movement, beginning her activism during the constitutional movement. In 1907, Sadigheh joined the women patriots in their march and in the boycotting of British and Russian products. In 1918, she opened the first girls' schools in her home in the city of Isfahan, but she was forced to close it after only three months, when she was arrested and imprisoned.

She opposed the cleric's enforcement of headscarves and vehemently fought their edict. In the city of Isfahan in central Iran, she established an organization, *Zanon'eh Iran* (*Woman of Iran*), and published a journal, *Zabaneh Zanan* (*Women's Language*). In her magazine, Sadigheh not only wrote against the hijab and advocated for women's rights but also debated politics, criticizing the king's policy of allowing British colonial actions against Iran.

Sadigeh Dawlatabadi

Awlam'eh Nesvaan (*Women's Universe*) magazine was the alumni publication of the American girls' school. Launched in 1921, it remained in circulation longer than any other women's publication of the period. The publisher, Navabeh Safavi, an American school graduate and journalist, wrote that the magazine focused only on "matters important to Iranian women." She put in place an innovative management style for the time, with the magazine supervised by an editorial board that included brave women activists of the day: Ms. Tabibeh Mirdamadi, Ma'sumeh Feili, Ashraf Nabavi, Farkhondeh Samii, Badr ol'Moluk Malekzadeh, and Homa Mahmoudi.

The clerics continued to provoke mobs against women activists and their male allies. In 1920, two high-ranking clerics, Zia'uddin Majd and Aboul-Hassan Tonekaboni, issued an edict calling on the faithful to fight women who were refusing proper hijab, arguing the hijab was fundamental to Islam.

In 1921, four women activists founded *Peyk'eh Sa'adat'eh Nesvan* (Women's Prosperity Courier). This organization was the first Iranian women's group to celebrate International Women's Day on March 8 of the same year. Two founders, Jamileh Sedighi and Shokat Rusta, were sentenced to four years imprisonment for their political affiliations with the Soviet Communist Party, but they were freed soon after the sentencing.

In 1921, Sadigheh Dolatabadi participated in the International Women's Congress in Berlin, Germany, and delivered a speech on behalf of Iranian women. She was the first Iranian woman to attend a meeting of the International Women's Congress, where she was dressed in the same style as Western women, without hijab.

While she was at the conference, Sadigheh received a letter from members of the Association of the Patriotic Women of Iran, asking her to appeal to individual European women representatives for support. However, none of the European women's organizations considered the Iranian women's movement worthy of their alliance and so gave them no support.

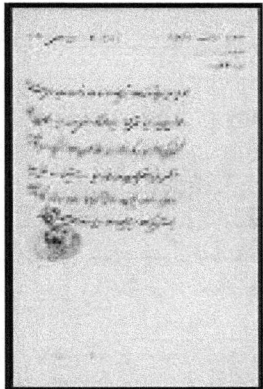

Letter from the Association of the Patriotic Women of Iran to Sadigheh Dowlatabadi in Europe. From Harvard University archives.

Sadigheh believed clerics used the hijab, which literally means "separation" in Arabic, to put a distance between "the creator" and women. Her opposition to the hijab was so strong that she had added the following statement in her will and testament, "When I die, I do not want and will not forgive any woman attending my funeral or memorial in a veil."

In 1980, the Khomeini regime ordered the destruction of Sadigeh Dawlatabadi's tomb. The reason: her last will and testament.

During her lifetime, Sadigheh said in an interview, "When I was arrested for the third time, the policeman told me, 'Lady you were born a hundred years too early,' and I replied, 'No, Sir, I was born a hundred years too late to help the women get their god-given rights back.'"

In 1926, two years before the Majlis passed a law giving women the choice to wear or not wear the hijab, Sadigeh attended the International Women's Conference in Paris. Upon her return to Iran, she went public in European attire without hijab.

Once again, the clerics went to the pulpit, demanding the faithful pour out onto the streets against women, which resulted in violence that left one person dead and twelve people injured.

In the debate in the Majlis on the enfranchisement of women, only the representative of the city of Hamadan dared to speak in support of the women. The clerics called his comments an abomination.

In 1926, an angry religious mob attacked Ms. Banu Namus, a member of the Ladies' Secret Society, pouring ash on her head and threatening to set her on fire. Her crime was opening the first girls' school in the city of Shiraz, in southern Iran. The school is still open today under her name.

While women took steps to educate girls and teach adult women and men to read and write, the clerical establishment continued to viciously oppose them. In 1927, they published a book, *The Response to Supporters of Emancipation*, with articles opposing women's emancipation.

By the 1930s, fourteen women's magazines in Iran debated women's rights, education, and the removal of the hijab. Women played an active part in politics, economics, and society, staging plays, holding auctions, and, if needed, selling their own jewelry to raise funds for schools, hospitals, and orphanages.

The women of Iran fought on two fronts against an internal threat. On one front, they were battling Shi'a clerical cronies for their equal rights and human dignity, and on the other front, they were fighting the external domination of British and Russian imperialism that not only robbed them of their wealth, but took away their sovereignty by supporting the clerical establishment.

They closely watched the actions of the new government and Majlis. They staged protests in front of the Majlis, and they made sure their representatives did their jobs and defended the homeland honorably. In a message to his bosses in London, the British ambassador said about the Ladies' Secret Society: "These women are all connected throughout the country and their network is very effective and unsettling for us."

Russia has always been the enemy for Iranians. Since Iran did not have the military to guard all her borders, local warriors defended the homeland. Amuni Mastan, a border guard commando, was one woman warrior.

Photographer Peter Jacks took this photo of Amuni Mastan, in the town of Aareem Savadkooh, in 1932.

CHAPTER TWELVE

America's Support and Empathy for Iranians (1911 – 1913)

UNTIL 1906, IRAN had had no system of governance to run the country. A regent carried out the wishes of the king and the clerical establishment, which ran the legal and social affairs of the land, according to *sharia*.

Most of the income of Iran went directly to the Russian and British governments, leading to widespread poverty among the Iranian people. The Iranian customs administration was under the control of Monsieur Joseph M. Naus, a Belgian administrator who took a cut off the top and then surrendered the taxes he collected from Iranian merchants to the Russians and the British.

In 1909, the new government had hired a French man, Monsieur Bizot, to establish an Iranian bank, but he, too, reported to the Russians and British Embassies and turned out to be ineffective, at best. The British and Russians were a major obstacle to the empowerment of the people and the establishment of a centralized Iranian constitutional government.

The Iranian revolutionary leaders adopted the Belgian constitution as a model for a constitutional monarchy. To establish a modern system of government, they understandably asked for the assistance of the United States.

Although there was no U.S. Embassy in Iran, nor any formal diplomatic relations between Iran and the United States, the revolutionary leaders dispatched two representatives to travel by carriage to the United States Embassy in Constantinople to submit their request for help.

Not for years, until 1944, during the middle of World War II, did the United States and Iran establish formal relations.

U.S. President William H. Taft was happy to respond favorably to the request for help from Iran and support the people of Iran. Eleven experts were handpicked and dispatched to Iran to set up a governmental system and train Iranians to manage their government of the people.

(left) American team sent to Iran (right) William Morgan Shuster

One trainer, accountant William Morgan Shuster, became outraged, seeing the unjust domination of Iran by the Russian and British governments. Taft had sent him to Iran to establish Iran's treasury and financial system. Working with Iranians, Shuster sympathized with their national struggle for sovereignty from the foreigners impeding their efforts for progress. The women of Iran particularly impressed him, with their patriotism and activism. He was aware of the Ladies' Secret Society and, as he wrote in his book, *The Strangling of Persia*,[1] he never met the women activists but he was aware of their existence.

After the success of the Constitutional Revolution of 1906, Iran was divided into two halves—northern and southern—in an Anglo-Russian convention held in St. Petersburg on August 31, 1907. While setting up the treasury, Shuster established a relationship with the members of the Majlis, not the foreign occupiers. His job clashed with British and Russian interests and they made every effort to thwart Iranians from taking control of their finance, treasury, and sovereignty.

---

1 Shuster, W. M., *The Strangling of Persia*, 190 -199.

The British Foreign Ministry wrote to the U.S. State Department complaining about Shuster's interference in Iran, which had been considered a British sphere of influence, and the British asked the United States to recall him from Iran.

In July 1911, Russia issued a third ultimatum, threatening the new government and Majlis and demanding the immediate dismissal of Shuster. It warned that, if Shuster was not kicked out of Iran, its troops would march on the capital. Iran had no military to defend herself.

On December 6, 1911, the Society of the Ladies of the Homeland sent a telegram to the Majlis, urging legislators not to give in to the Russian ultimatum and maintain their stance.

The Russian ultimatum aroused national protests, with the women of the Ladies' Secret Society leading marches and protests around the country. One day, they carried pistols under their heavy veils, as they marched to meet the president of the Majlis. They aimed their pistols at the MPs, warning them of dire consequences "if they wavered in their duties to uphold the liberty and dignity of the Persian people and the nation...."

The Ladies' Secret Society had quietly supported Mr. Shuster and the other ten American trainers who were building a secular government system for them. In his book, *The Strangling of Persia*, Shuster talks about the power and the influence of the women of Iran:

> ...It was at this time, when rumors were flying about Tehran that the Madjlis would yield to the threats and bribes which well-known Russians emissaries were employing with many of the deputies, that the Persian women performed the crowning act of the noble and patriotic part which thousands of their sex had been playing since Persia's Risorgimento began.
>
> Since 1907 the Persian women became almost at a bound the most progressive, not to say radical, in the world. It is not too much to say that without the powerful moral force of women the ill started and short-lived revolutionary movement, however well conducted by the Persian men, would have early paled into a mere disorganized protest. The women did much to keep the spirit of liberty alive. Having themselves suffered from a double form of oppression, political and social, they were the more eager to foment the great nationalist movement for the adoption of constitutional forms of government and the inclusion of western political, social, commercial and ethical codes.
>
> We of Europe and America, are long accustomed to the increasingly large role played by Western women in business, in the professions, in literature, in science, and in politics, but what shall we say of the veiled

women of the Near East who overnight become teachers, newspaper writers, founders of women's clubs and speakers on political subjects?

What, when we find them vigorously propagating the most progressive ideas of the Occident in a land until recently wrapped in the hush and gloom of centuries of despotism? Whence came their desire to play a part in the political and social regeneration of their country and their unwavering faith in political and social institutions? That it came and still exists there can be no possible doubt, and with it was born the discriminating intelligence which is as a rule acquired only by long years of practical experience.

The Persian women have given to the world a notable example of the ability of unsullied minds to assimilate rapidly an absolutely new idea, and with the élan of the crusader who has a vision, they early set to work to accomplish their ideals.

I had been fortunate enough shortly after reaching Persia to win the confidence of the National Assembly, or Madjlis, a body which fairly represented the hopes and aspirations of the great mass of the Persian people. This point gained, I was soon made aware that another great, though secret, influence was watching my work with jealous but kindly eyes. It was well known in Teheran that there were dozens of more or less secret societies among the Persian women, with a central organization by which they were controlled. To this day I know neither the names nor the faces of the leaders of this group, but in a hundred different ways I learned from time to time that I was being aided and supported by the patriotic fervor of thousands of the weaker sex.

A few examples may suffice. While sitting in my office one morning last summer, I was told that one of the Persian clerks in the treasury department wished to see me on an important matter. Information comes unexpectedly and from such curious sources in the Orient that no offer can be safely rejected. This young man came in. I had never seen him. We spoke in French, and after receiving permission to talk freely, with many apologies he said that his mother was our friend, that she had commissioned him to say that my wife should not pay a visit to the household of a certain Persian grandee, by whose family she had been invited, since he was an enemy to the constitutional government and my wife's visit would make the Persians suspect me. I thanked him, and at the time did not myself know of the contemplated call, but soon learned that it was planned, and, of course, advised against it.

On another, more recent occasion, a large crowd of poor women came to the Atabak Park to demonstrate against me because the treasury had been unable to pay the government pensions, on which there was over a million dollars then due. The available funds had been necessary for the volunteer troops who had been fighting against the ex-Shah. I sent one of my Persian secretaries to see these women and ask who had told them to come and make this demonstration. He returned mentioning the name of a famous reactionary grandee who was at the time well known to be favoring the cause of Mohammad Ali. I had then told that they would be given an answer on the following day if they dispersed quietly, which they did.

I then sent to one of the women's societies a simple explanation of our financial straits and the impossibility of paying these pensions because of the needs of the constitutional government, with a request that they prevent any further agitation against the treasury. Though it did not become possible to pay the pensions, there was never another demonstration by women on this account.

When the Russians threatened the Iranian government, it looked as if the Parliament was going to surrender and the Iranian women acted. Shuster wrote:

> With the dark days when the doubts came to be whispered as to whether the Majlis, or Parliament, would stand firm, the Persian women in their zeal for Liberty and their ardent love for their country, threw down the last barriers which distinguished their sex and gave striking evidence of their patriotic courage.

The Russians demanded the dismissal of the Americans, especially Shuster, and the money that they were not entitled to receive. The people were worried and wondering about the actions of their representatives and the honor of their country. Again wrote Shuster:

> The Persian women supplied the answer. Out from their walled courtyards and harems marched three hundred of that weak sex, with the flush of undying determination in their cheeks. They were clad in their plain black robes with nets of their white veil dropped over their faces. Many held pistols under their skirts or in the folds of their sleeves. Strait to the Majlis they went, and, gathered there, demanded of the president that he admit them all. What the grave deputies of the Land of the Lion and the Sun may have thought at this strange visitation is not recorded. The President consented to perceive a delegation of them. In his reception-hall, they confronted him, and lest he and his colleagues should doubt their meaning, these cloistered Persian mothers, wives and daughters exhibited threateningly their revolvers, tore aside their veils, and confessed their decision to kill their own husbands and sons, and leave behind their own dead bodies, if the deputies wavered in their duty to uphold the liberty and dignity of the Persian people and nation.

The women did not give up, became involved in both boycotting the import of foreign goods as well as raising funds for the establishment of the first National Bank of Iran. By selling their jewelry and dowries they financed the bank. The members of the Secret Union of Women published pamphlets and articles demanding men should give up their seats in "parliament" and let women run the country. With the victory of revolution and establishment of the constitution they expected equal opportunities and gender rights. None was granted in the constitution.

May we not exclaim: All honors to the veiled women of Persia! with the constraining traditions of the past around them, with the idea of absolute dependence upon the fancy and caprice of men ever before them, deprived of all opportunity, to educate themselves along modern ideals, they watched, guarded and rebuffed, they drank deep of the cup of freedom's desire, and offered up their daily contribution to their country's cause, watching its servants each moment with a mother's jealous eyes....

A few weeks later, with the consent of Ahmad Shah Qajar and the clerical establishment, the Russians bombed the Majlis (parliament), in a *coup d'état*, but the members of the Majlis would not surrender.

Despite the efforts of the patriotic women of Iran, protecting the Americans there to help them build a new constitutional government, the imperialists won, with the help of the Qajar Shah and clerics. The American advisors, including Shuster and his wife, left Iran in December 1911.

A year after his return home to the United States, Shuster published his book, *The Strangling of Persia*, dedicated to the Persian people, and he told the story of Europeans strangling Iran and her brave patriotic women.

He wrote; "With a knowledge of the facts of Persia's downfall, the scales drop from the eyes of the most incredulous, and it is clear that shows as the helpless victim of the wretched game of cards which a few European powers, with the skill of centuries of practice, still play with weaker nations as the stake, and the lives, honor and progress of whole races as the forfeit."[2]

In his foreword, Shuster wrote:

> Only the pen of a Macaulay or the brush of a Vereshchagin could adequately portray the rapidly shifting scenes attending the downfall

---

2 Ibid., 204.

of this ancient nation, scenes in which two powerful and presumably enlightened, Christian countries played fast and loose with truth, decency and law, one, at least, hesitating not even at the most barbarous cruelties to accomplish its political designs and to put Persia beyond hope of self-regeneration.

In his dedication to the people of Persia, he wrote:

> In the endeavor to repay in some slight measure the debt of gratitude imposed on me through their confidence in my purposes towards them and by their unwavering belief, under difficult and forbidding circumstances, in my desire to serve them for the regeneration of their nation, this book is dedicated by the author.

Under the Qajar dynasty, the Russians and the British constantly held Iran responsible for unaccountable amounts of debts they never considered paid. The bank of Iran was under British control and the new constitutional government had an empty treasury when Shuster established it.

The Association of the Ladies of the Homeland made a proposal to the Majlis to raise the funds to finance the National Bank of Iran, by cashing in their dowries from their husbands, their inheritance from their fathers, and the sale of the pieces their jewelry with enough money left over to help the government pay off its debts to Russia.

Bust of Howard Baskerville

Also critical of the British and Russian abuses of Iran and the Iranian people was Howard Baskerville, an American teacher in Iran, who joined his students in Tabriz, supporting the Constitutional Revolution of 1906. There, a Russian soldier killed him, and the teacher sacrificed his life for his students' futures. It was reported that 30,000 Iranians attended his funeral. Today, Baskerville is an Iranian hero, and a statue of him stands in the museum of the city of Tabriz.

Dr. Joseph Plum Cochran

Another American, Dr. Joseph Plum Cochran, established the first hospital in Iran in 1848, in the city of Oromia, in western Iran. He and his wife, Katherine, became citizens of Iran and raised their five children there. He also built a medical school to train Iranian doctors.

McCormick Hall, American College of Tehran, circa 1930.

Many Iranians were educated in a college that the Iranians called the "American College," because it was built in 1933 by Samuel Martin Jordan, a professor from New York University. Iranians called Professor Jordan the "father of modern education" in Iran.

CHAPTER THIRTEEN

The Communist Revolution, World War I, and the End of the Qajar Dynasty (1914 – 1926)

IN 1914, AT THE BEGINNING OF WORLD WAR I, as women were getting more involved in the socio-political affairs of the country, Iran came under the military occupation of British and Russian troops, even though the Iranian government had remained neutral during the European war.

Despite Iran's declared neutrality, she was dragged into World War I (and later, World War II as well). The Allies transferred arms and truck and tank convoys from Persian Gulf ports in the south to Russia in the north of the country, destroying transportation systems and roads in Iran.

Russian domination and interference in Iran ended for a short while, with the Bolshevik revolution of 1917 and the gradual withdrawal of Russian soldiers from Iranian territories. The vacuum gave the British government an opportunity to completely pull Iran into its colonial system. While short-lived, the Soviet policy of non-interference made them look like a better neighbor than Great Britain; therefore, Iranians directed their animosity against the British. The U.S. military completely withdrew from Iran at the end of World War I, following a British "declaration" that Iran was in its sphere of influence.

By the time the Great War ended, Iran had been devastated socially, economically, and structurally. Historical records reveal that the European occupying armies treated the people of Iran harshly. British and Russian soldiers had eaten their way through the country, overrunning farms and leaving silos and food storage houses empty. The British mil-

Communist Revolution, World War I, and End of the Qajars ~ 143

itary prevented the import of food to Iran.

The U.S. Chargé d'Affaires, Wallace Smith Murray, wrote a report in 1925 about the alimentation situation in Persia, in which he mentions the famine of 1917 to 1918 and states that one-third of the population of Persia had been "carried off" by starvation and the diseases that accompany malnutrition. He wrote:

> I could not believe my eyes. I had seen references to this famine in earlier reports, and was aware that this was a serious famine. But casualties of this magnitudes is another matter. The matter led me to make a careful search of the records of the Department of State for Persia during 1914-1919. It turned out to be a revelation. The records are immensely rich and previously unused. One by-product was a monograph on the history of Persia in World War I and its conquest by Great Britain. The other is this brief monograph on the famine-cum-genocide in Persia.

According to the book, *The Great Famine and Genocide in Persia 1917-1919*, by Dr. Mohammad Gholi Majd, millions of Iranians died of starvation and related malnutrition diseases.

The U.S. Ambassador in Great Britain wrote a telegram to Lord Curzon, the British foreign minister, who had lied to Iranians about the American support:

> The Secretary of State to the Ambassador in Great Britain (Davis)
> Washington, October 4, 1919/1 p.m.
>
> ...This was followed by other telegrams from the American Legation in Teheran indicating that the highest Persian officials openly stat-

ed that America had refused to aid Persians. In this connection you may remind his Lordship that the people of the United States have always been deeply interested in the welfare of Persia and during the recent terrible famine American Philanthropy on a generous scale, came to the relief of suffering Persians and did what it could to mitigate the unhappy conditions then existing...

Otherwise, few in the Western world talked about the famine that killed so many Iranians. The British Government has been unwilling to open documents related to that part of World War I history. The British government promised to pay reparation to Iran after the war. However, they reneged.

The war and its military occupation changed the nature and direction of the women's movement. The women had no choice but to tend the wounds of their occupied homeland, feeding her starving children. They had to shift their attention from issues of equal rights to charity and social work. Their fundraising efforts became charity events to save many children in orphanages from the famine.

Paris Peace Conference, 1919

On January 18, 1919, the Allies convened a Peace Conference at Versailles Palace outside Paris to establish the terms of peaceful coexistence. Iran sent two representatives: the minister of foreign affairs, Mr. Ansari, and a legal advisor, Mr. Foroqy, with a list of damages to present to the Allies for restitution. When they arrived at Versailles, the British representative made sure that the Iranians were refused entrance. The United States was the only country to stand by the Iranian representatives. U.S. Secretary of State George Lansing attempted to persuade the British government to allow the Iranian representatives the right to attend the talks and request reparation, but his efforts failed. Other European governments didn't support the Iranian representatives. Thus, the U.S. and Iran lost in their bid to win restitution for Iran.

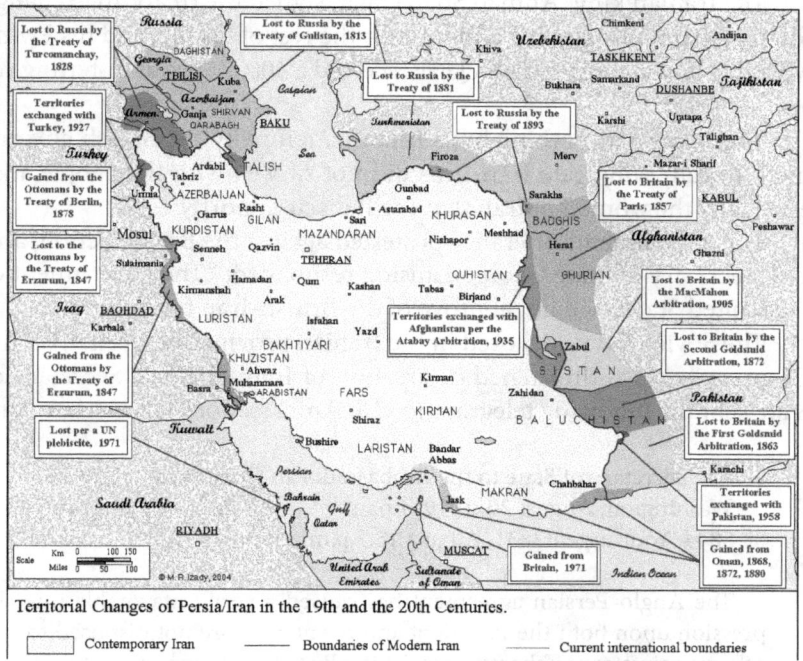

Territorial Changes of Persia/Iran in the 19th and the 20th Centuries.

In response, the Iranian delegation published booklets with its list of national demands, organized in three sections: political, economic, and legal.

The political demands were:

- Annulment of the 1907 St. Petersburg Treaty, in which the Russian and British governments divided Iran.
- Withdrawal of all military guards and personnel of foreign countries from Iranian territories.
- Return of all Iranian territories taken by Russia and Great Britain through occupation and intimidation.
- Return of the Western provinces of Kurdistan, Mosul, and Bakr, taken from Iran by the Ottomans.
- Return of Iran's Western borders to the Euphrates River.

On August 9, 1919, the British government proposed a treaty to the Iranian Prime Minister, Vosough Al-Doleh Qajar, which was later signed in London. In the proposal, initiated by the British Foreign Minister, Lord Curzon, Britain would pay the war reparations it had denied Iran at the Versailles conference, and in exchange, the British government would get total control of Iran's finance and military.

The Iranian king, Ahmad Shah Qajar, signed the treaty, in exchange for 15,000 pounds sterling a month for the rest of his life, and his Prime Minister Vosough Al-Doleh Qajar received a 400,000 pound sterling reward.[1]

The treaty was nothing but a brazen attempt by the British government to fully subjugate Iran. This did not sit well with the people and, especially the women of Iran that I will discuss shortly.

The governments of France protested against the British action, and U.S. Secretary of State George Lansing responded, "The government of the United States will not approve of the British-Iran treaty."

The Soviet Navy anchored in the Iranian province of Geelan, off the Caspian Sea, also threatened occupation of Iran. The U.S. Secretary of State sent the following telegram to U.S. Ambassador Davis in London.

> The Secretary of State to the Ambassador in Great Britain (Davis)
> Washington, August 20, 1919, 4 p.m.
> 5844. Your urgent 2831, August 18, 7 p.m.
>
> The Anglo-Persian agreement has caused a very unfavorable impression upon both the President and me and we are not disposed to ask our minister at Teheran to assist the British Government or to ask him to preserve a friendly attitude toward this agreement.
>
> At Paris I asked of Mr. Balfour three times that the Persians have an opportunity to be heard before the Council of Foreign Ministers because of their claims and boundaries and because their territory had been a battle ground. Mr. Balfour was rather abrupt in refusing to permit them to have a hearing. It now appears that at the time I made these requests Great Britain was engaged in a secret negotiations to gain at least economic control of Persia. The secretary employed and the silence observed seem contrary to the open and frank methods which ought to have prevailed and may well impair the bases of a peace inspired by friendliness. We cannot and will not do anything to encourage such secret negotiations or to assist in allaying the suspicion and dissatisfaction which we share as to an agreement negotiated in

---

1 "Anglo-Persian Agreement of 1919," *Encylopedia Iran*. http://www.iranicaonline.org/articles/anglo-persian-agreement-1919.

this manner.

> You will respond to Lord Curzon's request in this general sense.
> —Lansing

In Iran, the American Minister, John Lawrence Caldwell, sent a report to the U.S. State Department on August 28, 1919, that stated, "... Fierce protests by various groups and people in some provincial capitals, also markets closed to protest. Many Iranians believe that the acceptance of the contract means an end to Iran's independence...."

The response from Washington was:

> The Secretary of State to the minister in Persia (Caldwell)
> Washington, September 4, 1919, 5 p.m.
>
> You are instructed to deny both to Persian officials, and to anyone else interested in this matter, that America has not refused to aid Persia. You will also state that the United State has constantly and consistently showed its interest in the welfare of Persia and that the American Mission at Paris several times endeavored earnestly to secure a hearing for the Persian mission before the Peace Conference. The American Mission was surprised that it did not receive more support in this matter but the announcement of the new Anglo-Persian Treaty probably explained why the American Mission was unable to secure such hearing. It would appear also that the Persian Government at Tehran did not strongly support the efforts of its Mission at Paris.
>
> The government of the United States has learned with surprise of the recent Anglo-Persian Treaty which would be seen to indicate that Persia does not desire American support and cooperation in the future, in spite of the fact that the Persian delegates in Paris strongly and openly sought our assistance.
> —Lansing[2]

The ardent patriotic women of Iran were among the fierce protesters that U.S. Ambassador Caldwell spoke to Washington about. When the news of the betrayal by the British was revealed, there was a call for an urgent meeting of the board members of the Society of Patriotic Ladies of the Motherland, and they decided to advance their fight against British colonialism. Calling on their representatives to vote against the trea-

---

2 "Persia: Agreement Between Persia and the Great Britain," Breckinridge Long. http://images.library.wisc.edu/FRUS/EFacs/1919v02/reference/frus.frus1919v02.i0028.pdf.

ty, they demonstrated in front of the Majlis, writing articles, speaking on street corners and city parks, and distributing leaflets. They provided members of the Majlis the support of the constituency and the power to stand up against their colonizers.

The board members of the Society of Patriotic Ladies of the Motherland in 1921

The United States was the only country that came to Iran's aid. In a letter to the leader of the Majlis, the U.S. representative in Tehran, John Lawrence Caldwell, delivered the fledgling Iranian parliament the support that it needed to reject the British treaty and defend the country's sovereignty. This statement sealed the popularity of the United States in the hearts of Iranians for generations, until even today.

Slowly, the women resumed their political activities, rebuilding organizations such as the Society for the Welfare of Iranian Women, Women of Iran, Union of Women, Women's Efforts, and the Council of Women of the Center, followed by the Association of the Ladies of the Homeland. Even under foreign occupation and war, the members of the Association of the Messengers for Women's Prosperity celebrated International Women's Day in 1915 for the first time in the city of Rasht, while under the Russian occupation.

Marzieh Zarrabi was born in 1902 in the province of Geelan. In 1917, at the age of fifteen, she established the first girls' school in her province, and by 1919, she established the National Women's School. A year later, she established a third school in another town in her province of Geelan. In 1925, Marzieh published a new 24-page, 5x7-inch publication, *Eastern Women's Magazine*, with a mission to educate women about their rights. In a few years, more women joined her, writing articles and editorials in the magazine and volunteering to teach girls.

In 1919, Atefeh Tejaratchee made her first solo flight on a bi-plane, becoming Iran's first woman pilot. She encouraged her son to become an aerospace engineer.

The drawing on the cover of the magazine shows a woman, enlightened by the rays of knowledge, rocking a cradle with her left hand and holding the planet earth with her right hand.

Before they were sent back home, the American experts that President Taft had sent to Iran established a system of governance in the country. However, the war, famine, imperialist interference, and opposition by the Qajar Shahs and Shi'a clerical establishment prevented the implementation of their progressive plans to improve the country.

Iran had no middle-class, nor experienced political personalities, until the 1960s, when the generation of the young Iranians from the 1920s and 1930s entered society. Until then, almost all of the country's prime ministers and high-ranking decision makers continued to be royal members of the One Thousand Families of the Qajar elite.

Noor Al Hoda Mangeneh

Noor Al Hoda Mangeneh was born in 1901 to a family of the Qajar nobility and she received the best education, studying French and even learning to play the piano. She joined the women of the Ladies' Secret Society at a young age. In today's terms, Noor was an event planner and fundraiser for the organization. Being a member of nobility, she knew many women of means who paid handsomely to attend her fundraising events, even under the restrictions and threats of the clergy. She organized special events at her home, and women were allowed out of their homes in the late evening hours to attend. On the last night of the holy month of Ramadan in 1921, she sent out cards inviting women to a "wedding reception," a cover for a show she had produced. The women arrived, and the first and second acts of the show went well with the hostess at the piano. The guests were enjoying themselves when a dozen police officers, armed with bats and chains, kicked in the doors and barged into the house. They assaulted and insulted the women, destroyed Mangeneh's belongings and put an end to what they called "an illegal un-Islamic gathering."

Three months later, she succeeded in hosting the same show three nights in a row and raised the needed funds to build more adult education schools for women.

In the tradition of the times, Noor Al Hoda Mangeneh was married off at fifteen, though she divorced her husband shortly afterwards. She attended the American University in Beirut, majoring in psychology. Upon her return, she rejoined the women of the Ladies' Secret Society. She later became a member of the *Kanoon Banovaan* (The Lady's Center), at the Ministry of Education. She was another one of the many progressive Iranian women of the early twentieth century, who bravely stood up to the clerical establishment.

The push for educating girls continued. In September 1920, Badr Ol'Molook Bamdad established the first art school for girls. In 1923, she published a book, *Good Housekeeping*, that included a discussion on "democracy in Iran." The minister of education refused to publish the book, but the minister of war, Reza Khan Pahlavi, who became Shah two years later, had the Army publishing house publish the book.

In September 1935, Ms. Bamdad became one of the first ten female students to attend the newly-established Tehran University. In 1936, she established the first coed elementary school, making her the most despised woman by the clerical establishment. *Iranian Women from the Constitutional Revolution to the White Revolution* was among the many books she published

In February 1921, Reza Khan Pahlavi, a revolutionary-era champion, was named commander of the weak Iranian military. By October 1922, Ahmad Shah Qajar promoted him to the post of prime minister of Iran.

As Iran struggled with the post-World War I famine and the British and Russian occupation, the monarch of Iran, Ahmad Shah Qajar, an absentee king, was squandering money and time on women in Europe. Reza Khan Pahlavi unsuccessfully tried to convince intellectuals to replace the constitutional monarchy with a constitutional republic. The intellectuals agreed, however, to urge the Majlis to remove Ahmad Shah Qajar from the throne.

Only two members of the Qajar nobilities protested the decision. One was a woman: Ahmad Shah Qajar's mother, the powerful Queen Mother Malakeh Jahan, who even traveled from her home in Paris to the city of Najaf in modern-day Iraq to secure the support of the powerful Shi'a clerical leader who backed her son. The other was Prince Mohammed Mossadegh Ol'Saltaneh Qajar, a then member of the Majlis.

Sakineh Effat Shirazi was a scholar who dedicated her life to educating women. In 1920, she turned her home in Shiraz into a formal school for girls. Her name, Shirazi, means "of Shiraz." Four years later, her school became the first official government school for girls.

My own mother was born in 1921 into this era of advancement. My maternal grandparents gave her the name Parvin, meaning "north star." When my mother came of school age, the Iranian education system had just begun to develop, but my maternal grandmother sent her to the American Catholic boarding school which she had attended years earlier.

The author's mother

At the end of World War I, the Iranian treasury was empty and people were hungry. Prime Minister Reza Khan Pahlavi did not have the funds to build schools, but he had the wholehearted support of the Ladies' Secret Society. No longer secret, they publically marched in support of the new education initiatives, raising funds, building schools, and donating their family properties and homes to the school system. They also staffed the schools as volunteers and became the first teachers to formally educate the children of Iran, gladly and free of charge.

Fasih ol'Moluk Maram was one of the women who stepped up, raised funds, and built forty elementary and high schools for the government in 1921. She then founded the Teacher's College to staff the newly-established education system. Fasih ol'Moluk was a calligrapher and publisher of the *New Gift, Monthly Journal*.

* * *

In February 1923, a group of ignorant believers, urged by the clerical cabal, published a magazine against the women leaders, accusing them of witchcraft and deceit, rallying Muslims to save Islam by quashing the women. The next day, newspapers reported that hundreds of the members of the Society of the Patriotic Ladies of the Homeland went out in the morning, bought all the magazines they could find, piled them up in the main town square, and burned them in a bonfire.

Women were beginning to participate in the performing arts without fear of the ruling clerics. Qamar-Moluk Vaziri was born in 1905, one year before the ratification of the Constitutional Revolution of 1906. Her grandmother raised Qamar, whose name meant "moon" in Arabic, and she grew up hearing her grandmother singing prayers in private events for women in the women's section of the mosque. Qamar learned to sing and play the *tar*, a long-necked string instrument, from her grandmother.

Qamar-Moluk Vaziri

Under *sharia* of the time, women were not allowed to sing, dance, or appear on the stage, unless it was behind closed doors for an all-women audience.

In 1925, at the age of twenty, Qamar-Moluk Vaziri became the first Iranian woman to go on stage to perform at a concert, without wearing a hijab. The clergy went all out on the pulpit, damning her and calling her "a whore," "an abomination," "shameless," and many other names. However, she had the hearts of the faithful.

She began her performance by singing the song that a woman had sung in the park during the Constitutional Revolution of 1906. In short time, Qamar conquered the male-dominated world of performing arts and music and transformed Iranian society after 250 years of misogynistic clerical rule.

She said, "I went on stage without a hijab and performed during the times that women who went without a hijab would have been arrested and taken to prison."

Qamar dismantled barriers of fear and opened the stage to the talented women of Iran, including my sister, Nazila, who graduated from Tehran Conservatory as a soprano opera singer in 1972. Qamar became the first woman to sing on Iranian radio in 1919. She died at the age of 54, at the peak of her fame and popularity.

In October 1925, the Majlis voted to depose the absentee king, Ahmad Shah Qajar, and asked Prime Minister Reza Khan Pahlavi, who had campaigned for establishing a republic in Iran, to carry out the king's responsibilities temporarily, until a special session of the Majlis chose a new leader for Iran.

In December, the special session of the Majlis voted to end the Qajar dynasty and nominated Prime Minister Reza Khan Pahlavi to take the throne permanently, establishing the Pahlavi Dynasty. Only Prince Mohammed Mossadegh Ol'Saltaneh Qajar voted against the nomination.

Special session of the Majlis, November 1925

CHAPTER FOURTEEN

Reza Shah Pahlavi: Pro-Women and Patriot (1925 – 1941)

AT THE URGING of the women's movement in Iran, Reza Shah Pahlavi established an educational system for the children of Iran. He also established a foundation for higher education by building the University of Tehran, gradually staffed by Iranians who had been sent to study in universities in Europe and the United States. Slowly but surely, Iran began to have an educated citizenry.

In 1926, the newly-established Board of Education in Shiraz asked for six volunteers to transform the old religious boys' school into an elementary school for girls. Women stepped forward to renovate, paint, clean, and furnish the school with used, mismatched chairs and desks they had collected. The six women stayed on as volunteer principals and teachers, and they educated and protected the children for years, until the government was able to formally hire them and pay them.

Iran's treasury was empty and the Iranian bank was under British government control, and the British government prohibited the government of Iran to take charge. To manage his country, Reza Shah Pahlavi had no choice but to shut the bank down.

The treasury was looted, and Pahlavi did not have the needed funds to establish the Iranian National Bank. He asked the affluent bazaar merchants to invest in their country's bank by buying government bonds. However, Iranian merchants did not trust the government or the banking system and refused to cooperate.

Ignoring the rich merchants, the Association of Patriotic Women of the Homeland, who had previously proposed the establishment of an

Iranian-run bank, volunteered to be the bank's first investors. They offered their jewels, inheritance from their fathers, and alimonies cashed in from their husbands. The main investor was the very wealthy Princess Fakhr-Al-Dowleh Qajar, who could offer the rest of the funds needed for the bank.

Princess Fakhr-Al-Dowleh Qajar

According to *Anjoman* (*Association*) newspaper, a woman from the northeastern city of Mash'had sent a letter to the Majlis, saying, "This small piece of jewelry that I had saved for hard times, I send to the National Bank. I have nothing more to offer, than my life…"

That was how the women of Iran funded their National Bank in 1927.

* * *

Born in 1878, Bahar Khanum was a great musician and poet who played a variety of instruments. The clergy threatened her with excommunication for playing music and writing forbidden love songs. Also, a renowned chef, she wrote a cookbook that became a staple of Iranian households.

On February 23, 1928, the doors to Zoroastrian Cinema, the first movie theater for women which was staffed with female employees, opened in Iran.

That month, under pressure from the women's movement, the Majlis agreed to amend the constitution, elevating the status of women and removing them from the list of incompetents like minors, the mentally ill, and the criminally negligent. It also ratified a new dress code that adopted Western clothing styles, including short jackets and Stetson hats for men and, more importantly, hats for women, by removing heavy taxation on women's hats. This was one step the Majlis took to allow women to replace the chador and hijab with hats.

The amendment passed narrowly, but the choice to wear—or not wear—the dreaded chador, a symbol of slavery of women for three hundred years, had become the law of the land, despite the strong opposition of the clerical camp in the Majlis.

Having lost the vote, the clerical establishment resorted to outright violence against the women who wanted to follow the law and wear hats instead of the chador. Encouraged by clerics from the pulpit, vigilante mobs (hired for the purpose) took the law into their own hands and went into the streets to make sure that no woman dared leave her home without wearing a chador. The clergy intimidated government officials and put the fear of Allah into men if they allowed "their" women to go outside without the chador.

Organization for the Defense of the Human Rights of Iranian Women

In 1929, a group of educated women founded the Organization for the Defense of the Human Rights of Iranian Women. Women throughout the country overcame fear and refused the clerical demands that they wear the hijab, by any possible means.

In Shiraz, six women made colorful chadors of silk and taffeta. One morning, they gathered, wearing their new rainbow-colored taffeta chadors and went for a walk on the city's main street. They had agreed that if clerics stopped to admonish them, they would reply, "You demand that we wear hijabs. Why does it have to be only black?"

The six women walked halfway up the main street when a crowd began to gather. A cleric shouted at them, calling them "infidel whores." A mob gathered and, incited by the cleric, attacked and brutally beat the women. They were taken home with fractures to their skulls, arms, and legs.

Bad news kept arriving.

Eghbal Lahouri, a well-known Muslim poet, decided to encourage women around the country to stand up for Islam by wearing their chador. The aim was to divide women. In response to Lahouri, however, a group of male intellectuals decided to formally join the discussion of women's emancipation and support the emancipation movement. Men, such as Mirza-Abolghassem Azad, an activist intellectual, initiated the first Emancipation Society and other men supported its efforts.

Huma and Shams ol'Muluk Jahanbani were two leading feminist writers and speakers. Huma had organized a major demonstration by women outside the Majlis, demanding equal rights. A publisher and poet, she wrote constantly on women's issues. Shams ol'Muluk, a teacher in Tehran, was the first Iranian woman to teach, unveiled, in classes of a co-ed school that she had established.

Derakhshandeh Gohar-Naraghi, the wife of a member of a prominent family of the city of Kashan, convinced her husband to let her convert the old mosque of the city into an elementary girls' school in 1929. She personally supervised the construction of the elementary school and, six years later, built a high school next door to the old mosque, which by then had been converted into a thriving girls' school. She named the schools *Elm* (Knowledge).

* * *

The 1930s marked a period of great advancement for women in education and employment.

The United States, playing a key role in developing and supporting the goal of Iranian women toward female education, helped in that advancement. Chartered by the State University of New York, the American College of Tehran opened in 1930. It was one of numerous colleges and secondary schools that American organizations and churches built across Iran. These schools educated many ordinary Iranians, including many members of my family.

In October 1930, the government of Iran sent a woman, Sara Heidari, to France as its first Iranian woman diplomat. On November 5, 1930, Badri Vaziri, a violinist, played in the country's first orchestra for women. The event was significant because Ms. Vaziri was the granddaughter of Bibi Khanum Estarabadi, the activist who had fought for women's rights in the 1860s, while she was a tutor to the royal harem. In 1961, Ms. Vaziri became the director of the Tehran Conservatory of the Performing Arts, from whence my sister graduated as an opera singer in 1971.

On January 19, 1931, Mohammad Reza Shah Pahlavi dispatched the first group of female high school graduates to Europe for higher education.

That year, women successfully persuaded the Majlis to approve a new civil code that gave women new rights, including a limited conditional right to file for divorce and a change to the minimum age for marriage: from nine to fifteen for girls, and from fifteen to eighteen for boys. The civil code was secular, but family laws were still under the domain of *sharia*.

The number of women's organizations in the Ladies' Secret Society had grown, and they started a new campaign against the country's inhumane *sharia* by marching, writing, and speaking publicly for the rights of women and pressuring the Majlis to amend the unjust laws.

The clergy stood at the pulpit every Friday and denounced the new legislative amendments that improved the lives of women and girls. They worked overtime to turn the ignorant faithful against progress and women's rights.

As Iranians became educated, the influence of the old twin establishment had begun to diminish and it was losing its battle for control of the people. The clerics began attacking the reputation of Reza Shah Pahlavi, accusing him of being a traitor for forcing Western modernity on the Iranian people. They called him a dictator for enforcing laws that the clerics opposed.

With the invitation of the Ladies' Secret Society, the Congress of Oriental Women opened in Tehran in 1932 and made recommendations to improve the lives of women. One of the Iranian speakers, Ms. Iran Erani, declared socialism was the only way to secure the rights of women.

Iranian women reiterated their demand to the Majlis for emancipation and electoral reform. They were refused—for the third time.

Disappointed by the Majlis and knowing the clergy would block ratification of their proposed legislative reforms, women activists asked the king, Reza Shah Pahlavi, to intervene and he promised to take action.

One year later, in February 1934, the minister of education established the independent *Kanoun'eh Banuvan* (The Ladies Association), to implement the reforms recommended by the women's organizations. With the power of the state, The Ladies Association helped women achieve many of their demands. Mrs. Hajar Tarbiat, a respected constitutional activist, became the first chairwoman of The Ladies Association, helping to bring many of the women's dreams to reality.

Reza Shah Pahlavi established a national education system to educate all Iranian children, regardless of their gender. On cue, irate clerics took to their pulpits, accusing Reza Sha Pahlavi of apostasy and threatening him with a *fatwa*.

The Communist and Marxist parties also opposed The Ladies Association, alleging "royal interference in the country's social affairs."

In 1935, the first Iranian movie starring a woman, *Dokhtar'eh Lur* (*The Lur Girl*), opened in movie theaters. It was about the Lurs, the people of my ancestry who are the ancient Iranian Meds of the Zagros Mountains in western Iran. The wife of a camera operator played the lead, and she became an overnight star. The clergy responded by accusing the camera operator of every imaginable sin. They failed, however, to keep the devout away from the theaters to see the movie.

That year, the Majlis passed an amendment to the constitution, granting religious minorities in Iran the freedom to practice their religions, however they wished, without the interference or restriction of the government. The clerical establishment had viciously discriminated against religious minorities and segregated them from society. They told the ignorant faithful that any non-Muslim was of a lower caste and therefore, "untouchable," or *najis* (religiously dirty). They forbade Zoroastrians, Christians, Jews, and even non-Shi'a Muslims from any public display of their faiths.

In 1933, the women's organizations held a conference in Tehran and reiterated their demands for reforms in the country's electoral rights. They presented a recommendation to the Majlis, but influential clergy members of the Majlis strongly opposed the change and prevented it from being presented on the floor. Once again, the country's leaders refused stand up for women's equal participation in the governance of their own country.

Parvin Etesami was one of the women who protested through her poetry. Parvin was born in 1907 and began writing poetry around age seven. She attended the Iran Bethel, an American school for girls in Tehran, and graduated from the American Girls College in Tehran in 1924. Parvin learned classical Persian literature from her father. Like my mother and many Iranian women, she had been named Parvin, meaning North Star—the guiding star in the sky.

Parvin Etesami

She rewrote Western literary pieces that her father had translated, in the style of Persian poetry. By 1931, literary magazines published Parvin's poetry, and she published her first book of poetry in 1935.

Parvin was married to a cousin of her father, but the marriage lasted only ten weeks. In 1938, she worked at the library of *Danesh-Saraay'eh Aali* (The Teacher Education College) in Tehran. Her second book was published after her death in 1941 at the age of thirty-five. Her poetry consisted of 209 verses, written in many styles of Persian poetry. Her sudden death shocked the country and especially, women activists.

According to Heshmat Moayyad, a professor of Persian at the University of Chicago with a speciality in Sufi literature, Parvin Etesami's book, *Safar'eh ashk* (*Journey of a Tear*), is among the finest lyrical poetry ever written in Persian. During her short life, Parvin managed to achieve great fame among Iranians. Her poetry follows the classical Persian tradition in form and substance. Parvin's poems were about the pain of being a woman deprived of her human dignity. In one of her poems, she wrote, "A woman lives and dies in a cage."

* * *

The core principal goal of the Ladies' Secret Society in the national conference of 1910 was the education of women, children and adults. As time went by, their numbers and power grew.

By 1934, Effat Tejaratchi was a student in the pilot school of the country's newly-established National Airline. She flew a Tiger-Mouse plane and, on October 20, 1940, she made the first of many solo flights.

After graduating, like other women, she taught at the same school. In 1936, she had received an invitation to be tutor to the queen, but she refused.

Abolition of Mandatory Hijab

In 1934, the Association of Patriotic Women of Iran concluded that without the government's enforcement of the amendment to the country's dress code, ratified by the Majlis on February 23, 1928, they would not be able to refuse wearing the cleric-enforced mandatory hijab.

On January 7, 1936, Reza Shah Pahlavi called for the enforcement of the 1928 law and abolition of the clergy-mandated dress code, the hijab. To stop the clergy from further intimidation, he made execution of the law mandatory and barred women from wearing hijab in public. By doing this, Reza Shah Pahlavi became the target of clerical wrath, and they fell just short of issuing a *fatwa* against him.

The members of the wealthy and influential Qajar family, who had a historic relationship with the clergy, expressed their opposition to Reza Shah Pahlavi, calling him a dictator. Even the country's Tudeh Communist Party, supported by the Soviet intelligence agency, the KGB, began calling him a dictator.

That year, not only was a national education system established to educate boys and girls equally, but Tehran University allowed the first women to enroll as students. Amineh Pakravan was the university's first female lecturer, along with Dr. Fatimah Sayyah, the first woman to become a professor.

(left) Reza Shah Pahlavi attends the graduation of women from the Teacher Education college. (right) The women graduates, 1936

On January 8, 1936, Reza Shah Pahlavi attended the first graduation ceremony of the Teacher Education College, with his wife and two daughters, all three women dressed in Western attire, not wearing the hijab. The women graduates also attended without hijab. For the first time in 360 years, Iran had a queen who attended an official event with the king, handing the graduates their diplomas.

In his opening speech, Reza Shah Pahlavi made a promise to the women activists who had stopped his car and given him their list of demands. He stood by the Iranian women's emancipation movement, saying:

> We should not forget that half of our country's population was unaccounted for, that half of our country's skilled forces were unemployed. Women did not figure in any statistics as though they were creatures of a different kind and were not among the population of Iran. I am not given to pretense and don't wish to compare today with the days gone by but ladies, you should consider this a great day and use the opportunities that you now have for the good of your country.
>
> You, my sisters and daughters, entering society, and having taken steps toward your own and your nation's prosperity, know that it is your duty to work for the betterment of your country. The prosperity of the future is in your hands. You shall be the educators of the next generation and it is through you as good educators that good individuals shall be generated.

The media reported that stores sold 50,000 women's hats in the days after the speech.

164 ео The Ladies' Secret Society

1935 celebration of the removal of the hijab, in the city of Shiraz

After four hundred years of clergy domination, one hundred years of struggle for equal rights, and betrayal after betrayal by the leaders of the constitutional movement, the women of Iran deserved to have the power of the Shah behind them. The emancipation of women had officially begun. An end to the clerical intimidation and harassment of women was on the horizon.

The opening of the first Girl Scouts of Iran by Reza Shah Pahlavi in 1939

The first women students entered the new Tehran University. They included:

Shams al'Moluk Mosaheb
Mehrangiz Manuchehrian
Zahra Eskandari

Batul Samei
Tosey Haeri
Shayesteh Sadegh
Taj Muluk Nakhaei
Forough and Zahra Kia
Badr al Muluk Bamdad
Shahzadeh Kavousi
Saraj al Nesa, a student from India.

In 1937, the Marriage Act eliminated some clerical control over family laws, by finally including them in the country's civil code, making it mandatory to register marriages, divorces, births, and deaths in government notary offices. Also that year, women pushed for passage of the law changing the girls' marriage age, from nine to fifteen, enforceable by the government and making noncompliance punishable by law.

The first graduates of a dressmaking and millinery school in Tehran

Shortly after the emancipation of women, Mr. Hambarson, a well-known tailor in Tehran, opened a school for women to learn the art of dressmaking and millinery. The next morning, a long line of women stood at the door of his school, to learn the craft and become independent. Thirteen women were hired that day.

The first three Iranian women—center middle row—graduates of the American college in Tehran, 1936

The first women graduates from the University of Tehran, including a foreign student from India, in 1940

CHAPTER FIFTEEN

Cold War and Iranian Women (1940 – 1946)

In March 1939, the United States diplomat James Byrnes demanded at a council meeting in the League of Nations to give Iran a chance to also be heard.

The 1940s brought a new world war to Iran by the old European imperialists. This time, they not only occupied Iran, but destroyed the infrastructure and the railroads that the great patriot Reza Shah Pahlavi had built by levying a small tax on sugar. They removed him as the leader that Iran needed to implement the goals of the Constitutional Revolution of 1906.

In 1941, despite declaring neutrality, the allies reoccupied Iran, to save Russia via a "back door."

The British were not happy with Reza Shah Pahlavi because he would not capitulate to their unfair colonialist practices. He fought for a new and fair contract for the petroleum they had been purchasing for practically nothing. As a part of this ruse, the British labeled him a fascist, noting that, in 1933, he had required that his country's name remain Iran, as it had been for two thousand years, and not Persia, as the Greeks had called us. Persia is the name of only one province in Iran. The British prime minister Churchill accused him of being a fascist and friend of Hitler to convince U.S. President Roosevelt to agree to the removal of the Iranian patriotic and progressive king and sent him into exile.

Reza Shah Pahlavi did not hold any degrees or scholastic achievements, since there wasn't any education system available to Iranians when he was growing up. Moreover, he was not a member of the royal One Thousand Family elite and had never traveled out of Iran. He had come from among the people ignored by the government. He was a patriot and visionary who listened to the people and wanted Iran to be the educated, sovereign, prosperous, and modern country that the constitutionalists had fought to achieve.

Before his forced exile, it is said Reza Shah Pahlavi asked President Roosevelt to secure the sovereignty of Iran after the end of the war and to prohibit the Russians and British from their continued occupation.

The second destruction of Iran under the Allies' military machine 1942 – 1943 (Photo from warfarehistorynetwork.com)

After the British ousting of Reza Shah Pahlavi, a group of high-ranking ayatollahs made a proposal to the British minister in Iran, Sir Reader William Bullard, to replace him with a Qajar prince living in London. They argued that a Qajar king would be a better partner for both the British and the clerics.

In 1941, Reza Shah Pahlavi's 22-year-old son, Mohammad Reza Pahlavi, took the throne, despite the objections of the clerical establishment. He was young, European-educated, and inexperienced, with his country under military occupation by the countries that had deposed his father.

As many Iranians said: "He was a young lamb among the wolves. Let us hope he grows up to become a wolf."

When World War II ended, Iran was on the verge of another famine. In its Marshall Plan to help rebuild countries destroyed by World War II, the United States gave Iran a $10 million grant of agricultural support, despite protests from the British and Soviet governments.

The Allies called Iran the "Victory Bridge," and while the Tehran Treaty called for the departure of Allied forces at war's end, the Soviet military continued marching farther into Iran after U.S. forces left and the British Navy retreated into the Persian Gulf.

The Allied leaders at Tehran conference, from November 28 to December 1, 1943

In 1946, President Harry S. Truman, who had just taken office as President of the United States, sent a cable to Soviet ruler Joseph Stalin, giving the Soviet forces six weeks to evacuate Iranian territories, per the terms of the treaty. The Soviet forces left Iran in five weeks, and President Truman became the historical savior of Iran.

The Soviets, however, left behind a rebellious group of Iranians indoctrinated and trained by the Soviet intelligence agency, the KGB, to overthrow the Iranian government in favor of Russian re-domination of Iran behind the Iron Curtain. Although the Iranian military quashed the uprising immediately, Communist sympathizers in Iran created the Tudeh Party (the Party of Masses) to wage guerilla warfare in Iran, starting with the assassination of prime ministers and intellectuals along with the bombing of banks and police stations.

The Tudeh Party continued its underground terrorism and anti-government, anti-American propaganda campaigns guided by the KGB, via the Russian Embassy. The Cold War had begun in Iran.

With the support of the Soviet Union, the Tudeh Party's Women's League had become the most organized of the women's organizations.

Huma Houshmandar, a communist activist, published a pamphlet, *Our Awakening*. In 1949, the Women's League changed its name to the Organization of Democratic Women and opened branches in the major Iranian cities where the Soviets had consular offices. After World War II, the Organization of Democratic Women changed its name again, this time, to the Organization of Progressive Women, and it tirelessly worked for electoral rights.

The Cold War put Iranians at a crossroads that prevented the establishment of the modernity for which they had fought so hard. Of the two imperialist occupiers of pre-war Iran, the Soviets would not let go of Iran and its long-time policy of using the country to access the Persian Gulf. The British had financial problems as a result of World War II and, therefore, relinquished the security of energy transportation in the Persian Gulf to the United States.

While Iranians hated the British and Russian soldiers in their country during the first and second world wars, American soldiers were popular. They were friendly, ate their own food, and did not take food that belonged to Iranians.

My maternal great aunt Muluk told the story of meeting a Russian soldier who grabbed her and slammed her against a wall in an effort to steal her groceries. Seven-months pregnant, she feared losing her baby, between the wall and the Russian soldier's boots, so she gave him her bag of food and begged him to take his boot off her back.

In contrast, Iranians respected Americans because they handed out candy and chewing gum to children and cans of sardines to grownups. My maternal great grandmother who had back problems received her first bottle of aspirin from an American military officer. She never forgot his kindness, and every time she repeated the story for us, she always added, "God bless Americans."

The British worked to keep their apportionment of the Iranian oil and gas industries, using the Cold War to further their interests. World War II had prompted women activists to shift their priorities to charity work, such as raising funds to fight poverty among women and children and caring for the injured Iranian civilians and soldiers from World War II.

Iran paid a hefty economic price with the end of World War II, as it did after the end of World War I, and it simply could not afford a recovery. The U.S. Marshall Plan helped reduce the suffering of yet another famine through a $10 million grant, but it wasn't enough. The British-owned Anglo-Iranian Oil Company refused to pay Iran's small share of oil revenues, and the British government, which owned 51 percent of the Anglo-Iranian Oil Company stocks, refused to address the protests of the Iranian government.

The British had signed a 50-year treaty, creating the Anglo-Iranian Oil Company, in 1901. In a 1933 renegotiation for a larger share of the revenue, the British made the treaty conditional on extending the contract to 90 years.

Iran was in chaos, marked by post-war destruction and poverty. The clerical establishment was up in arms, holding the Shah responsible for the "ungodly" behavior of the women's organizations demanding their rights. The Soviet-directed Communist Tudeh Party exploited the post-war disorder and nationwide poverty to set the stage for a Russian takeover. The National Front Party was a minority party in the Parliament headed by Prince Mohammed Mossadegh Ol'Saltaneh Qajar, who opposed every project the prime ministers proposed.

Between 1946 and 1965, there were four assassination attempts against the king, Mohammad Reza Shah Pahlavi, and three prime ministers were assassinated, their killers driven to violence through clergy *fatwas*.

Shah Mohammad Reza Shah Pahlavi and King Geroge

In 1948, disappointed by the management of the English-controlled Anglo-Iranian Oil Company, the young Shah traveled to London to personally appeal to the British Prime Minister for payment of Iran's shares. The British government treated him royally, but he received a polite, heavy-handed colonialist "no" to his requests.

The next year, in December 1949, the Shah decided to go to Washington, D.C., to make Iran's case and win U.S. support for Iran to get its share of oil income from the British government and the Anglo-Iranian Oil Company. He also asked for help against Soviet aggression in Iran. He even personally appealed to former First Lady Eleanor Roosevelt for her support.

President Truman said he could not influence the British government or the Anglo-Iranian Oil Company, but he agreed to support the Iranian military against the Soviet aggression. On December 30, 1949, President Truman and the young Shah of Iran issued a joint statement, affirming U.S. support and military assistance to Iran.

**(left) Eleanor Roosevelt greets Shah Mohammad Reza Shah Pahlavi.
(right) President Truman speaks with the Shah.**

In a joint statement, President Truman declared:

> ...A serious threat to international peace and security anywhere in the world is of direct concern to the United States. As long ago as December 1, 1943, when President Roosevelt, Prime Minister Churchill, and Marshal Stalin signed the Three Power Declaration at Tehran, the United States made clear its desire for the maintenance of the independence and integrity of Iran. The great interest of the United States in this regard has been repeatedly affirmed in its foreign policy declarations and the United States Government intends to continue that policy to help free peoples everywhere in the maintenance of their freedom wherever the aid which it is able to provide can be effective.

British Prime Minister Winston Churchill and Soviet leader Stalin were not happy with the statement.

Meanwhile, back in Tehran, the minority leader of the Majlis, Mohammed Mossadegh Ol' Saltaneh Qajar and two of his friends, established a political party with a platform that appeased the clerics. The National Front Party also advocated for nationalization of the Iranian oil industry.

(In 1979, National Front Party leaders refused the prime minister position that the Shah offered them and then, shockingly, announced their support for the Ayatollah Khomeini, living in exile in Paris, and denounced Shapour Bakhtiar, a National Front Party leadership member who had accepted the Prime Minister position to save Iran from the clergy. Shapour Bakhtiar was a son of the Bakhtiari Lur tribe of Iran. He was rooted in Iran's ancient tribes, whose members are considered the most patriotic of Iranians and who hold a negative view of the Shi'a clergy, whom they never allowed to interfere in their lifestyles.)

The nationalization of Iran's oil had been the subject of national discussion by Reza Shah Pahlavi since before World War II. With American support and recent British mistreatment, Mohammad Reza Shah Pahlavi decided to choose a prime minister who would attempt nationalization of the Anglo-Iranian Oil Company (AIOC) and guarantee the sovereignty of Iran.

The man he thought would be perfect to carry out the task was none other than Mohammed Mossadegh Ol'Saltaneh Qajar, a patriotic but stubborn older statesman and leader of the minority party in the Majlis. He was a Qajar prince and a wealthy feudal lord with a princely attitude that helped him when dealing with imperialists. Mossadegh had a Juris Doctorate degree from the University of Neuchâtel in Switzerland. Respectful of education, Iranians called him called him "Dr. Mossadegh," because he had a doctorate degree in law. Importantly, he hated the British domination of Iran. As chairman of the new National Front Party with ties to the clergy establishment, he was the perfect choice.

As a Qajar prince, Mossadegh had a friendly relationship with the clergy, especially the clergy members of the Majlis, including the most powerful of the clerics, Ayatollah Kashani, a close friend and confidant. It was an alliance that the Shah, as a young, non-Qajar king who challenged the power and influence of the clergy, did not have.

The Shah appointed the prince as prime minister in hopes of nationalizing the oil industry and removing the British hold on Iran's destiny. The Majlis and the Senate confirmed his appointment with a large majority.

During the 18 months of negotiations, the British government imposed economic sanctions and an international embargo on Iranian oil, in an effort to starve the people and pressure the Shah and Mossadegh into succumbing to the demands of the AIOC. Meanwhile, the Soviet Union took advantage of the country's poverty and political uncertainty to promote Communism and foment unrest and chaos, attempting to ripen Iran for a Russian takeover.

While Prime Minister Mohammed Mossadegh defended Iran's rights and sovereignty at The International Court of Justice in Holland and then at the United Nations, the British government pressured Iran, politically and economically. Historical records show that the British constantly pressured the Shah to fire his Prime Minister, which he refused to do.

President Truman and Prime Minister Mossadegh

The United States stood by Iran and supported Prime Minister Mossadegh Qajar. President Truman invited him to Washington, D.C., after his speech in defense of nationalization of Iranian oil industries to the United Nations. Rejecting the British case against Iran, Truman gave him a stately welcome, complete with medical appointments at Bethesda Naval Hospital for seizures he was suffering. The U.S. Congress honored him with meetings and luncheons. President and Mrs. Truman hosted a dinner for him at the White House, and U.S. Secretary of State Dean Acheson had numerous meetings with him.

The American government gave the Iranian Prime Minister their full support and millions of dollars in aid and loans that Mohammed Mossadegh had requested to fill Iran's empty treasury and save Iranians from starvation. The aid provided in order to give him time to negotiate a fair contract with the British Oil company. Meanwhile, politicians in the British Parliament and House of Lords delivered speeches, railing against the great betrayal by the United States for supporting Iran, not the United Kingdom.

The U.S. media went all out in its support of the Iranian prime minister, giving him a hero's welcome, with his picture on the cover of *Time* magazine as "man of the year." The British media criticized its American counterpart for supporting Iran and abandoning the United Kingdom.

The U.S. came to Iran's aid again and acted as a broker, negotiating a new and fair contract with a very reluctant Anglo-Iranian Oil Company and the British government.

However, Prime Minister Mossadegh rejected the contract, while the treasury was empty and poverty was rampant.

Taking advantage of the pain and poverty of Iranians during the post-war decade of the 1950s, the Communist Tudeh Party began recruiting young Iranian women to join their ranks. In their publications, they promised women equal rights under communism. However, there was a condition. They had to first commit to communist ideology.

Women continued to grow in all fields of education and to excel in arts and sciences, while they were denied basic legal and civil rights under the family laws. On Feb. 28, 1950, Mansureh Atabaki became chief editor of *Zohr'eh Zan* (*Women's Mid-day*) magazine. The first Iranian mezzo-soprano opera singer, Evlyn Baghcheban, graduated from Tehran Music Conservatory in 1950. She was one of the first singers to perform in the new Tehran Rudaki Opera House.

The 1950s was to be a post-war period of peace and recovery, but the original goals of the constitutional movement were no longer the topic of discussion. Equal rights, patriotism, freedom, and respect for human dignity were pushed aside, as internal Cold War ideologies began to tear the country apart. The Soviets wanted to regain domination that American support had managed to sever in their backyard. The clerics wanted their power back and domination over the Iranian people, who wanted equal rights and freedom from religion.

Although the women of Iran had lost a great ally and advocate in Reza Shah Pahlavi, they continued their war against the draconian power-mongering of the clerics and the interference of the European imperialists in the internal affairs of their country. They continued their struggle by forming the National Women's Society and the Council of Iranian Women in 1942 to oppose polygamy, legal under *sharia*.

During his term, from 1951 to 1953, Prime Minister Mohammed Mossadegh refused to deal with the issue of women's rights. Nonetheless, women were determined to exercise what rights they had.

Badri Teymourtash became the first woman dentist in Iran and opened a practice. Later, in 1960, she established the College of Dentistry in the city of Mashhad in northeastern Iran.

Monir Mehran (Asfia) was a sportswoman who founded the first sports center for women and published a sports magazine with her husband in 1943. She was also the first woman sportscaster in Iran.

In 1943, Hajar Tarbiat, Safieh Firuz, and many other women established a political party, *Hezb'eh Zanan* (The Women's Party), which did not do well electorally because many women joined the mixed-gender Democratic Party of Iran.

Professor Shams ol'Moluk Mosahab received a doctorate in Persian literature from Tehran University in 1944 and became the second woman senator, after spending three decades as a member of academia. She wrote and translated numerous books. She passed away in 1997.

In 1944, Meimanat Chubak, an attorney, became the first woman legal investigator, and Iran Alam became the first female professor in the faculty of medicine at the University of Tehran.

Fatimah Sayyah, the first woman appointed to professorship in Iran, was born in 1902. In 1943, Tehran University appointed her chairperson of the department of Russian literature. She was the first woman to represent Iran in the United Nations in Geneva. In 1945, she attended the Congress for Peace and Women in France. She was one of the founding members of the Iranian Writers' Union. She died in 1987.

Nosrat ol'Moluk Kashanchi was born in 1914 and married off at the age of eleven. By seventeen, she had passed the university entrance exam and entered medical school. She became the first woman legal medical advisor in Iran in 1946. That same year, actress Mahin Oskouei became Iran's first female theater director.

Efat ol'Moluk Khajenuri, a member of the Society of the Patriotic Women, founded the first Girls' Industrial Arts School in 1921. In 1946, she transferred the college to the Ministry of Culture, which renamed it the Khajenuri School of Fine Arts, after the activist.

Born in 1925, Raziyeh Shabani was the first woman political prisoner in contemporary Iran. The government arrested and imprisoned her in 1946, accusing her of sabotage as a member of the Communist Party. In response, a group of women activists published a journal of the Women's Party of Iran (*Hezb'eh Zanan'eh Iran*).

Alenush Tarian studied physics in Tehran University and graduated in 1947. She was sent to France to continue her studies, and in 1955, she received her doctorate degree. For a year, Alenush was a student of the French scientist Marie Curie.

On May 14, 1946, the Council of Iranian Women organized a demonstration in front of the Majlis, demanding emancipation. They received no response and were accused of having been "incited by someone behind the scenes."

CHAPTER SIXTEEN

Women Lawyers and the Fight for Enfranchisement (1947 – 1963)

IRANIAN WOMEN continued fighting for their rights amid wayward ideological disruptions. They would not take their eyes off their main goal of total equal rights—a fact that was the bane of the clerical establishment.

The number of educated women in Iran had increased and so had their demands. Education was no longer the issue, because they had achieved that important goal and the government had taken up the task of educating its citizenry. Women had become a part of the nation's brain trust. They were journalists and prominent activists, and they held the power of the pen. Now, they aimed to remove *sharia* from the lives of women, especially underprivileged women.

Women pushed against any barrier they could in athletics, including getting into swim suits. They established the first women's swim team in 1947.

In 1951, the board members of the National Women's Society reached the conclusion that it was essential to be a part of the political process to achieve their goals. They had tried to overturn laws against women through the parliamentary process, but the clerical members of the Majlis thwarted their efforts at every turn.

They went to the office of Prime Minister Mossadegh, asking him to present legislation to the Majlis giving women enfranchisement, but he refused to support them.

In February 1950, Ms. Sadigheh Dolatabadi, a prominent intellectual and woman activist, unsuccessfully tried to meet with Prime Minister Mossadegh to discuss women's rights. Three months later, she wrote a letter to the prime minister, asking him to include electoral rights for women in a new amendment he was submitting to the Majlis.

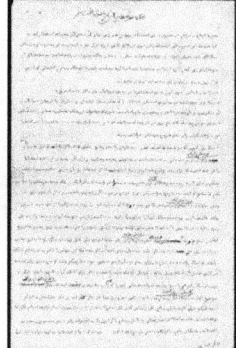

The edited draft of Sadigheh Dolatabadi's letter. Photo from the archives of Harvard University.

In the letter, Ms. Dolatabadi wrote:

> Since the constitutional revolution the laws of the land have ignored the rights of women. In the beginning women were considered minors, criminals, and mentally incompetent, however, the 1928 session of Majlis finally removed that insult against the women of Iran. Unfortunately, nothing much has changed during the last 50 years. We have stood by you and supported you in the Majlis and we now expect that as the Prime Minister you will stand by us...

Under pressure from women activists, Prime Minister Mohammed Mossadegh reluctantly agreed to include the issue in new legislation, but only granted women a provincial electoral right and only in his first draft of the amendment. The amendment provoked the expected uproar from clerical members of the Majlis, including Ayatollah Kashani, the prime minister's closest political ally.

Ayatollah Kashani and Prime Minister Mohammed Mossadegh Ol'Saltaneh Qajar meet at the prime minister's house. The prime minister would often do business from his bed.

The prime minister removed the electoral rights of women from his proposed amendment, and the issue became null and void. Although women gave it their all, protesting in front of the Majlis, they lost to the Qajar prince and powerful clerics once again.

Disappointed by a prime minister who had turned his back on them, women leaders requested an audience with the young Mohammad Reza Shah Pahlavi and asked for his support for the electoral vote legislation in the Majlis. The Shah was on their side, but when he brought up the subject of women's enfranchisement, the clerics refused a debate on the issue. From the pulpit they attacked the Shah, referring to him as an atheist and dictator for even mentioning the issue of women's emancipation.

Despite setbacks, women were making progress. On February 17, 1954, Ms. Ma'sumeh Moghadam was the first civilian to jump free-fall and receive a parachutist's license.

Born in 1891, Shams ol'Moluk Mosahab joined the team of teachers of the Ladies' Secret Society when she was fifteen. In 1916, she sold her inheritance and rented a house, founding the *Dushizegan* (Young Ladies) School two years later. Like most of the activists of the Ladies' Secret Society, she remained a volunteer teacher. Mosahab became a journalist and in February 1955, she began publishing the monthly journal, *Zendegi'eh Roosta'i* (*Village Life*). She was among the first women to enter the University of Tehran, and she was one of the first two women to become a senator in 1963. Shams ol'Moluk married her husband, under the condition that he would not interfere in her activism.

No longer underground, the new generation of the Ladies' Secret Society began to make inroads in visual arts, such as movies and theaters during the 1950s. However, success was not easy for women human rights activists. In 1955, activists such as Mehrangeez Dowlatshahi established the *Rah'eh No* (The New Path) organization and a year later, Safieh Feerouz established the Women's League of Supporters of the Declaration of Human Rights.

In the 1950s, the high-ranking ayatollahs, unhappy about losing their power and influence (especially on women's issues), organized and financed a group of firebrand assassins who called themselves the Muslim Brotherhood. Navob Safavi was the leader of the posse who carried out the assassination of the intellectuals and political figures of Iranian society, whom the high-ranking ayatollahs deplored.

From the beginning, the Ladies' Secret Society protected their girl students from the threats of the clerics. They transported them to school, kept them overnight, and began their education at young ages. Born in 1909, Jamileh Roshdiyeh founded the first kindergarten and the first school to have a bus service. In 1959, she founded the first boarding house to protect female university students from local clerics' threats. In 1957, Pari Khanum became the first woman driver of an 18-wheeler.

In 1957, the women's organizations decided to join forces for the battles ahead. The Organization for the Cooperation of Women's Associations was established with fifteen member organizations joining forces. They knew it would be an uphill battle, but this time, they were determined to fight the clergy to the bitter end, no matter how long it would take.

The business luncheon of the Association of Women Lawyers, 1957

Their list of issues was long, but their main goal was political emancipation, which women were determined to achieve. The new prime minister agreed to submit their legislation again to the nineteenth Majlis, but he also faced strong opposition from the clerical members. Ayatollah Falsafi shouted his opposition to the women and the prime minister. Ayatollah Boroudjerdi even threatened the government for allowing women to hold a Women's Day parade in Tehran.

The women went back to Mohammad Reza Shah for his support, but he only promised to try supporting them on the local municipality councils. Before he could take action, the high-ranking ayatollahs, including Ayatollah Khomeini, sent him a warning: "If you act, you may not be here to carry out the action..." The warning worked. The Shah did not act.

Senator Mehrangiz Manouchehrian (1905-2000) was born a year before the signing of the new constitution, in the city of Mashhad. She graduated from the French Catholic School, Jeanne d'Arc, and began teaching at the school. In 1939, she graduated from the teacher training college, majoring in philosophy and education. She was among the first fourteen women to enter the law school at the University of Tehran in 1946. She married her professor, Dr. Hosseini-Nejad, and opened a law practice after her graduation. She later received a doctorate of Juris Prudence and in 1959, Dr. Mehrangiz Manuchehrian, Esq., became the first woman member of the Iranian Senate, appointed by Mohammad Reza Shah Pahlavi in October 1966. According to the constitution of 1906, the king was given the right to appoint half of the members of the Senate with the approval of the Majlis.

Senator Mehrangiz Manuchehrian

During her three terms as a member of the Senate, Manuchehrian tried to resign twice. The first time was over her proposed legislation on the rights of underage orphans that she finally passed through the Senate, although that, too, was refused by the clergy in the Majlis. The second resignation was a result of the prime minister's refusal to implement a law that would allow the government to issue passports to women without the written consent of their husbands. The Shah rejected both resignations.

The Senate refused to debate the bill when the clergy did not approve Dr. Manuchehrian's proposed family protection legislation and the prime minister was too intimidated by the power of the ayatollahs to support it. One of the more problematic issues was her proposed abolition of polygamy.

However, the women representatives of the Majlis, in the lower house, offered a compromise and submitted her legislation with a few changes that would not put forward all of the reforms that Senator Manuchehrian wanted, but the legislation would pass as a first-step effort.

Women's organizations protested in front of the palace, demanding support for the emancipation of women, in 1961

Journalist Parvin Ardalan wrote, "They knew that polygamy would not be easy to reverse, after all it was a man's right that they would be taking away. So, they agreed to allow polygamy but only with the permission of the wife."

The legislation, the Family Protection Act of 1967, passed in the Majlis. A small majority of the MPs voted for it. The Senate had no choice but to ratify it. The women had accomplished one big step and made plans to revisit the issue the next year.

Mehrangiz Manuchehrian was an advocate of reform and criticized the laws of the theocratic hierarchy against women, children, and the individual rights of citizens. In 1949 she wrote a book, *Criticism of the Constitution of Iran on the Legal Right of Women*, but the government prohibited its publication. After the 1967 ratification of her legislation, her book, *The Family Protection Law*, was published and became a bestseller.

She never hesitated to argue against the men who opposed her legislation on the rights of women and children. She was once sent into exile when she argued with her boss, the minister of justice, who did not want to support an amendment to the existing anti-woman laws.

Senator Manuchehrian was a committed activist of progressive ideals, an internationally known Iranian woman, and a member of the American Society of International Law, the International Communication Committee of National Organization of American Women, the Inter-Parliamentary Union, and the International Alliance of Women Lawyers. She founded the National Union of the Iranian Women Lawyers.

In 1967, Senator Manuchehrian was elected director of the International Alliance of Women Lawyers. In 1968, she received the United Nation's Peace Award. In 1971, she was the recipient of the Peace Award by the Center for World Peace. Mehrangiz Manuchehrian was a licensed lawyer, a senator, an advocate for the Center for the Guidance of Children, and a professor of criminal law. She attended twenty-three United Nation conferences on the issues of women and children and published forty-two books written or translated by her.

In a speech at the American Women Lawyers conference in Virginia she said, "The UN Declaration of Human Rights is not without discrimination against women, because in the very first article it states, 'All human beings are born free and equal in dignity and rights. They are endowed with reason and conscience and should act towards one another in a spirit of brotherhood.' I am proposing to the United Nations to add the word 'sisterhood' to that sentence also."

(left) A meeting of the executive council of the International Council of Women in Tehran, 1966.
(right) Iranian delegation in the International Council of Women.

Senator Manuchehrian was one of the first women lawyers of Iran to work hard to make it possible for women to attend law school. She passed legislation to reform the university's discriminatory policies against women and passed a bill to promote nutritional programs for children in schools in Iran.

This is how Parvin Ardalan, a journalist-activist, describes Senator Manuchehrian in an article entitled, "The Women's Movement in a Game of 'Snakes and Ladders:'"

> The Family Protection Act was drawn up by a lawyer by the name of Mehrangiz Manouchehrian, who was the first female senator in the

Iranian parliament. She was not merely a lawyer but had a tremendous command of the materials of the law.

She was both a feminist and a conscientious opponent of legal discrimination against women. Though she was in the position of power, she championed women's issues. She founded a non-governmental organization, The Association for Women Lawyers, and by virtue of winning the International Prize for Human Rights, she achieved international recognition.

The Association of Women Lawyers was the most active of all women's organizations and the only one to survive the upheaval of the clergy's 1979 takeover of Iran. So far, it has continued to defend human rights, especially women and children's rights, in Iran.

(left) Dr. Farrokhrou Parsa dressed in her ministerial formals while serving as secretary of education, and (right) as a defendant accused of "spreading vice on earth and fighting God" by the cleric's Islamic Revolutionary Court

Farrokhrou Parsa was born in 1910, in the city of Qom, the Shi'a Vatican of Iran, where her mother, Fakhrafagh Parsa, was sent into exile. Her mother was a journalist and activist for the equal rights of women and her father was also a journalist.

As a child, she attended the public school that her mother had fought to establish. In 1941, she received her Bachelor of Science and entered the University of Tehran medical school, where she graduated at the top of her class in 1949. She married her sweetheart, colonel Shirih-Shokhan, in the same year. Although a medical doctor, Farrokhrou Parsa chose to be an educator; she followed in the footsteps of the Ladies' Secret Society, and her own mother, in educating the new generations.

After graduation, she applied and got a job at the Ministry of Education. In 1953, she established the Society of Women Teachers.

In 1959, she became the first female managing director of the administrative department of Tehran National University. A few of the men in power and the usual members of the clergy opposed her appointment, but she survived the ordeal and kept the position.

In May 1964, she won the election and became one of the first five female members of the Majlis.

Dr. Farrokhrou Parsa was the first Iranian woman to become a member of the cabinet, after five hundred years, in 1967. As the Secretary of Education, she realized the dream that three generations of Iranian women, including her own mother, had fought for.

In the early morning of May 8, 1980, Dr. Farrokhrou Parsa was executed by the order of Ayatollah Khomeini. Her crime: "corruption against Allah and promotion of prostitution in the Ministry of Education."

Before she was killed, she wrote to her children. Her letter read:

> ...I am a doctor and know that death is no more than a second, and I welcome it happily. I am not willing to wear a chador or hijab on my head just to live a few more years. I refuse to invalidate 50 years of struggles for the equality of women and men, by saying that I am sorry and regretful. I refuse to even take one step backward....

She was survived by her husband and four children.

Nayereh Saidi

The next generations of leaders of the constitutionalist Ladies' Secret Society like Nayereh Saidi continued the struggle. Nayereh was a poet, writer, and translator, who became one of the first female members of the Majlis. She published the lady's journal, *Banu*, in 1943. Representative Neyereh Saidi was the first Iranian woman to receive the UNESCO prize.

Parvin Sufi began teaching in 1943 after receiving her Jurist doctorate from a university in Paris. She was elected to the Majlis on September 1969, and soon after she was offered a cabinet position by the Prime Minister. She became the first woman Minister of Interior.

Taniya Ashut, an Iranian pianist, received the first prize at the French Conservatory, on June 30, 1958. She also won international prizes in Geneva and Munich.

Instead of going to school, many women obtained new trade licenses, now available to women, to start their own businesses. Mahin Afshar sold some of her dowry to fund a transportation brokerage that she started, becoming the first international businesswoman in Iran. In 1958, she received the first trade license issued to a woman by the government of Iran.

Soghra Azarmi

Dr. Soghra Azarmi was born in 1912, in the city of Kermonshah. She was my mother's cousin and also graduated from American Catholic School in the city of Hamadan, at the age of fifteen. After graduation, the American Catholic School hired her to teach the elementary school classes. While teaching, Soghra continued her higher education at the same American school, so as to be able to teach at the high school level.

In 1931, she applied for a certificate to open a school with support from the American school and she received it to teach the same curriculum. Five years later, she applied to the American college in Tehran and was able to breeze through her studies, receiving her bachelor's degree within only three years.

Dr. Azarmi graduated from the University of Tehran Medical School in 1946 and received a scholarship for an internship at the University of Chicago hospital. While in Chicago, she met Professor Hesabi, an Iranian physicist, and married him. Two years later, she returned home to begin working as Iran's first and foremost cytopathologist. However, upon her return, her husband demanded that she wear a chador and stop working. Dr. Azarmi ended their marriage.

In 1956, she was appointed director of the Tehran University hospital. Later, she joined the Johns Hopkins Hospital Cancer Research Institute in Baltimore for two years and upon her return to Iran, she began working as the head of the Cancer Research Institute, while teaching at the University of Tehran's Medical School.

Aside from the activities and positions that she held, Dr. Azarmi never stopped supporting many of the women's health clinics in the poor neighborhoods in cities throughout Iran. She was one of the first women medical students at the University of Tehran, the first Iranian cytopathologist, and the first director of the first cancer research institute in Iran.

She died in February 1972 from breast cancer. It had taken her a long time to become a medical doctor because there had been no medical school in Iran, but she made her mark.

Shams ol'Zoha Neshat was born in 1915. Her father was Mirza Safi Ali-Shah, an elite Sufi philosopher, and she was also a renowned poet, artist, and painter. I had the honor of having been one of her students. Shams was an internationally known artist and received many awards for her paintings, including the Royal Belgian Art Award, American Art Award and the Harvard University gold medal during the 1950s and 1960s.

Maryam Firouz

Maryam Firouz (1912-2005) was one of the many princesses in the Qajar One Thousand Families. After graduating from a French Catholic school, she was married to another member of the Qajar royalty and she divorced ten years later, after her father's death.

She was wealthy, influential, and hated the Pahlavi Shah. Eventually, she joined the Communist Tudeh Party and married Nooreddin Kianoori, the nephew of Ayatollah Khomeini and the leader of Iran's Tudeh Party. Her activism in the Communist Party made her famous inside and outside of Iran. The European media gave her the title of the "Red Princess." In the 1953 coup, she was an instrumental intermediary between her cousin, Prime Minister Mohammed Ol'Saltaneh Mossadegh, and the Tudeh Communist Party.

After World War II and the two assassination attempts against Mohammad Reza Shah Pahlavi at the hands of a member of the Tudeh Party, she and her husband fled to the Soviet Union, later moving to East Germany to continue their opposition to the Pahlavi Shah and the United States. One year before his takeover, Maryam Firouz praised Ayatollah Khomeini and called him the most important supporter of women's rights in our history.

In 1979, after the Islamic revolution, Maryam Firouz and her husband, Kianoori, returned to Iran and did not approve of what they saw. When the Red Princess and her husband criticized the regime they had previously supported, they were arrested, imprisoned, and tortured.

Later, in February 1988, Kianoori wrote a letter to Ali Khamenei, the Supreme Leader of the Islamic regime, and protested the ongoing and brutal tortures in their prisons:

> My wife, Maryam, was so tortured and flogged so severely, that seven years on, she is still suffering from the pain. They slapped her in the face and hit her on the head so much that she has lost her hearing and all these physical tortures while calling her names such as whore, bitch and flesh-peddler. Allow me to add this last bit of disgraceful behavior, that my wife Maryam was a 70-year-old woman at that time.

A few years later, Iranian authorities released Maryam Firouz from prison but put her under house arrest. She spent the rest of her life writing a book, *Shining Faces*, about average apolitical people who had helped her along the way, out of pure humanity and without any expectations.

In January 2005, the Red Princess died at the age of 95 in her home in Tehran.

* * *

In 1921, after the famine of World War I, the population of Iran was approximately ten million people, most of whom were peasants. By1978, the population of Iran was 32 million, illiteracy was coming to an end, and the economy was flourishing. Women comprised 33 percent of university students, and there were two million women in the workforce, including 190,000 professionals with university degrees. There were women truck drivers, police officers, business persons, actresses, artists, scientists, mayors of small cities and villages, and farmers. Women had risen in politics, with nine judges, 333 leaders in local councils, twenty-two legislators in the Majlis, two politicians in the Senate, and one ambassador.

I was the first woman to become managing director in the notoriously corrupt Customs Administration in 1978.

Mehrangeez Dowlatshahi

Mehrangeez Dowlatshahi (1917–2008) was born into an influential Qajar family. She attended the Zoroastrian elementary school and the American high school. In 1938, she traveled to Germany for her higher education in philosophy and sociology, where she received her PhD and returned home after World War II in 1946. While in Europe, she married an engineer named Mozafar Fee.

She held many positions but the most important of all was the establishment of the Women's Association for a New Path (WANP). In 1958, Mehrangeez joined a group of men to establish the "Center for Progress" that became an important political organization in Iran. In May 1960, she became a founding member of the New Iran Party, and made an important speech at the opening of the first Iranian political party. In 1968, thanks to her persistence, the women's organization of the New Iran Party was added to Iran's first political party. In 1969, she became her party's candidate and a member of the Majlis representing her home city of Kermanshah. She served three terms and established the women's caucus at the Majlis to help push for the implementation of the family protection laws and they succeeded. She represented Iran and the women of Iran in many of the international organizations and conferences.

Ms. Dowlatshahi became the first Iranian woman to represent her country as an ambassador to Denmark.

After the 1979 Islamist revolution, she moved to France, and in 2001, she wrote a book, *Society, Government, and the Movement of the Iranian Women*.

Mahnaz Afkhami

Mahnaz Afkhami, the first president of the Iranian Women Organization and the first Secretary of the Department of Women's Affairs, wrote:

> ...Iranian women's ability to control their lives at mid-century was conditioned by the strong, deep-rooted, and systematic opposition of the conservative Muslim clergy and other conservative forces, many within the government, to their efforts to gain rights. The clergy's attitude to women's rights was also a key factor in their persistent opposition to the Pahlavi regime...

Pari Zangeneh

Born in 1939, in the city of Kermanshah, Iran, Pari Zangeneh was one of the first generation of women opera singers in Iran. She began her studies in music as a young girl and later she graduated from Tehran Music Conservatory, as an opera singer. Afterwards, she attended the Vienna Conservatory and graduated from there. Pari became a famous opera singer, performing internationally. Her recording of lullabies from different countries in their traditional languages became world famous. In 1972, she lost her sight in an automobile accident, but it did not stop her from performing. For the first time, she recorded Iranian folk songs. She became an activist for the rights of the sight-impaired in Iran and wrote a book, *Beyond Darkness*, published in 2008. My sister, Nazila, one of the youngest women opera singers who attended the Vienna Conservatory before 1979, remained in Europe after the Khomeini takeover.

Forough, a poet, artist, and rebel

Forough Farrokhzad (1935-1967) was born on January 5, 1935, in Tehran, into a middle-class family of seven. Despite her family's objection, she dropped out of high school and married a cousin at the age of sixteen. Three years later, she separated from her husband, giving him custody of their son.

Forough wanted to pursue her dream of becoming a poet, and in 1955, she succeeded in publishing her first book of poetry, *Aseer* (*The Captive*), establishing her as a major literary talent. In 1956, she published a second collection of poems. The publication of her third book, *Oseeyaan* (*Rebellion*), made her a household name and a poet of great acclaim.

But poetry was not enough for Forough, who made a documentary movie about the leper colony in Iran in 1962. She won many international awards for her short film, *Khaaneh Siaah Ast* (*The House is Black*). Her documentary impacted Queen Farah deeply, who established a modern village with health and comfort facilities to help lepers.

By 1963, Forough had become an international icon and the subject of many biographical short films by UNESCO. Italian filmmaker Bernardo Bertolucci has made a movie about her life.

Over the next two years, she published two more collections of her poetry; but, on Monday, February 14, 1967, while Forough was driving to visit her mother, her car struck a wall and she was killed from injuries to the head.

In her poems, she talked about the plight of Iranian women and a society that was harshly intolerant of her lifestyle and life choices.

Call to Arms

Only you, O Iranian woman, have remained
In bonds of wretchedness, misfortune, and cruelty,
If you want these bonds broken,
grasp the skirt of obstinacy.

Do not relent because of pleasing promises,
never submit to tyranny,
become a flood of anger, hate and pain,
excise the heavy stone of cruelty.
It is your warm embracing bosom
that nurtures proud and pompous man,
it is your joyous smile that bestows
on his heart warmth and vigor.

For that person who is your creation,
to enjoy preference and superiority is shameful,
woman, take action because a world
awaits and is in tune with you.

Sleeping in a dark grave is happier for you
than this abject servitude and misfortune,
where is that proud man? Tell him
to bow his head henceforth at your threshold.
Where is that proud man? Tell him to get up
because a woman is here rising to battle him,
her words are the truth, in which cause
she will never shed tears out of weakness.

Jinous Mahmoudi Nemat (1929-1981) was a physicist who became the first director of the office of meteorology in Iran and later the president of the meteorology college. She represented Iran in the international meteorologist conferences.

Jinous Mahmoudi Nemat

The Islamist regime called her an apostate and executed her at the age of fifty-two for "crimes against Allah," because she wouldn't renounce her faith, as a Baha'i.

* * *

The mission of the Ladies' Secret Society, begun in the mid-nineteenth century, educating young girls and adult women, continued after the Constitutional Revolution of 1906, and its work eventually paid off. A new generation of women believed they had to get educated and participate in the affairs of the country.

My father, the first feminist in my life, was proud of his three daughters. His advice to me and my sisters was simple: "If you want to be a sovereign individual, not just wives but partners of your husbands, you must be able to be economically independent, and since you are not members of the One Thousand Families, it will not be possible unless you strive to be three professional women with the best education."

As a high school student, I wrote a series of articles in the weekly publication, *Etelaa'aat'eh Banovon* (*Women's News*), including a commentary about the unfair treatment of teenage girls by their parents and the rules of society.

In the 1960s, when my generation of women entered society, there was no need for the word "secret" in the empowerment we were forging in the spirit of the Ladies' Secret Society.

We were not only reading and writing, but we had opportunities to become highly educated women, with strong voices to stand up for our rights.

There were many highly qualified women university graduates in the workforce. The women of Iran had become educated and influential in all occupations. The activists had grown in numbers and had become powerful.

Women were more organized and politically involved, standing on the streets, blocking the Shah's car, marching to the office of the prime minister, standing in front of the Parliament and the Palace of the Shah, unequivocally demanding their emancipation. They campaigned for their human rights even by meeting with the more moderate clerics, when necessary.

Yet, Iranian women still lived under *sharia,* manipulated by clergy who continually worked to deprive them of human and civil rights. They could not win custody of their children after they reached a certain age or travel and work without the permission of the male guardians in their lives. Men could divorce their wives when they wished, without even their knowledge. Daughters inherited half of what sons inherited. Polygamy and temporary marriages remained legal. The law of the land included religiously-sanctioned prostitution of poor women and many other injustices.

By the early 1960s women were convinced they should have electoral rights. Pressure mounted on the prime minister and the Majlis, not only from women, but also from many men, who finally—and formally—joined the movement.

To assert their power in a gesture of civil disobedience, hundreds of thousands of Iranian women around the country went to the election polls in February 1960. Knowing election officials wouldn't count their votes, they still cast their votes in ballot boxes, as a symbol of their determination to realize emancipation from the Shi'a clergy.

In 1961, Ms. Monir Vakili, the first internationally-known Iranian opera singer, established an opera company and pushed for the construction of an opera house.

Meanwhile, three more organizations joined the High Council of the Organization of Iranian Women, and they invited the Shah's twin sister, Princess Ashraf Pahlavi, a feminist, to join them.

The High Council of the Organization of Iranian Women began focusing on a fundraising project to support their political activism. A few years later, they changed the name to the Organization of Iranian Women.

Finally, that year, the new government of Prime Minister Ali Mansur established a rule, allowing women to participate in local council elections. In May 1962, Ms. Hakimi announced her candidacy for the Isfahan city council, but she was barred from registration.

The next year, in September 1963, Ayatollah Khomeini sent a telegram to the Shah and politely complained that the government had not followed the laws of Islam by giving women the right to vote in local and national elections. He wrote:

> This troublesome issue has disturbed many of the Islamic *Ulema* (clerical scholars). I would like to remind His Majesty that the interest of the country lies only in the preservation of the Islamic canons. Please order the government to remove all the programs that are offensive to the holy Islam, so our Muslim nation will pray for you.

The women were undeterred. On January 7, 1963, following the barring of Ms. Hakimi from registering for council election in Isfahan, the High Council of the Organization of Iranian Women staged a national protest, winning the support of the people to the total enfranchisement of women in the upcoming referendum.

The High Council of the Organization of Iranian Women protested in front of the office of Prime Minister Asdollah Alam, to get him to enforce the new provincial law. Under pressure from the city of Qom, where Khomeini and other high-ranking clerics lived, the prime minister canceled his support.

On December 10th, the Association of Women Lawyers issued a statement criticizing the government's lack of courage in enforcing the laws of the land.

The clergy would not retreat. They opposed the law and called it unconstitutional and in defiance of *sharia* law. From the pulpits, they called on the faithful to rise up against the infidels, and on January 22, 1963, they organized a major demonstration that became uncontrollable, resulting in many injured and arrested.

Nevertheless, women would not give up. The next day, a group of women's organizations called for a peaceful demonstration against the members of the Majlis who had voted against the enfranchisement of women. Teachers, high school students, the National Iranian Oil Company and bank employees, and thousands of shopkeepers participated in the rally. A group of teachers and office workers held a one-day strike.

Three days later, on January 26, 1963, the Shah called for a national referendum on a set of social, economic and political proposals called the White Revolution. The referendum called for the right of ownership of land for the peasants by abolition of feudalism. Women became the main activists for its approval, for one of the proposed changes was an amendment to the constitution of 1906, revising the electoral laws to grant women enfranchisement.

Following the success of the referendum, in February of that year, the Majlis ratified the revision with a majority of the legislators. The women secured zero votes from the clergy.

With the majority vote of the Majlis (parliament), including women, the Majlis removed the Article 13 laws that barred women from exercising their right to political participation by crossing it out and replacing the word "male" from Article 6 and Article 9 with the words "all citizens." On March 3, 1963, following 353 years, of struggle, the women of Iran became politically enfranchised.

Women fought hard to succeed and when the time came, they campaigned for their candidates and lined up to vote.

It took the clerics just a matter of months to rally their followers to fight back.

In June 1963, during the Islamic holy month of Ramadan, Ayatollah Khomeini called on his followers to rise up against the White Revolution and the referendum for women's rights. Khomeini issued a *fatwa* that proclaimed; "women's enfranchisement equals prostitution."

The *fatwa* amounted to an assassination order.

From the pulpit, Khomeini led uprisings in Tehran and Qom, resulting in bloody clashes between the police and his followers. The uprisings continued, and no amount of negotiation convinced Khomeini to stop the destruction that resulted in murder, injuries, and arrests. To establish peace and order, Prime Minister Hassan Ali Mansour ordered Khomeini's arrest. He was tried in the court of law for ordering assassinations, and a long list of other crimes, including instigating uprisings, violence and public destruction of properties. Khomeini was found guilty and sentenced to death by the court. A group of clerics went to the prime minister, asking for clemency. Ayatollah Shariatmadari, a respected peaceful cleric, went to the Shah and asked him to grant Khomeini an amnesty. Ayatollah Shariatmadari asked that Ayatollah Khomeini be sent out of the county to exile, in order to establish peace in the country. The Shah accepted the offer and Khomeini was exiled to Turkey.

The Communist Tudeh Party went on a propaganda rampage, calling the Shah a dictator and the detainees, political prisoners.

Not long after, one of Khomeini's followers assassinated Prime Minister Hassan Ali Mansur in front of the Majlis. He belonged to the *Ikhwan ol'Muslimin* – the Muslim Brotherhood. When arrested, he said he killed the prime minister for signing a treaty with the United States.

* * *

With the clergy inciting uprisings against women, Iranian men stood by the country's brave women activists. On August 27, 1963, they convened the Congress of the Free Men and Free Women to choose male and female candidates for the upcoming Majlis elections. In the following month's elections of the twenty-first Majlis, six women won more votes than their male opponents.

The Shah appointed Dr. Mehrangiz Manuchehrian and Professor Shams ol'Moluk Mosahab as Iran's first female senators, receiving the approval of the Majlis in a wide majority.

Meanwhile, according to a declassified CIA report, in November 1963, Khomeini sent a message to President Kennedy asking for U.S. support to replace the Shah with him. The CIA report said:

> Khomeini explained that he was not opposed to American interests in Iran. On the contrary, he thought the American presence was necessary as a counterbalance to Soviet and possibly British influence. Khomeini also explained his belief in close cooperation between Islam and other world religions, particularly Christendom.

The White Revolution had also ended feudalism in Iran, eroding clerical wealth and power in the country.

The Shi'a clergy, including Ayatollah Khomeini, have always been a part of the feudal lords who ruled Iran. Starting with the Safavid dynasty, they owned land and peasants. The clerics used a system of *waqf*, a form of endowments to religious institutions, along with *khums* and *zakat*, sharia law taxation on the people of Iran. When the people voted to end feudalism, the Shi'a clergy led by Ayatollah Khomeini became angry at the Shah and attacked him in sermons from the pulpit.

In 1965, following another uprising incited by Khomeini against women and the end of feudalism in Iran, the U.S. State Department reported:

> Khomeini says he has opposed the emancipation of women under present circumstances, stating that emancipation without education is meaningless.

Iranians were shocked by the United States' response in support of the clerical power. The U.S. never looked at the constitution of Iran to see if education was the law; no one questioned the fact that illiterate men were voting legally, so why not women? Neither did they mention the fact that Iranian women were educated.

Unfortunately, Mr. William G. Miller of The State Department Bureau of Intelligence and Research misrepresented the issue in a multipage report that he sent to the office of Secretary of State Dean Rusk in 1965. Mr. Miller wrote:

> Part of the conflict between the regime on the one hand and the religiously-oriented masses on the other is over the pace and means of carrying out reforms. The clergy has under great pressure grudgingly recognized that reforms in Iranian society must be made. Khomeini says he is not opposed to land distribution and that land distribution is consistent with Islam if just compensation is made. He has opposed, for example, the emancipation of women under present circumstances stating that emancipation without education is meaningless. In almost every instance the principle of a particular reform has been accepted, the challenge has come over methodology. The clergy by its training and philosophical outlook is tradition-bound. The basic changes implicit in some of the Shah's reforms, such as land distribution, require adaptations that will markedly alter the whole religious structure. "What will the position of the *ulama* be without the *waqf*?" is the kind of question that has deep philosophical and religious implications for

the *ulama* and Iran as a whole. That there has been opposition on the part of the *ulama* is inevitable. But within the traditional structure, the power of the *ulama* might have been used to justify and institutionalize the changes taking place.[1]

To assert his power, Khomeini issued *fatwas*, calling for the assassination of any opponent. He threatened and intimidated women, men, Majlis members, authorities, cabinet members, the Shah, and the United States of America over every step the people of Iran took to establish complete separation of religion and government, even though Iran was following the principles set forth in the human rights proclamation of Cyrus the Great, not Western culture.

Women were ready to take their place in the political arena once the new law took effect. They had their candidates to promote for the upcoming election, succeeded in sending five women to the Majlis, and installed a few more in other positions around the country.

The first five

Hadjar Tarbiat was born in 1906, in Tabriz. She began teaching in small home schools, then founded an elementary school and later, a high school, using new teaching methods. In 1963, she became a member of parliament from Tabriz.

In 1964, Morasa Kohrugi was the first Iranian woman to win an election and she became the mayor of her small town, Nosud, in western Iran.

On June 24, 1965, Ghodsieh Hedjazi, a lawyer, became the first female prosecutor in the Ministry of Justice when she brought charges against a man for theft and fraud, on June 24, 1965.

The success of the first elections encouraged women activists to or-

---

1 http://www.pugwash.org/reports/rc/me/tehran2006/tehran2006-report.htm.

ganize a support system, establishing an Election Committee to help more women run for political office. The goal was not only to increase the number of women representatives in the Majlis and Senate but also to encourage and support women political candidates in rural villages and towns.

Campaign and Election Committee

On October 16, 1966, women representatives met in a seminar to prioritize women's issues, where they made a list of issues they planned to introduce and pass in the Majlis. Health, education, employment, and family laws topped the list. Following the seminar, on October 24, Senator Manuchehrian introduced legislation making family law secular, but the clergy rejected it, and they threatened to excommunicate her as a *kafir*, a nonbeliever.

By 1970, the number of women MPs had grown to eight, and the support group concentrated on winning more seats in the Majlis every election—just what the clergy feared. Empowered rural women had also begun quietly winning in more local, village, city council, and mayoral elections without any fanfare.

* * *

Women's activism did not end with politics. Women pursued advancement in the arts and other fields.

To be a prima ballerina, Aida Ahmadzadeh and her husband, Nejad Ahmadzadeh, established the Iranian National Ballet Company in November 1966.

By request of the Shah, the Majlis ratified a constitutional amendment on August 23, 1967, giving the Queen the right of regency in the event of the Shah's death, while the Crown Prince was not of age.

Ayatollah Khomeini denounced the action and declared it against Islamic laws.

Mahnaz Afkhami, a women's rights activist, became secretary general of the *Sazmaneh Zanoneh Iran*, the Organization of Iranian Women.

With determined activism and the support of women, Senator Manuchehrian presented the family protection legislation to the Senate in 1967, but it was opposed by some of the senators who were threatened by the clergy.

However, the issue was pursued by the women's caucus of the Majlis, after a deal was made with the prime minister. The Family Protection Law was ratified in the lower house of the Majlis in September 1968 but not before some changes were made by the cleric members. Under the new law, divorce was referred to the family court and was no longer the sole right of men. The age for marriage was set to 18 years for girls and 21 for boys.

The last phase of the implementation of women's equal rights was the total secularization of the family laws and the use of the judiciary for setting up family courts. Senator Manuchehrian wrote and ratified the law in the Senate in the same year. Under this law, the women of Iran had earned the right to become judges in the family courts.

This was the beginning of a holy *jihad* by the clergy establishment. The women of Iran and the Shah faced the wrath of clerics, led by Ayatollah Khomeini who made a famous speech from the pulpit, damning the Shah for supporting the women of Iran. He did not direct his anger and assault on women, because he did not consider them worthy of mention.

The first class of Iranian women judges

Following protests, clerics took action with a drastic response, writing threats in *fatwas* by Ayatollah Khomeini, declaring the act heretical.

The clergy took to the pulpits and called on the faithful to demonstrate against the Shah, America (as they called the United States), and women. Demonstrations became violent and the police intervened. Every successful step made by women enraged the clerical establishment and made its leaders fear they would lose their power by losing control over the women and children of Iran.

The young generation of women finally made it into all branches of the Iranian Armed Forces and passed their training with excellence.

Akram Monfared and Sāsān-dokht Sasani, the first female Iranian Air Force pilots, in 1967. At the age of 20, Sasani became the youngest female pilot and Monfared graduated at the top of her class in flight numbers.

However, the struggle for complete emancipation continued in the Majlis and the Senate. Women would not give up and that year the Organization of Iranian Women encouraged lawmakers to expand the

Family Protection Act. One more step was taken toward the amendment of family laws on child custody, the joint ownership of the family assets, and the right of women to receive a passport without the written consent of their husband or father. The enactment of these changes in the family protection laws took two more years to become a reality for Iranian society.

Elaheh Azodi, 1968 Miss Teen International

The Organization of Iranian Women amended their charter in 1973 to include defending women's health, family, and social rights, to achieve complete equality in society and under the law. The changes to the charter transformed the women's movement from a grassroots human rights movement and organization into a social work advocacy and a governmental auxiliary organization. The Organization of Iranian Women (OIW) became involved in the healthcare and education systems, instead of remaining a gang of independent activist women standing for gender equality, ready to fight an opposition they knew would not be defeated easily.

When Khomeini began his revolution, no women's organization existed to oppose him or to argue against Marxist-Islamist books, such as *Fatima is Fatima* and *Western Struck*, which supported the gender apartheid policies that the people had defeated in the Constitutional Revolution of 1906. The field was wide open for the new doctrine of Red Shi'ism to rise and influence a generation that was newly educated but intellectually aimless and lost in society.

The great women who had fought for 70 years were either dead or had become too old and the younger generation was absent from the arena of ideas. We were all too busy getting degrees, working, building a carrier, and running our families when the old enemy struck back in 1979.

It was not easy to eradicate over 300 years of the Shi'a clerical power and influence. They had established a vast foundation, creating a whole auxiliary of fake Arab culture in the minds of the illiterate poor nation of Iran, and had done so for centuries. They had vast networking centers in the mosques, with a hundred thousand clerical members and seminaries ready to follow their leadership. The mosque was also wealthy for they collected Islamic taxation: *khums* and *zakat*. They had also collected monthly stipends from the government since the Safavid era, excluding the fifty years of the Zand era.

Even after the Constitutional Revolution of 1906, the clerical establishment used *sharia* to keep women and children hostage. They forced changes in the adopted Belgian constitution to allow the membership of clerics in the parliamentary system that helped them keep their influence in the laws of the land, hence guaranteeing their hold on the juggernaut of the nation, no matter how hard women worked to bypass their power.

The clergy targeted the United States, blaming American culture for corrupting the God-fearing Muslim nation of Iran by influencing women to challenge Allah's laws by asking for equal rights, and by teaching young Iranians about human rights and the separation of mosque and government.

The Shi'a clerical establishment hated the United States not because of U.S. foreign intervention or Iranian patriotism. Historically, the clergy in Iran had had an amicable understanding with the Russian and British "colonization" of Iran for over a century. As a matter of fact, there is even an old joke among the Iranians that goes, "If you lift the clergy's turban you will see a stamp on their foreheads saying, 'Made in England.'"

The Iranian clergy never opposed the Russian occupation of Iran and never protested against their massacre of Muslims in Central Asia or Chechnya.

In one speech, Khomeini said, "We are not afraid of America's military might, we want to keep out the influence of their 'culture' that is corrupting the Muslim nation."

Aside from the clergy's frustration over losing its constituency to education, economic prosperity, and the activism of women, the KGB wanted Iran back behind the Iron Curtain.

KGB-style anti-American propaganda began after World War II, when Truman forced Stalin to leave Iranian territory. However, anti-Shah propaganda began in the mid-1950s, continuing through the next decade. The propaganda portrayed the United States as capitalist and thus imperialist, with the Shah labeled a "stooge of the imperialist." There was no mention of 150 years of Russian imperialism against Iran.

Dissemination of disinformation was endless and continuous. Accusations circulated, such as the idea that the United States was burying its nuclear waste in the Iranian desert with the blessing of the Shah. Another trope chronicled the story of an American working in Iran who supposedly refused donated blood from an Iranian for his dying child.

The CIA and the British MI6 organized a coup in 1953 against Mossadegh, with little mention of the Anglo-Iranian Oil Company. The British officer in charge of the coup, Anthony Cavendish, said, "Prime Minister Mossadegh was removed through skillful planning by SIS, a branch of British MI6, with very little help from CIA. The truth is that the CIA took very little part in the business, except in the financial phase."

At a cabinet meeting on August 25, 1953, Prime Minister Churchill said, "It would be easy for the Americans, by the expenditure of a small amount of money, to keep all the benefits of many years of British work in Persia."[2]

The first young generation of Iranians that Reza Shah Pahlavi had sent to Europe for education during the 1930s were the first non-Qajar educated Iranians who joined the government.

Farangees Yeganegi

Farangees Yeganegi (1916- 2010), an important member of the Ladies' Secret Society, spent her life in the service of Iran and the country's women. For many years, Mrs. Yeganegi was president of the High Council of Iranian Women. In 1956, she and her husband built the Library of Ancient Iranian Culture in Tehran, containing 12,000 books and thousands of research documents. The Islamic regime refused to continue

---

2 Elm, *Oil Power, and Principle, Iran's oil Nationalization and its aftermath.*

funding the upkeep of the library, but hailing from a prominent Iranian Zoroastrian family, Mrs. Yeganegi secured financial support from the Zoroastrians, which continues to support the library today.

The primary means of advancement for women was still education, in most cases involving simple literacy skills followed by vocational and job-oriented skills in the rural parts of the country. In 1966, Mrs. Yeganegi established the Iranian National Handicrafts Center, a semi-independent government organization, to create a market for Iranian handicrafts and help the economic growth of rural villages and tribes. She was my first boss.

The mother of my college roommate in California, she offered me a job when I returned to Iran after graduation, warning me the salary was not much, but the work would be rewarding and the realization of my duty as an Iranian woman.

She told me, "You are paying forward to the society that gave you opportunity and the scholarship. This job will help the economic conditions of the poor rural women, and you are well-suited to take it up."

From ancient times, Iranian women have produced the goods of cottage industries, but in the twentieth century, only Iranians bought those goods, providing meager finances to a family. In my first job, I was sales manager at the Iranian National Handicrafts Center.

Five years later, I was selling $80 million in Iranian handicrafts, mostly made by tribal and village women, to many Western countries in wholesale and retail businesses in the heart of New York City and Paris. All of the sales income went to the artisans and craftspeople, and we were able to create other cottage industries to make usable twentieth-century marketable products, from silk fabrics to needlework, leatherwork, pottery, and other handicrafts.

Queen Farah Pahlavi was the best promoter of Iranian crafts inside the country and abroad. She had her dresses designed and made in Iran, mostly with needlework, silk batik, or brocades made by village and tribeswomen. She even promoted homemade clothes by having her family wear handcrafted clothes—needlework vests and ties for the Shah and her sons and dresses for her daughters and her—made by women from the Baluchi tribes in southeastern Iran, at the border of Afghanistan and Pakistan. Her presents to foreign dignitaries included traditional crafts made by Iranian artisans and artists.

The Iranian National Handicrafts Center created a rural class of economically independent women in the remote villages of Iran. When Khomeini took over in 1979, he closed most of the center's activities.

Queen Farah Pahlavi dressed her family (left) and herself (center and right) in handcrafted clothes made by traditional artisans and young Iranian fashion designers.

Masomeh Soltan was born in Tehran in 1945. She married a bus driver at the age of nineteen and, a few years later, she became the first woman interstate bus driver.

Parvin Darabi was Iran's first woman electronic engineer. In the 1970s, she was the first Iranian woman to work as a computer technician in Iran.

The members of the Organization of Iranian Women hailed from all of the country's religions. Dr. Mehri Rasekh, a prominent member of the Bahai community, and Ms. Shamsi Hekmat, a Jewish educator, were on the central council of the Organization of Iranian Women.

Ms. Farangees Yeganegi, a prominent Zoroastrian feminist, was appointed first secretary of the high council and later, deputy secretary general of the Organization of Iranian Women.

Other appointed members were university professors Parvin Buzari, Fakhri Amin, Vida Behnam, and, another member of the Baha'i faith, Nikchehreh Mohseni.

In the 1970s, the Organization of Iranian Women finally succeeded to win the women's right to assume custody of their children if the child's father died. The guardianship of paternal grandparents and the clergy was removed. On December 21, 1972, Robabeh Najafizadeh, an activist woman, made history by becoming the first public prosecutor in the small city of Miyaneh in northwestern Iran.

During the 1970s, Iranian women were exceeding in all fields—as nuclear scientists, truck drivers, international beauty contestants, and comprising nearly 40% of the University students.

1972 candidates for Miss Teen Iran

An article in the *Keyhan* daily evening newspaper about the women who were one-fourth of the scientists working in Iranian nuclear energy research in the 1970s

The 1970s saw the height of the Cold War, with Iran at the heart of that war. Soviet policy was to push the United States out of the Middle East and win back the Iranian colony they had lost after World War II. For the anti-American Shi'a clerical establishment, the goal was to return Iran to the Qajar era and establish the clergy-shah powerbase, written in 1695 by Mullah-Bashi Mohammad Taghee Madjlesi under the Safavid Shah Soltan Hosein. They wanted the Russians and British back in control, and they wanted to keep the country's citizenry poor and illiterate. One strategy of Communist-Islamist propaganda was to make the Shah a symbol of the evil United States in Iran.

The Communist Tudeh Party, supported by the Soviets and directed by its KGB intelligence agency, had one goal: to kick the U.S. out of Iran. The Islamist-Marxist *Mojahedeen E Kalq* (also known as the MEK, or now, the National Iranian Resistance Council, NIRC) was a terrorist organization trained by Palestinians and financed by Libyan dictator Moammar Gaddafi, with close ties to the KGB. Its goal was to kill as many Americans as it could in Iran to force the United States to leave.

The campus of Tehran University on a fall day in the 1970s

Slowly, a new generation of young, educated, middle-class youth, raised in a secular system and non-Qajar, replaced the older generation of Qajars that had been the governing class of Iran. They assumed leadership positions in government and willingly worked with women on issues related to social, cultural, and economic development.

By 1975, the Organization of Iranian Women had built a network of 349 branches in Iran, with two thousand paid specialists in its legal, childcare, and family planning sections in 120 centers throughout the country. The organization's budget had grown tenfold, not counting volunteer services, in-kind donations, and charitable contributions. Work in the areas of literacy, general education, and vocational training continued.

The Iranian mission to the United Nations Commission on the Status of Women proposed a program that had been developed in Iran, the International Research and Training Institute for the Advancement of Women. The UN General Assembly adopted the proposed plan in 1975 for the first conference to be held in 1980 and hosted by Iran. The Organization of Iranian Women volunteered Iran as the permanent host for the main office of the UN's International Research and Training Institute for the Advancement of Women. Unfortunately, Iranian women had lost to the clergy by 1980, and the first conference on the International Research and Training Institute for the Advancement of Women never took place in Tehran.

Shohreh Nikpour became the second Iranian to become Miss Teenage International in 1975.

The Organization of Iranian Women urged the government to establish a Department of Women's Affairs that would be responsible for the health, social welfare, job training, and education of the women of Iran.

In December 1975, Prime Minister Amir-Abbas Hoveida added the Department of Women's Affairs to his cabinet and appointed Mahnaz Afkhami, the past president of the Organization of Iranian Women, as the department's minister. Ms. Afkhami became the second woman member of the Iranian cabinet.

Although the department had proposed no changes, nor implemented full secularization of family law, the clergy—namely, Ayatollah Khomeini—reacted frantically as usual, calling for demonstrations and uprisings throughout the country. The clergy called the establishment of the Department of Women's Affairs and the appointment of Ms. Afkhami an act of heresy. The Department of Women's Affairs was to secure funding in the government budget to improve the socioeconomic life of poorer women.

Women representatives and senators made a few more small steps forward in changing the laws. The Majlis made progress on the law requiring that a woman get her husband's permission if she wanted a passport, reforming the law so that a husband's consent was required only once for a woman to travel. In 1977, abortion became legal on demand for unmarried women; married women had to have the consent of their husbands.

Maliheh Farshid

In 1978, Maliheh Farshid, an architect, was awarded the job to design the Sports Complex in the city of Ahvaz, in southern Iran. She planned to have the complex ready for the 1984 Olympics, which Iran had been designated to host.

Queen Farah Pahlavi

Farah Diba, the daughter of a middle-class single mother in Iran, grew up among ordinary people and became Farah Pahlavi, the people's working queen. She was comfortable among the people and made sure that government officials heard their voices. Over the advice of her security team, she chose to deliver her children at a free women's clinic run by the Organization of Iranian Women.

In 1978, the Shah chose Farah Pahlavi as regent, despite the protests of the Shi'a clergy establishment. After 300 years, an Iranian queen had been appointed guardian of her children, including the crown prince and heir to the throne, with a voice on the country's issues.

By unifying their organizations, the women of Iran began a new chapter in their movement. Slowly, the activists abandoned to the government issues of human rights and opposition to clerical power. They started pushing for specific services for women, including free health care, child care, economic support, job training, and legal and social protections.

Grassroots activism around the country diminished. The new generation of the Ladies' Secret Society was largely educated and included professional, middle-class women who passed the torch to the government's Department of Women's Affairs. The Organization of Iranian Women became the government's auxiliary organization. By 1978, there was no grassroots activist watchdog organization to stand up to the return of the clerical cabal.

CHAPTER SEVENTEEN

Red Shi'ism and Clergy Takeover (1978 – 1979)

IN THE 1960S, some of the students who went overseas for education in Europe and the United States came from clerical and religious families. The young male students disapproved of Western social culture and stayed away from it. However, they did become involved in the Socialist-Marxist movements, especially in France. Hence, when they returned home, they became tools for Khomeini's Hezbollah, with the communist movement members opposing the policies of the government.

Slowly, they crafted their own ideology: a combination of Shi'a dogma and Marxist doctrine, both of which were against modernity, human rights, women's rights, individual freedom, and democracy. To some, what they created was analogous to black liberation theology in the United States. This ideological hybrid grew in Iran in the 1970s.

These young, newly-educated Iranians began advocating for the replacement of "Western civilization," symbolized by the United States, in an ideology that they called "Red Shi'ism," with the red symbolizing Marxism. Among their leaders were men by the names of Ali Shariati, Jalal Al-e Ahmad, Khalil Maleki and others.

Ali Shariati was the son of a cleric in a small town in the province of Khorasan in northeastern Iran and a first-generation university graduate in his family. A student at Tehran University, he earned his PhD in theology and divinity and received a two-year scholarship to continue his studies in France.

Shariati was young and charming. He wore ties and tailor-made

Western suits. He had attended university, not a seminary, and finished his graduate studies in France. He was a gifted writer and public speaker, who spoke standing behind a podium, not from a pulpit.

Ali Shariati

Shariati developed a brand of Red Shi'ism that promised an international revolution for social justice, through *sharia*. His Islamic reformation movement was an ideological combination of the Marxist socialism that he had absorbed in France and *sharia* that his father had taught him. He believed in a *jihad*, or struggle, against corrupt Western modernity.

He attracted a generation of young, educated followers from poor, uneducated older and sometimes illiterate families. The youth did not want to return to living in the shadow of ignorance, yet they could not find their place in modern society. They did not believe in the clerical establishment, but they believed in their religion. They did not approve of the clergy-tradition lifestyles, but they resented the new modernism that they did not quite understand and did not fit into. They were book-educated but not intellectual—and that made them easy prey.

Shariati connected with this new generation, who in many ways had biographies that resembled his own. In 1974, he published a book, *Fatima is Fatima*, named after a daughter of the Prophet Mohammad. In it, as well as in speeches and other books, he glorified traditional views of Islam on women, rejecting the women of modernity and Western values of equal rights. He called American women's culture corrupt, and he argued that Iranian women were confused and needed guidance. He did not address serious issues of human rights and, with the fading of women's rights organizations, there were no women activists to challenge him and force him to debate. A year later, Shariati died of cancer in London at the age of 44. His ideology of Red Shi'ism survived, however, inspiring a generation of young Iranian men who would become followers of Ayatollah Khomeini in 1978.

From Red Shi'ism rose a man, Jalal Al-e Ahmad, whose father was a member of the clergy. After World War II, Jalal joined the pro-Soviet Communist Party and supported the Russian takeover of Iran. Initially, he belonged to a secular group, Third Force, created by former members of the Communist Tudeh Party who opposed the Russian influence in their party and the affairs of Iran. The Third Force remained loyal to Marxist ideology. Jalal gradually began to believe that Iranian politics should be defined by Islamic leadership, especially after the rise of Ayatollah Khomeini in 1963 and Khomeini's opposition to the enfranchisement of women.

Simin Daneshvar and her husband, Jalal Al-e Ahmad

Jalal Al-e Ahmad wrote an anti-American bestseller, *Gharb-zadeh'gee* (*Westoxification*), which advocated for a doctrine similar to Shariati's Red Shi'ism. It condemned Western civilization as corrupt, advocating for a movement, International Islamic Social Justice, to replace Western civilization.

In 1949, when Jalal married a modern Iranian woman, Simin Daneshvar, who did not wear hijab, his father disowned him and never stepped into their home.

Ms. Daneshvar was the first woman fiction writer and storyteller in a post-Qajar Islamic Iran. A year after marrying her husband, she received her PhD in Persian literature from Tehran University.

Soon after, Simin received a Fulbright scholarship to study writing at Stanford University and, from 1951 to 1953 while in the United States, she published numerous essays, short stories, and two books in English.

Her bestseller *Sovashon* (*A Persian Requiem*), a story of bloodshed in Iran during WWII, was more widely read and loved than any of her husband's books.

Simin has said that she opposed her husband's ideology, but later, during the 1979 revolution, she said in an interview that she was willing to wear the chador or hijab to advance democracy. So she wore the chador, but with the Islamic revolution, she lost the freedoms and equal rights that her sister-activists had worked so hard to provide her and other Iranian women over the previous century.

A brand of anti-Western Islamist-Marxism grew within this small band of self-styled 1960s Iranian elites and they created cults, such as the *Mujahidin E Khalq* or MEK. They used "Western civilization" to target the United States, not Europe. They exempted European imperialists from their anti-West propaganda because Europeans had historically supported the Shi'a establishment.

In the 1970s, the Organization of Iranian Women established Women's Family Health Centers with branches around the country, supported by influential women. The government health department provided gynecologists, nurses, midwives, and free medical supplies for birth control. These family health centers became more popular with women than government health clinics. A joint effort by the Organization of Iranian Women and various ministries allowed women seven months of maternity leave with full pay and established government-subsidized daycare facilities for children age two or less.

The Organization of Iranian Women made the mistake of trying to accommodate the clergy by framing their progress for women under the umbrella of Islam, even citing the Qur'an if it suited their arguments. To minimize opposition from the clergy, the organization curtailed the expansion of family centers in many cities and included religious instruction and Qur'an reading classes in some family centers.

As usual, they received very little support from the clerical establishment or the new Red Shi'ism of younger Islamist-Marxist intellectuals, such as Ali Shariati and Jalal Al-e Ahmad, who even approved of *seegheh* or temporary marriage, a form of religiously-legalized prostitution meant to accommodate men's sexual appetite.

Women made up 39 percent of the university students and 25 percent of the workforce, which included 690,000 professionals with university degrees. I was one of those women from the new generation, just starting my journey to make my homeland prosperous and progressive.

By 1979, the women of Iran had succeeded in making dramatic social, political, and economic change for over sixteen million women. According to a report by the Organization of Iranian Women, "On the eve of the Islamic Revolution, nearly 2 million women were gainfully employed in public and private sectors, 187,928 women were studying in various branches of Iran's universities, and of nearly 150,000 women employees of the government, 1666 occupied managerial positions. There were 22 Majlis parliament deputies and two Senators in the Senate, one ambassador, three deputy ministers, one provincial governor, five mayors, and 333 town and city council members were women." Moreover, the Organization of Iranian Women had 349 branches, 113 centers, and covered 55 other organizations dealing with women's and children's welfare and health.

In April 1979, Azam Sepehr-Khadem, editor-in-chief of the *Iran Post Journal*, opened a branch of the Association of Women Writers and Journalists in Iran, not realizing that she—and the women of Iran—would soon be deprived of career and freedom.

In the 1970s, the grassroots component of the struggle had faded away as activists' attention was diverted from the *human rights* of women to the *welfare* of women. That interrupted the historical continuity of the women's movement against the power of the clerical establishment.

Instead of staying the course as independent, grassroots activists for equal rights, the Organization of Iranian Women left the battleground and forgot the enemy was still waging a war on women. They did not realize their traditional activism was needed for generations to come to protect their advances.

The old clerical ideology of political Islamism and the new ideology of Marxist-Islamism were brewing up the glorification of subservient women in hijab.

The Cold War coalition of Islamists and communists prevented the Iranian people from enjoying the kind of free society for which they had fought for a hundred years to achieve. Our society was in a constant war of ideologies that incessantly pitted us against each other.

Through the Russian Embassy and its historical influence and knowledge of Iranian society, some women of the new middle class were attracted to the Tudeh Party, Iran's Communist party, demanding the establishment of communism. In an effort to overthrow the government, numerous Islamist-Marxist cults, such as *Mojahedeen E Khalq*, (the *Jihadists* of Masses), known today as the National Iranian Resistance Council, the *Fedayeen E Khalq*, the Maoists, and the old clergy establishment waged active disruptions, assassinations, sabotage, bank robberies, and police station bombings.

The year 1978 was the peak of the Cold War. Iran was an easy battleground for her northern imperialist neighbor. The Islamists feared the Iranian people, especially women and their successful movements for equality and freedom. The Iranian left, which the KGB had essentially controlled for over fifty years, was not popular among Iranians because of their economic prosperity and education. Many left-leaning Iranians and young teenagers had joined Islamic reformation cults and movements, even with their Soviet-inspired anti-America and anti-Shah propaganda.

As usual, the United States was naïve and uninformed about this brewing ideological war.

Ayatollah Khomeini had never given up on the support of the United States in his revolution, even after the assassination of President John F. Kennedy and the absence of a response from President Johnson to his letter seeking support. Khomeini continued his ever-louder opposition to the Shah, particularly on every progressive action taken, mostly led by women. Documents in the Carter Library reveal that Khomeini was not one of the important members of opposition to the Shah, although he was the loudest.

Shockingly, President Carter chose a loud, fanatic cleric to take Iran's destiny backward, triggering a militant Islamic movement around the world.

Khomeini had also cultivated supporters inside various U.S. government agencies, such as William G. Miller, a high-ranking official at the State Department's Bureau of Intelligence and Research, who supported him.

In his original message to President Jimmy Carter, Khomeini had promised, "America's interests and citizens in Iran would be protected under my rule."

CIA records show that in 1978 and 1979, President Carter and Ayatollah Khomeini negotiated on the terms of agreement for replacing the secular Iranian monarch, Mohammad Reza Shah Pahlavi, a longtime ally of the United States, with Khomeini, the zealot cleric.

Philip Stoddard, head of the State Department Intelligence Bureau at the time, said, "We would do a disservice to Khomeini to consider him simply as a symbol of segregated education and an opponent to women's rights."

In Tehran, U.S. Ambassador William Sullivan met with the secret Islamic Revolutionary Council on January 24, 1979, including Ayatollah Mousavi Ardebili. In a report, Mr. Sullivan said the cleric seemed "reasonable." He was a more forceful type among the clergy, but he was "no fanatic," he wrote. Ayatollah Ardebili became the chief justice in Khomeini's Islamic Republic of Iran, ordering the execution of tens of thousands of political opponents.

Ambassador Sullivan, however, never met with the women representatives of the Majlis, nor with any of the women senators to hear their views.

According to U.S. documents, available in the U.S. Library of Congress, Khomeini's attitude was collaborative. In his secret message of January 27, 1979, he proposed this deal to President Carter:

> Iranian military leaders will listen to you, but the Iranian people follow my 'orders.' You prevent the military from any coup against my takeover and I will restore stability back to the country, ending the unrest.

In his "first-person" message, he noted: "It is advisable that you recommend to the army not to follow [Prime Minister] Bakhtiar."

In January 1979, President Carter dispatched Robert E. Huyser, a U.S. Air Force General, on a secret mission to Tehran to carry out Khomeini's demand of neutralizing the Iranian military opposition, preventing a coup against Khomeini's Islamic regime.

According to a BBC report,[1] chronicling the contents of newly released CIA documents, Khomeini sent President Carter a personal message, saying, "You will see that we are not in any particular animosity with the Americans."

He pledged his Islamic Republic would be "a humanitarian one, which will benefit the cause of peace and tranquility for all mankind."

The BBC article said, "...the documents show more nuanced U.S. behavior behind-the-scenes. Only two days after the Shah departed Tehran, the U.S. told a Khomeini envoy that they were—in principle—open to the idea of changing the Iranian constitution, effectively abolishing the monarchy. The U.S. gave Khomeini a key piece of information—Iranian military leaders were flexible about their political future." President Carter agreed not only to remove the leadership, but also to change the 1906 constitution of Iran that women had fought so hard to realize.

On January 20, 1979, British Ambassador to Iran Anthony Parsons wrote that he had no doubt that the masses of people in Iran wanted "Khomeini's prescription of an Islamic Republic."

Western media outlets reported that one million Iranians marched for Khomeini. They ignored the fact that the population of Iran was 35 million people at the time and therefore 34 million, or the overwhelm-

---

1 "Two Weeks in January: America's secret engagement with Khomeini," BBC, http://www.bbc.com/news/world-us-canada-36431160.

ing majority, did not trust the clergy, especially Khomeini, and supported a separation of religion and government. The rallying cry of "prosperity, modernity, and sovereignty" in their homeland was ignored. Do the math. Only about three percent of the Iranian people marched for Khomeini, assuming all the marchers were Iranians. The demonstrations were composed, at least in part, of Afghan refugees paid to march.

In a recording on the plane returning to Iran in 1979, a Western reporter asked Ayatollah Khomeini, "How do you feel going back to Iran after all these years in exile?"

In Persian, Khomeini responded, "*Hichie*," which means, "Nothing." Nothing.

His translator hesitated and asked Khomeini if he was sure of that statement.

"Yes, I am sure!" he said, angrily. "Tell her, *hichie*."

The translator didn't. He told the reporter, "His eminence has no comment."

* * *

Although the National Front Party was a secular political party, it had close connections to the clergy. The funders of the National Front Party were almost all members of the Qajar's One Thousand Families, including Prime Minister Mohammed Mossadegh Ol'Saltaneh Qajar, who was a prince, the leader of the party, and a minority legislator in the Majlis.

Many ideological organizations, such as The National Front Party, the communist Tudeh Party, the *Mojahedin E Khalq* cult and others were under the erroneous impression that Khomeini was an idling, old cleric and he, too, could be easily eliminated, paving the way for them to take over. His anti-Shah, anti-America stance was sufficient for them to ignore who he was in reality and what the consequences of his emergence would be on Iranian society, the country, and the whole world.

Obviously, the main propaganda campaign of the Khomeinist ideology was to make the Western world think that it was the people who wanted him, and the problem with the women of Iran, as Ali Shariati had put it, "was the corrupt western [sic] culture imposed on the Iranian society and women by America," through the Shah, of course.

The Khomeinist movement blamed the United States for teaching the women of Iran to fight for freedom and equality. In fact, they had been waging this battle for one hundred years, as an intuitive right that most human beings seek. Unfortunately, the Western media listened to Khomeini and his gang of campaign leaders and viewed the issue as an "exotic" expression of "Orientalism."

The American elite fell for Khomeini's propaganda and concluded that the Shah was dragging the Iranian people kicking and screaming into modernity despite their wishes, and as a result, America was guilty of supporting him. Somehow, Westerners did not bother to ask: what women would want to live in slavery?

Using the pulpit as its weapon, Khomeini's campaign circulated its talking points through a network of mosques across Iran, teaching the uninformed to obey their rules and turn a deaf ear to the opposition movement.

The propaganda campaign convinced some of my employees at the Custom's Administration to work for Khomeini's campaign, and these campaign workers told me that the local mosques handed out stacks of money to activists who paid illegal Afghan laborers, standing on the street corners waiting for construction and landscaping jobs, to actually march for Khomeini. The going rate, I was told, was the equivalent amount of $15 and a coupon for a shish kabob meal. Few asked: who provided Khomeini with the tens of millions of dollars of funding that he pumped into his campaign?

On February 1, 1979, Khomeini returned to Iran after 14 years of exile.

The same people who argued against my negative opinion of Khomeini changed their minds a few months after their man took over. At the time, I was in Europe and they wrote me expressing guilt and regret over what they had helped do to their homeland, wishing they had listened to me. I have kept their letters.

Ms. Afkhami, director of the Foundation for Iranian Studies, wrote about the women who marched for Khomeini:

> Whenever women activists asked for clarification of positions on specific issues of women's rights and status, they were accused of introducing secondary issues, and admonished to maintain the unity of rank and purpose against the government. The mobilization efforts launched by women activists in the preceding decades combined with the revolution's misleading assertions about the status of women were instrumental in drawing women to the demonstrations.

In 1980, the regime adopted an internal war of intimidation, taking control of the two preeminent daily evening publications and closing the rest. Next, it banned all political parties and ideologies.

After his takeover, Ayatollah Khomeini appointed Ayatollah Sadeq Khalkhali as the supreme prosecutor and judge, tasked with implementing *sharia*. Ayatollah Khalkhali ordered the arrest and summary execution of the country's top government employees and thousands of its educated, professional intellectuals.

Khomeini announced the "economy belongs to asses."

Iranians started calling Ayatollah Khalkhali "the hanging judge." Over the next decade, the regime waged a bloody war with Iraq on the direct order of Ayatollah Khomeini and it conducted summary executions of tens of thousands of young, innocent Iranians, mostly teenagers, fooled by the MEK, Black Marxists, Red Shi'ism Islamist-Leninist cults, which had helped Khomeini ascend to power.

Khomeini took the opportunity to keep Iran at war with Iraq for eight years, while he established his total control over Iran. *The Guardian* reported the death toll of the war was an estimated one million Iranians and 250,000 to 500,000 Iraqis. He left a shocked, demoralized and bankrupt Iran when he died of a heart attack on June 3rd, 1989.

In his first acts, Khomeini cracked down on women. Except for a few Western feminists, such as Simone de Beauvoir and Kate Millett, the Western elites who had been critical of the Shah did not support Iranian women when they protested.

Intellectuals, such as French socialist Michel Foucault, had invested much of their ideological hopes and dreams in Khomeini. They romanticized the Islamic people's revolution. While Khomeini was in exile in France, they had aided and advised him on how to handle the Western media. When he took over with their support, they said nothing to oppose the atrocities he was committing. In these people's eyes, Khomeini could do no wrong and even the massacre of innocent men, women, and teenagers appeared justifiable to them. Their ideology took precedence over their humanity.

To defend themselves and cover up for Khomeini, socialists Marc Kravetz and Foucault even blamed young Iranian women for the crime of acting like free Western women! They were essentially saying, "How dare Iranian women want to be free individuals?" The Western elites, who so vehemently fight for progressive ideals in their own societies, refused to advocate for the same values in Iran and, to make matters worse, they actively supported the regressive, archaic, and patriarchal oppression of women in Iran.

Knowing that as public intellectuals they had acted hastily and out of ideological fervor, they claimed the issue was more complicated than we, as women in Iran, were able to decipher. They claimed that if Iranian women had not worn provocative miniskirts and makeup, Khomeini would not have had to implement a crackdown on them. In an article in *Le Matin de Paris*, Catherine Clement confidently alleged: "…Women also supported Khomeini…"

French socialists even argued in favor of Khomeini. They published an article in *Le Monde* that stated, "The veil is not exactly a sign of oppression, it allows women to affirm their role as activists, equal to that of men…"!

But they did not answer the question that Iranian women asked, "In that case, why don't you wear the hijab?"

In an article protesting the discrimination against Iranian women, Atoussa H., an Iranian intellectual in Paris, hurt by the arrogant and dismissive responses of the left, wrote, "It seems that for the Western Left, which lacks humanism, Islam is desirable…"

Original photo of Iranian women protests.

Edited photo by the Code Pink organization. Code Pink founder Medea Benjamin is the third person from the left.

In recent years, Iranian women have received little support from their Western sisters, and some Western women organizations have even sent emissaries to Iran to actively work with the oppressors of Iranian women.

As discussed earlier, Code Pink, an organization based in Washington, D.C., promotes itself as a movement dedicated to peace and women's rights. In fact, Code Pink has opposed the activism of Iranian women for years, one time taking a photo of Iranian women demonstrating at Tehran University against forced hijab and editing it to insert the faces of their own happy-go-lucky women over the unhappy faces of Iranian women. This was not only a misrepresentation of the facts but a horrifying act of betrayal by some American women who were hypocritically conveying the message to the ruling cleric that American women are happy with gender apartheid against Iranian women.

In 1965, Khomeini had said, "The abolition of the veil was one of the darkest moments of the history of Islam."

In 1978, in his audiotapes, recorded in Paris and smuggled into Iran, Khomeini repeatedly lied to the people, denying any intention of subjugating women. That was why a few hundred thousand women, who naïvely believed him, marched in his support.

In interviews and speeches from exile in Neophile-le-Château, France, Khomeini denied he was a misogynist.

Although the Western media chose to believe him, a huge majority of women activists in Iran did not. They were career women like me. Many men supported us. At home, my father was disgusted by the blatant lies of Khomeini.

On November 17, 1978, Khomeini told the British newspaper, *The Guardian*, "In the Islamic Republic, women will participate in the elections and will have total equality with men." When he took over Iran, his tune changed dramatically and he announced, "Women must obey *sharia* laws without any argument."

Iranian activist Reyhaneh Noshiravani wrote, "…Khomeini abrogated the Family Protection Law in its entirety on February 26, 1979 and officially launched its cultural revolution, which involved the purging of all western [sic] influences from Iranian society. The Islamization of women's status becomes the cornerstone of this program."

It now seems that the reported one million people who marched for Khomeini were paid or somehow mesmerized to take leave of their rational faculties, while thirty-four million people remained silent, thinking that the revolutionary movement was just a passing fad.

In the 1990s, the regime increased its campaign of kidnapping, torturing, and killing intellectuals and opposition leaders. Iranians call that period the "Chain Murdering Era." The Revolutionary Guard carried out planned assassinations of over one hundred opposition leaders across Europe, mostly unreported by governments or the international media. In one assassination, the regime murdered Shapour Bakhtiar, the last prime minister of Iran, in Paris. In another, it killed Fereidoun Farrokhzad, the popular host of a TV program, who had fled to Germany.

By 1998, the regime thought it had successfully wiped out the country's old guard and modernity-loving patriots, establishing the rule of fear in the country. But that year, university students from the generation that the regime had raised, rose up in protest against the regime. They wanted modernity, democracy, and equal rights, not a dogmatic and doctrinal dictatorship.

CHAPTER EIGHTEEN

Women Lose the War to the Clergy (1979)

O N FEBRUARY 12, 1979, the constitutional revolution's progress was halted by the establishment of an Islamic Republic in Iran.

Less than one month later, on March 5, 1979, Khomeini banned women from being judges in a single declaration and abolished the Family Protection Laws in April. Khomeini said the existing secular laws were in breach of *sharia* and therefore they had to be abolished. The new regime ordered women who worked in government, like me, to observe the new Islamic dress code of hijab, covering every strand of our hair with a black scarf and shrouding our bodies in a black gown, or be fired.

On March 8, 1979, International Women's Day, about 100,000 women gathered at Tehran University, according to media estimates, and marched across the city toward the Ministry of Justice for a sit-in. I was there with my young daughter, my mother, and maternal grandmother.

That morning, my grandmother, in her eighties, had insisted that we go and protest to stop this *na-mard*, "little man," who was pushing our country's daughters back to the dark ages, whereas her generation had fought against such oppression. Four generations of our family went to stand firm against the "little man's" law.

The protesters could not hear the speakers because the government had sabotaged their microphones. Still, the crowds grew by the minute as we marched and shouted, "Freedom is universal, not Western and not Eastern."

Suddenly, a mob of vigilantes armed with bats, chains, whips, and batons attacked the women, beating them and sending many women to nearby hospitals. However, the crowd was determined to reach the Ministry of Justice. We reached the steps of the courthouse.

Pelted by rain and snow, women continued to march in the anti-oppression demonstrations over the coming days, men joining them to try to shield the women demonstrators from the regime's hoodlums.

Harkening back to the days of the Ladies' Secret Society, the women of Iran came together in historic solidarity against the country's new theocratic dictatorship.[1] It was emotionally moving to see the women believers feel the clergy had betrayed them by making hijab mandatory. They joined their secular sisters to protect the right of women to choose whether they want to wear hijab or not. They marched so their daughters could have equality and choice. These women felt betrayed.

In another sit-in against Khomeini's new laws of gender apartheid, women lawyers and judges, fired by the regime, went on strike in the

---

1 "March 8, 1979 Iranian Women March Against Hijab and Islamic Laws," Arjang Sepasi, https://www.youtube.com/watch?v=pxGYLk92edY

lobby of the Ministry of Justice. Unlike the days before the revolution, only one woman from the Embassy of France taped a report, now posted on YouTube.[2] The TV camera teams of the international media did not show up on any one of the days.

Sit-in by women lawyers and judges, fired by the regime, at the Ministry of Justice

After a few weeks of demonstrations, the protests ended with many more women injured by the hired hoodlums and thugs. The women protesters arrived at the bitter conclusion that the regime had reduced them to second-class citizenship by force. There was no international court to file a petition for justice, no Western media holding the regime accountable, no support from the United Nations, and no way out.

The leaders of Western democracies chose to remain silent in response to the new regime's blatant obstruction of human rights. The Western media did not cover the women's march as they had covered pro-Khomeini marches and they did not criticize Khomeini as they had criticized the Shah. The United Nations did not protest the degradation of women by the new regime in Iran.

On March 29, 1979, Khomeini announced that Iran would become a gender-segregated society, starting with sports arenas and beaches. Later, the regime passed laws completely banning women from attending

---

[2] "Iran Tehran: Women march March 8, 1979 against compulsory Hijab," Narges Ghaffari, https://www.youtube.com/watch?v=jqrPoPYZfc0.

sports events.

After a "referendum" on April 1, 1979, the new regime declared the establishment of the Islamic Republic of Iran and in December 1979, their Clerical Assembly drafted a new constitution for Iran based on *sharia*, with Ayatollah Khomeini as the supreme leader with total control over the judicial, executive, and legislative branches of government.

Iran was in chaos, with no law and order, and suffering under the power of armed thugs and hoodlums trained by Palestinian leader Yasser Arafat and Hezbollah—with full authority to kill.

Under the direct declaration of Khomeini, the age of marriage for girls was reduced from eighteen to thirteen, with the father's right to reduce it further to nine.

When the Assembly of Islamic Experts was drafting the new constitution for the Islamic Republic, only one woman, Monireh Gorjee, was symbolically present and she never spoke to oppose the application of *sharia* against the women of Iran.

Under the new constitution, the women of Iran became the slaves of men. The constitution included a number of disturbing provisions:

- Women and children are the property of men with limited rights.
- The value of a woman's life is one-half the value of a man's life.
- The testimony of one man is equal to the testimony of two women.
- Daughters get half the inheritance that sons get.
- A woman does not have the right to divorce her husband.
- A man can divorce his wife any time he wishes, even without her knowledge.
- Men are allowed to marry four "permanent" wives and as many temporary wives as they wish.
- Women cannot travel, work, go to school, or even leave the house without the permission of their husbands or fathers.
- A woman must live where her husband decides.
- Mothers do not get custody of their children after sons reach the age of two and daughters reach the age of seven, in the case of divorce.
- Children belong to their father, as soon as they are born.
- A husband can take children away from their mother and have another woman raise the child.
- A widow does not get custody of her children after the death of her husband. Paternal grandparents or paternal relatives get custody of the children and the mother has no right of visitation.
- If a father does not have any family, a local cleric takes custody of the woman's children, as well as the family assets and possessions.

- The age of criminal responsibility, under article 1210(1) of Iran's Civil Code, is set at fifteen for boys, but only nine for girls.
- The law sanctions marriage of girls at the age of thirteen, but gives fathers the right to sell their daughters at the age of nine.
- In the case of inheritance, an older widow with grown children only gets one-eighth of the value of a dwelling.

Ayatollah Khomeini also required that child brides live at the home of their husbands *before* they reach puberty.

To justify its gross violations of women's human rights, the regime used women as a political tool, establishing an "Islamic women's movement" to sanction its new regime of gender apartheid.

In early March 1979, the regime set up the Foundation of *Mostazafeen* (the Foundation for the Disadvantaged) and asked women to join. Poorer, uneducated women, who had marched on the streets for the revolution, participated in hopes the Ayatollah would perform a miracle. The foundation took the women's jewelry but failed to help them. The same foundation has controlled Iranian banks and industry, estimated at 20% of the economy.

Meanwhile, women protesters, including millions of teachers, government and non-government employees, university students, professors, professionals, and activists, resolved to remain unified to win back their rights and oppose the new regime.

In December 1979, the secular women activists announced they would hold a Unity Conference of Women to oppose the regime. Political parties on the left and the Islamist authorities on the right opposed them. A day before the conference, the government cut off the electricity to the auditorium where the conference was going to be held and members of the Islamist-Marxist MEK, now called the National Iranian Resistance Council, infiltrated the crowd to disrupt the speakers. However, the women persisted and had their conference.

The regime responded to the women's conference by establishing the Society of Women for Islamic Revolution, led by Azam Taleghani, the daughter of Ayatollah Taleghani, otherwise known as the "Communist Ayatollah." Ms. Taleghani wrote a letter, warning the leadership of the revolution not to make the hijab compulsory, but her appeal went un-heard. In 1980, wrapped in Islamic attire, Ms. Taleghani represented Iran at the United Nations Commission on the Status of Women in Thailand.

To pretend it was pro-women, the regime also handpicked three women to become members of its Islamic Council. All three women came from powerful, high-ranking clergy families in the new regime.

The regime changed the name of the secular National Women's Day of March 8, 1979, to another date and called it Fatima Day, after the daughter of the Prophet Muhammad. Zahra Rahnavard, the wife of Mousavi, the new president of Iran, adopted more conservative Islamic practices and wore three layers of hijab, taking control of *Etteleat Banovan* (*Ladies' News*) a popular magazine. Fereshteh Rafsandjani, daughter of clergy member, Hashemi Rafsanjani, took over another women's magazine, to promote *sharia* among less-educated women.

The government dispatched women to international women's conferences, wrapped in total Islamic hijab in the style of the Qajar era, with three layers of covering, to tell the international community that the rules of gender apartheid were what the women of Iran wanted.

In the summer of 1980, Prime Minister Mohammad-Ali Rajai hammered the last nail into the coffin of Iranian women's human rights, introducing a law demanding compulsory hijab to the Islamic Council, which passed it by acclamation. To carry out the law, the Islamic Council created a cadre of hijab police, made up of women checking other women's hijabs on the street and in public places to make sure they were abiding by the law of not showing even a single strand of hair.

These women came from two groups: family members of the ruling clergy and some opportunist members of the Marxist-Islamist Red Shi'ism ideology who had become torchbearers for the regime. The foot-soldiers were mostly the poorer, less-educated women who had been promised rewards.

Uniforms established for women

On February 11, 1980, one year after the regime's takeover, the clergy established an armed female militia to police women and keep them under control. Most of the militia women were members of the Islamist-Marxist cults, with a modified hijab that they had designed for battle.

When the United Nations Women's Conference opened in Denmark in 1980, Shahin Tabatabai, daughter of a cleric, represented Iranian women dressed in full hijab. Another Iranian woman, "Islamic scholar" Laleh Bakhtiar, living in the United Kingdom, attended the conference as an independent observer. She did not criticize the new clerical regime's anti-women policies and even sanctioned the stoning of women, calling adultery the worse possible crime a woman could commit.

Khomeini knew that it would be extremely difficult to enforce his Islamist ideological regime on the Iranian people, especially on women. Therefore, he goaded Iraqi dictator Saddam Hussein who foolishly attacked Iran and gave Khomeini a perfect opportunity to engage the country in a long, bloody, and brutal war from September 1980 to August 1988, which would give him greater leeway in internal affairs.

Khomeini promoted the revival of an extremist ideology of Islam, called the *Velayate Fagheeh*, or the jurisprudence of the clergy, written by Mullah Mohammad Taghi Madjlesie, the Lebanese Shi'a cleric that the Safavids had imported into Iran in 1695.

Khomeini imposed this doctrine with full force, giving women the same social, legal, and economic status as minor children, convicted criminals, and people with mental illnesses, all of them under the custody of men, and all according to *sharia*.

The color of women's uniforms was drab and dark. The Islamist-Marxist cults designed the uniform to establish militant uniformity in its cult-like brand of Red Shi'ism, or Marxist-Islamist Shi'ism. Even today, with the exception of the leader's wife, Maryam Radjavi, who wore French-designed silk uniforms in happy, bright colors with matching headscarf, the female followers of the National Resistance Council of Iran—the former *Mojahedin E-Khalq* cult—wore identical drab uniforms.

The father or paternal grandfather was given authority on all matters, including the authority to marry their nine-year-old daughters to any man. Men were given the right to marry four wives and countless temporary wives and divorce their wives at will. There was a return to the Qajar era of harems, a repeal of family laws, and the abolition of population control policies and family planning centers. The country's population of 35 million grew to 80 million in just over thirty years, without any economic planning to care for the burgeoning population.

According to the dress code set by the clergy, women had to wear black and men had to wear white. Psychologically, the clergy were communicating that women are sinful and evil and therefore should wear dark colors, while men wear white as a symbol of innocence and should be aware of the deceitful nature of women.

Photo by Shirin Neshat

Clergy, appointed by the Supreme Leader, won management over the universities. They separated men and women in classrooms, with women on one side and men on the other side. A few years later, professors taught male and female students sitting in segregated classrooms. Currently, women are only taught by female professors and men are only taught by male professors.

The Islamic Council also passed the law of *Qesas*, or "Retribution." Women who failed to observe the clergy-demanded hijab faced a punishment of seventy-four lashes and, in adultery cases, women and men faced death by stoning, with women, in practice, punished much more often and with greater severity than men.

Atefeh Rajabi Sahaaleh would have been educated and become an independent woman. However, under *sharia* law, her impoverished grandmother was allowed to marry her off at the age of nine to a fifty-four-year-old Afghan man. After she gave birth to twins at the age of fourteen, her husband accused her of prostitution and the head cleric in their small town of Neka in northern Iran sentenced her to death. The regime executed her in 2004, at the age of sixteen.

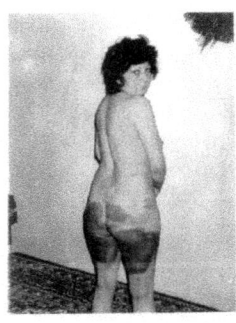  

(left) She was flogged fifty times for attending a birthday party. (middle) Working with Iranian women activists, Lord Avebury issued this booklet in an attempt to expose the injustices that Iranians faced. (right) The cover of *Paris Match* Magazine.

In 1994, Lord Avebury, chairman of the Parliamentary Human Rights Group in the British House of Lords, issued a report documenting his work with Iranian women activists.

One Iranian woman was sixteen when her husband accused her of adultery, and her plight with the justice system was featured on the cover of French magazine *Paris Match*.

The regime began to enforce harsh and severe *sharia* against women and children, under the pretext of guarding the country's religious and revolutionary values. (The clerical establishment has continued to refuse any and all reforms that have any semblance of bringing civil rights back to Iran.)

The constitution, written by Khomeini in 1979, is considered divine rule by the clergy and therefore, unchangeable by any man.[3]

The "reformists faction" had claimed that it would try changing the anti-women laws, but it has proven to be unwilling and unable to bring about any changes for the betterment of women and children. In fact, the clergy hierarchy has continued passing more oppressive, abusive laws against children and poor women. They claim that the laws of Allah are irreformable.

The clergy's war against modernism crushed women in their pursuit of equal rights and also dehumanized half the population, forcing them into chains through a regime of punishment and torture. The clergy won uneducated men over by seducing them with the power to rule over half of the society. In this way, the clergy won absolute power over the people.

(left) Women, armed against women, enforce compulsory hijab laws. (right) Plain-clothed hijab police officers stop women on the street and punish them for not wearing "proper" hijab.

In the summer of 1980, the regime implemented a communist-style program, Guardians of Orthodox Islamic Culture, to indoctrinate underprivileged women and defeat the women's movement completely. It hired and trained less-educated women as hijab police with power over educated, middle-class women.

Five years later, the regime barred women in colleges from studying a number of selected majors, including law and sciences, while establishing a center for religious studies where it recommended that women

---

3 *Encyclopedia Iranica*.

enroll.

The policies of discrimination against women and children were sanctioned as *sharia* and thus, mandatory. However, these supposedly irrevocable laws have been repeatedly changed and revoked, based on political interests.

War refugees (photo from Iranian historical photographs site)

During the Iran-Iraq war, from 1980 to 1988, the women and children of Iran suffered the most under what they called "petro-poverty," losing providers for their families in the forced war. Mothers lost their young sons when the military seized them to be minesweepers; many women and children who fled their homes in war zones become homeless.

Khomeini died in 1989 shortly after the end of the war, leaving a nightmare for women who became caregivers to their sons, the nation's wounded and disabled as boy-soldiers. After his death, the regime allowed women to enter the job market because of the devastating loss of one million young men and boys. That year, the clergy reinstated part of the family planning protection program to slow the increasing birth rate which had spun out of control after the regime took over in 1979.

According to reports from the Islamic regime, today there are over half a million homeless and "nameless" children on the streets of Tehran. These children are born out of *siqeh*, or the temporary marriages that the regime allowed under *sharia*. *Siqeh* amounts to clergy-sanctioned prostitution which, combined with clergy-enforced poverty on women, makes women powerless in these "marriages." According to *sharia*, only fathers can apply for a child's birth certificate. But under *sharia* rules, men do not have any parental responsibilities to babies conceived in *siqeh*. Because their mothers are not allowed to register their babies legally, these children do not exist in the eyes of the clerical establishment regime in Iran.

A New Generation and an Old War

In the early 1990s, women began to make a comeback in defiance of the clerics' anti-women laws. Their goal this time was to present a free alternative to the clergy's policy through civil disobedience and activism. In 1994, the Iranian delegation to the fourth United Nations World Conference on Women in Beijing opposed the progressive programs at the conference, especially those related to laws governing women and families. Meanwhile, it was at this conference that Hillary Clinton, leading the U.S. delegation, declared, "Women's rights are human rights."

The 1990s became the era of publishing women's magazines again.

From March 2 to March 5, 1995, Iranian women film directors held their first festival since 1979 in the city of Shiraz, as another gesture of civil disobedience.

Recognizing the pressure placed on them by the women's display of opposition, the regime pretended to listen to the women.

In the 1996 Islamic Council elections, fourteen women members of the ruling clergy families were "elected" in another superficial effort by the regime to pretend women's voices were important.

Clerics who were only educated in *sharia* had hijacked the justice system. They allowed educated women lawyers to become "legal consultants" in special family courts and administrative justice courts, but they gave them no legal or judicial rights.

"Portrait of My Brother" by Iranian artist Clara Akbar

In March 1996, a well-known Iranian artist and miniature painter, Clara Abkar, died at the age of eighty-one. Ms. Abkar was honored by UNESCO as one of the most important etchers of the twentieth century. In 1916, she had painted an artwork called, "Portrait of My Brother," which was sold in a London auction house in April 1989.

Soon after, Fa'ezeh Hashemi, the daughter of the clerical president, Ali-Akbar Hashemi-Rafsanjani, started hosting sports matches for Muslim women in Asia. In October 1996, women athletes were finally able to compete in the first public event—with a women-only audience.

The next month, the regime appointed Zahra Sadr-Azam Nuri as mayor of one of Tehran's districts. She was Tehran's first woman mayor. In 1997, Iran's poet laureate, Simin Behbahani, was nominated for the Nobel Prize in Literature.

That year, out of necessity, the Majlis passed legislation that allowed women to work six hours a day. Ayatollah Mohammad Khatami, touted as a pro-women's rights reformer, was elected with 65 percent of the female and youth vote. He appointed a female advisor on women's issues, only to go back on his word because a cleric, Ayatollah Mazaheri, opposed Iran joining the United Nations Convention on Elimination of all Forms of Discrimination Against Women (CEDAW) on the grounds that it breached *sharia*.

President Mohammad Khatami preaching to a group of children in Iran. The boys have notebooks in front of them, but the girls, their bodies shrouded in tight headscarves and gowns, have paper flowers in front of them. The Western media touted President Khatami as a "reformist," but he never repealed the country's system of gender apartheid.

In 1997, Shirin Ebadi, an attorney, received the Human Rights Watch award for her activities for the human rights of women in Iran. The same year, eighteen-year-old Samira Makhmalbof directed a movie, *The Apple*, becoming one of the world's youngest professional film directors. Women pushed for child custody rights, but the regime agreed only to have a lawyer present in court during child custody cases.

Ms. Badro' Zaman Qarib

On February 1, 1997, Iran's department of higher education chose *Farhang'eh Soghdi (Soghdi Culture)*, the first dictionary of the ancient Persian language spoken by some of the most prominent tribes in Central Asia, as the book of the year. Written by Badro' Zaman Qarib, an Iranian linguistics scholar, it gained international recognition.

A new generation of women, inspired by the work of the Ladies' Secret Society and Iran's powerful women's movement, commemorated June 12, 1998, the historical day of struggle for women's equality in Iran, as a National Day of Solidarity. Two days later, on June 14, 1998, the regime inaugurated the first Women's Police Academy. With growing ranks of women political prisoners, the regime trained policewomen to arrest members of the women's opposition movement. On October 11, 1998, a group of women journalists formed the first post-Islamic Union of Women Journalists, overcoming numerous obstacles from the regime.

Farzaneh Sharafbafi, an Iranian businesswoman with a PhD in aerospace, became the first woman professor of engineering and aeronautics. In July 2017, Iran Air named her chief executive officer of Iran Air, the first woman named to that position.

Mina Rahbari and Tusi Ha'eri became the first women broadcasters at a Tehran radio station in post-Islamic revolution Iran.

The opposition lost many souls, like Parvaneh Majd Eskandari, born on March 14, 1938, the year after the women of Iran won the right to choose whether or not to wear the hijab. The Shi'a clergy have had a long history of assassinations to remove obstacles from their path. With the death of Khomeini and the end of the bloody Iran-Iraq war, the clerical powerbase grew increasingly insecure. It revived its brutal policy of eliminating activists, intellectuals, and opposition leaders, no matter where they were—inside the country or outside.

In the 1950s, Parvaneh had been a student activist and a member of the Iranian Nationalist Party, opposing the Shah. While a student activist, she had met and married her husband, Daryoush Forouhar. Parvaneh became a teacher and in 1979, she and her husband supported Khomeini, only to be very disappointed when Khomeini's promises turned out to be nothing but lies. As nationalists, Parvaneh and her husband bravely spoke out against Khomeini and his oppressive un-Iranian laws.

Parvaneh Majd Eskandari

In November 1998, Parvaneh and her husband were found brutally murdered in their home. She had been stabbed twenty-five times. Parvaneh had predicted their murder at the hands of the clergy in an interview with a human rights reporter: "We are living in fear of being killed. Every night when we go to bed we thank God for getting through another day."

The Majlis passed two new restrictions on women, removing their images from the media and imposing the gender apartheid law of segregation on women in hospital wards, putting the lives of women in peril when medical services were not available in the women's section.

In a 1999 uprising at Tehran University, students held up placards with one word, "REFERENDUM," both in Persian and English, demanding support for regime change and calling on the international community to support them. It was simply a peaceful protest against the ruling dictators. The students called for the empowerment of the people through the disempowerment of the regime.

The popular Ayatollah Kazemeini Boroujerdi preached for separation of religion from the government. He advocated for the unalienable right of the individual to hold personal religious beliefs and to exercise freedom of speech and worship. Ayatollah Broudjerdi was violently attacked in the pulpit, arrested, defrocked, and sentenced to life in prison in 2006. He is now under house arrest. His followers have been arrested or are in hiding.

A respected cleric, Saïd Mohsen Saïdzadeh, presented a new interpretation of *sharia* on the grounds that the old interpretations were, in fact, against Islam. He was arrested, defrocked, and imprisoned.

On July 7, 1999, male and female students at Tehran University began a peaceful demonstration in support of a professor who had been fired by the cleric who led the university. By the end of the first day, the protest had become an uprising for civil rights and human rights—including freedom of speech—that President Khatami had promised but never delivered.

The uprising spread through universities nationwide. The Revolutionary Guard and its auxiliary militia, the Basij forces, attacked the students on campus and in the dormitories, killing dozens of students. The government closed the universities on July 14, 1999 to end the uprising. According to reports, dozens were also injured, and over 1,700 protesters were arrested and imprisoned.

More than six hundred female medical students at an all-female university in the religious center of Qom protested in front of the Ministry of Health in Tehran saying that they had been deprived of proper medical training because of a lack of female professors which were required to teach women students. To the ruling clerics, the medical school was the ideal example of an Islamic institution, women training female doctors for female patients, but its model had failed miserably at the hands of clerics.

In 2000, director Samira Makhmalbof won the Cannes Film Festival award for her feature film, *The Blackboard*. For the first time since 1979, Iranian women attempted to celebrate International Women's Day on March 8, 2000, in Tehran's City Park. Police barred them from the park.

In Iran, many Iranians were devastated by the news that Muslim extremists had killed thousands of Americans in the 9/11 attacks. Women activists organized a candlelight vigil and on September 18, 2001, thousands of Iranians gathered in town squares to express their solidarity with the United States. They carried white candles and white flowers, symbolizing peace and friendship. Agents of the Revolutionary Guard attacked the crowds and forced them to disperse.

With the permission of the regime, a group of women activists participated in the April 2002 conference of the Gunda Werner Institute of Heinrich-Böll-Stiftung, an organization promoting feminism and gender democracy, in Berlin. During the conference, Ms. Lahiji and Ms. Kar courageously argued that religious domination of Iranian civil law had seriously denied women their rights. Upon their return home, the Ministry of Intelligence arrested and imprisoned them for "acting against the internal security of the state and disparaging the holy order of the Islamic Republic."

That day, the regime closed eighteen reformist newspapers.

On March 8, 2002, a group of women planned to celebrate International Women's Day for the first time in Tehran's Laleh ("Tulip") Park and local parks around the country. Thousands of women participated, calling for equality, peace, and justice.

In 2002, women protested across the country

The auxiliary Basij forces beat and arrested many demonstrators.

The same year, six female representatives from the Islamic Council proposed that Iran become a signatory to the Convention on the Elimination of all Forms of Discrimination Against Women. The men on the Islamic Council reprimanded them and refused to follow their recommendation.

New statistics showed that women made up 60 percent of the university students.

On July 11, 2003, agents of the Ministry of Intelligence brutally tortured, beat, and killed Ziba (Zahra) Kazemi, while interrogating the 54-year-old Iranian-Canadian photojournalist. She had traveled home to Iran to visit her eighty-year-old mother and the regime had arrested her for the crime of taking a few photographs of students protesting in front of Tehran's notorious Evin Prison. The prison has become noteworthy as a holding pen for the Islamic regime's political prisoners since 1979. It was sarcastically called "Evin University" because prison officials house so many students and intellectuals there.

Ziba (Zahra) Kazemi

The official Islamic regime report claimed Ziba died as a result of a stroke. She was buried immediately and without an autopsy, despite the Canadian government's repeated requests for an autopsy. The regime refused to allow her mother or any loved ones to see her body. Her son and the Canadian government demanded the body be returned to her family in Canada, but their request remains unanswered to this day. The coroner who examined her body said the cause of death was that her skull and almost every other bone in her body had been broken or crushed. When he spoke of his findings, he, too, was forced to flee Iran, fearing for his and his family's safety and life.

The Women's Cultural Centre, protesting violence against women, announced a celebration of International Women's Day on March 8, 2003. However, the Islamic Revolutionary Court proclaimed the gathering illegal and ordered the arrest of the two women organizers.

A coalition of religious and secular women demanded an end to the ban on women running for president and staged a sit-in protest in front of President Khatami's office. He did not respond to their appeal.

Iranian women love soccer, which they call football, and they want to cheer their team in World Cup matches, but authorities of the regime have banned them from attending any sports events. One of my teenage cousins cut her beautiful long hair to wear a boy's cap and clothes to attend soccer games with her father. Iranian teenage girls gather outside stadiums, chanting, "Down with the mullahs!"

The shame of discrimination has been worse when World Cup matches are in Iran. In an Iran-Ireland match in November 2001, and later in an Iran-Japan match in 2004, the regime's theocrats allowed Irish and Japanese women inside stadiums to cheer their national teams, but they banned Iranian women, forcing them to stay on the streets outside the stadium's gates.

1976 women's soccer team

During the Iran-Bahrain soccer match in 2006, hundreds of young women gathered in front of the Tehran Azadi (which ironically means "Freedom") Stadium and forced their way through the metal gates into the stadium in time to watch the second half of the game and cheer their Iranian team.

That year, Iranian film director Jafar Panahi made an international award-winning film, *Off-side*, a re-enacted documentary that captured the story of the Iranian women banned from entering Azadi Stadium to watch the Iran-Bahrain match. Later, an Iranian-British journalist, Nisha Susan, wrote:

> In Iran, everyone's jubilant that their football team has made it to the finals, but only men were allowed to enter the celebrations at the, hello, hilarious name, Azadi (freedom) stadium. The Football Federation

announced in advance, 'In this ceremony only men are allowed to be present and the women who like the national team are asked to avoid coming to the Azadi, [Freedom] Stadium.'

They still protest today with Iranian men carrying and hanging banners outside the stadium saying, "Honk if you are an Iranian woman and you love football."

Iranian men, fathers, husbands, and brothers also want women to be able to watch the games. Many take their women relatives, spouses, and friends into stadiums disguised as boys. They demonstrate with signs, arguing that women should be allowed in stadiums.

In a column in a feminist online magazine, *The Ladies Finger*, journalist and author Nisha Susan wrote:

> Women have not been allowed to watch football in Iran since 1979. Iranian women have registered their protests in hordes over the years, every time Iranians had a major international victory women protested by honking their car horns, taking off their veils and breaking into the stadium. Lots of grave foreign policy sorts have been writing about

football as the barometer, canary in the coal mine and other such metaphors for gauging the true state of Iranian politics.[4]

With the unholy restrictions, women have formed a soccer team that competes internationally, looking like scarecrows in headscarves, long-sleeved tunic jerseys, and ankle-length pants, but they are committed not to give up.

Women in Iran believe the international community fails to support their acts of civil disobedience, making it easier for the intolerant, misogynist clergy to further deprive them of participation in sports. Nisha notes, "…the Iranian women's team was disqualified from the London Olympics for wearing hijabs on the field. Jolly multiculturalism."

Shirin Ebadi receives the Nobel Peace Prize in 2003.

---

4 Susan, *The Ladies Finger* (June 20, 2013), http://theladiesfinger.com/author/nisha-susan/.

In late 2003, a group of human rights organizations criticized the Noble Peace Prize Committee for not recognizing the One Million Signature movement led by Iranian women. The committee offered the prize to one Iranian woman, not the movement of all Iranian women. On October 10, 2003, Iranian attorney and women's rights activist Shirin Ebadi received the Nobel Peace Prize "for her successful human rights activities to improve the status of women and children under *sharia* law." Shirin comes from the generation of women who enjoyed the rights won by three generations of women activists over one hundred years of struggle, including the work of her feminist sisters in the Ladies' Secret Society. Before the Khomeinist revolution, she had become one of the first women judges. Then the regime removed her from the bench—just because she was a woman.

At the 2004 Asia Pacific NGO Forum of Beijing +10, Iranian journalist Fariba Davoudi Mohajer delivered a powerful speech on the injustices women journalists face in Iran:

> My country—Iran—and many countries in the region are in the grips of the serious peril of patriarchal culture, which takes away innovation and activity from society and obstructs the real participation of women. However, never—except for very few instances—did the governing culture allow women to move up towards the posts of manager, editor, or director in the media in which they worked. The patriarchal culture governing the media made the growth of women dependent on the decisions of men and drew invisible ceilings to cap the progress of women to ensure that the media's senior management positions would always be out of their reach. As a result, women had no say at the decision-making levels and as a consequence the issue of "women in Iran's press" did not get the attention it was due, as the decision for what article to print, where to print it and how was one made exclusively by men.
>
> All our efforts to have a permanent page for women's issues in newspapers were unfruitful. All our efforts for getting permits for publications especially for women were unfruitful, except in a handful of cases which passed through special filters.
>
> All our efforts so we could write what we wanted about women's issues without the final supervision of men did not get us anywhere desirable. The only newspaper that did have a page allocated to women was suspended, and the director of the next newspaper was not willing to allocate a page to the issue.
>
> This is not a desired state to be in when you aim to publicize women's issues and bring it from the sidelines to forefront of the social

discussion. Our other aims were to boost the awareness of women through the media, establish a two-way connection with the public and influence public opinion to build norms which redefine the role for women.

I believe that there is a collective decision throughout the world to exclude women from macro decision-making processes, and thus their presence in the most important means in this regards—-namely the media—has been limited. The United Nations can never publicize women's issues without a variety of media. It can never talk about women's rights until it has adopted practical plans for female journalists and how news relating to women should be reflected in the media. Without advertisement, tools of the United Nations cannot influence public opinion and make the changes required to reestablish the rights of women.

In my country, we have the best, most professional, and bravest women journalists, women who have made the most changes with the least facilities. Women who have consistently and constantly written to change backward interpretations and traditional roles. They have been influential in reversing or stopping governmental actions (for example in regard to executions). They have expressed the necessities and have at times forced the bettering of women's conditions.

Today we female journalists write about women ministers, women lawyers, women judges, and honor killings, and try to continue with our work without losing heart. Women journalists, like all other Iranian women, lack four essential elements, which must be analyzed and addressed.

What is certain is that to achieve these goals we require tools, resources and agents of change. We cannot create change unless we have these three elements at hand, and unfortunately, we have none.

The agents of change are all men. The officials of political parties and groups, media, press, television and radio managers and directors are all men. Men write our school books and men write the laws. Men pay us our wages, and in short, men hinder our drive towards change.

On International Women's Day, March 8, 2004, Iranian women opened the first women's library named after one of the most prominent women activists of the former generation, Sedigheh Dolatabadi. This was one more step taken by the Cultural Center of Women to guarantee women free access to knowledge. As a function of the library's activities, the Cultural Center of Women also established the Dolat-Abadi Award, given to women's studies books.

In June 2005, the first Iranian woman climber, Laleh Keshavarz, reached the top of Mount Everest.

On International Women's Day 2005, women activists organized another peaceful gathering to commemorate the day in parks around the country and, again, paramilitary forces attacked, dispersed, and arrested them.

On June 12, 2005, women activists of religious and secular beliefs united again in another demonstration. Their demands included giving women equal rights in marriage, changing the minimum legal age of marriage for girls from nine to eighteen, granting women equal rights for women as witnesses, banning polygamy, and providing women with equal rights to divorce and joint custody of children after divorce. Revolutionary Guard forces attacked, once again arresting and dispersing them.

 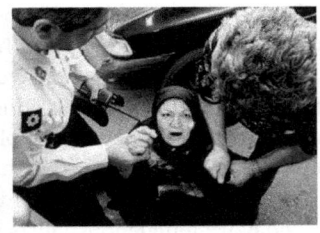

Three months later, thousands of women gathered in front of the University of Tehran, and American actor Sean Penn, meeting in town with the ruling clergy, attended the rally. He lost his camera when paramilitary forces attacked the crowd of women. The women asked him to take their message to America, but their pleas were mostly ignored.

Women in front of the University of Tehran, chanting, "We condemn all discriminations!" (Source: Kossof.com)

In celebration of the forbidden International Women's Day, on March 8, 2006, thousands of women activists gathered at Tehran's Daneshjo Park. Many prominent members from the older generation of women's activists, including the great poet laureate Simin Behbahani, spoke to the crowd. Revolutionary Guard paramilitary forces attacked the women—beating, arresting, and hauling many of them to prison, including Simin, then eighty years old. Men had joined the protests to help protect the women from attack, but the Revolutionary Guard attacked them too, beating and imprisoning them.

A woman protestor holds a sign with "woman," written in Persian, behind the red bars of a prison cell, describing the plight of women of Iran.

On June 9, 2006, Amnesty International issued a statement calling for an end to discrimination against women in Iran, urging Iranian authorities to ensure the safety of protesters at a peaceful demonstration scheduled for three days later, in compliance with international standards of human rights.

In 2006, journalist Marguerite Del Giudice spent some time in Iran, researching and writing a *National Geographic* article in which she wrote in bold letters:

> An irony is that the Islamic revolution – which at times is referred to as the "second Arab invasion"—appears to have strengthened the very ties to the antiquity that it tried so hard to sever.[5]

A young Iranian woman stands at the foot of the column in Persepolis wishing to reclaim her heritage.

---

5 *National Geographic*, August 2008.

CHAPTER NINETEEN

The One Million Signature Campaign (2006—2008)

ALMOST ONE HUNDRED YEARS after the advent of the Ladies' Secret Society, the women of Iran faced a dire situation. They needed to launch another movement.

They had exhaustively tried to influence reform through civil disobedience and obedience, writing, reasoning, and voting for "reformists." For demonstrating and marching they were imprisoned, tortured and raped. The clergy responded not by peaceful means and concessions but retaliation, including more repressive laws against women and children.

Women activists decided to petition the hierarchy of the Islamic regime for a just and equal society and organized an effort to hold another protest. On June 12, 2006, a united women's organization held a peaceful protest march in Tehran, in their first attempt to educate the public and engage with them. These women were able to distribute 5,000 pamphlets that explained *sharia* in simple language, so ordinary people could learn about the dangers of the clerics' laws.

Revolutionary Guard paramilitary forces attacked, injuring many and arresting eighteen women who later received sentences of four months to three years in prison, twenty to thirty lashes, and $200 in fines, equal to about a family's monthly income.

On June 15, 2006, Amnesty International issued a public statement, condemning the regime's response:

> Amnesty International condemns the Iranian security forces' violent disruption of a peaceful demonstration on 12 June, by women and men advocating an end to legal discrimination against women in Iran. Police, including a large unit of police officers reportedly moved in as soon as the demonstration began and immediately started beating the protestors with batons in order to force them to disperse. They detained scores of demonstrators, on 13 June 2006, Minister of Justice and Spokesman for the Judiciary Jamal Karimi-Rad stated that 70 people had been arrested, 42 were women, and 28 men, for participating in what he alleged was an illegal demonstration. When questioned about the beatings by police, he said, "If there was any beating, it will be reviewed." Some of those detained, are reported to have been released.
>
> Amnesty International believes that those detained may be prisoners of conscience, detained solely for the peaceful exercise of their internationally recognized right to freedom of expression and association. If so, they should be released immediately and unconditionally. Amnesty International is also calling for a prompt, thorough, and impartial investigation into the excessive force used against the demonstrators. Anyone found responsible for abuse should be brought to justice promptly and fairly.

Despite the violence of the regime, ordinary citizens responded positively to the pamphlets, motivating women activists to launch a petition drive. After lengthy deliberation, they decided to announce the creation of an effort, a One Million Signatures Campaign to End Discrimination Against Women and Children.

Two months later, on August 27, 2006, the women's groups officially announced the inception of the petition campaign, calling for one million signatures to end discrimination in Iran and reform the country's laws. One hundred well-known and prominent women, including poet laureate Simin Behbahani and the lawyer Shirin Ebadi, offered their complete support to the "Founding Ladies of 54," a group of women activists of the younger generation.

Some of the "Founding 54" women on the One Million Signatures Committee

The next month, activists in the city of Tabriz were the first to join the campaign, and they organized committees for training, fundraising, and public relations. The following month, women activists in the city of Isfahan launched a branch of the campaign, followed that month by women in the city of Hamadan and the city of Gorgan. A few days later, women from the city of Zanjon announced their support. By late November 2006, sixty campaign activists hosted a training seminar for volunteers in the city of Karadj and formally joined the campaign. By year's end, women in the city of Yazd joined; and a women's group, *Roghieh Chehr Azad*, and thirty other women's organizations from the city of Kermanshah established their One Million Signature campaign. In mid-December 2006, the campaign held its first general membership meeting in Tehran. That day, the regime arrested an activist, Zeynab Peyghambar-zadeh, while she was collecting signatures in one of Tehran's busy subway stations.

By the end of December 2006, women's organizations in a majority of cities had announced their membership in the One Million Signature Campaign. They trained volunteers and the movement's founding members had a website up and running.

"The websites are our loudspeakers for collecting signatures and running workshops and enable us to organize and discuss theoretical issues with the people," said Mahasti Ganjavi, a founding member.

The movement quickly received international recognition. Shahla

Lahiji, the publisher of *Roshangaran* (*The Intellectuals*), received the 2006 IPA Prize—Freedom to Publish Award—in recognition of her courage as one of the first female publishers in Islamic Republic Iran.

21st century Ladies' Secret Society, photographed by Raha Askarizadeh, during a secret meeting in Tehran.

On January 25, 2007, organizations such as the Feminist School, Change for Equality, and Men for Equality established their own One Million Signatures websites. Two activists, and Mansoureh Shojaee, were arrested and banned from traveling while collecting signatures in late January 2007.

The next month, an international organization, the Women's Learning Partnership, issued a statement in support of the Iranian women's campaign for one million signatures. Women in the holy city of Mashhad held a training workshop for volunteers and announced their city's membership in the campaign.

On February 24, 2007, the ancient Iranian mother's day, a new organization called the Mourning Mothers Committee, made up of women whose children had been killed by the regime, held its first meeting in Tehran and joined the petition drive. The women of the city of Rasht joined the petition effort late that month.

On the third day of March 2007, the regime arrested twenty-eight women members of the campaign and held them for months without bail, accusing them of unlawful assembly. Some of them were later freed, but others were sentenced to from three months to three years in prison. The regime sentenced others to lashing.

The next day, women of the province of Kurdistan held a seminar for the One Million Signature Campaign in the city of Soleymaniyeh in Kurdistan. Soon after, Iranian women in London held a photo exhibition on the One Million Signature Campaign, in support of their sisters inside Iran.

One Million Signatures to Change the Discriminatory Laws

Campaign leaders organized a public meeting in Tehran on March 14. The women held their third membership meeting in Tehran in April 2016 to discuss the relationship between the campaign's political parties and social movements.

Meanwhile, the arrests continued. The regime arrested five members of the campaign—Nahid Keshavarz, Sara Imanian, Sara's husband, Homayoun Nami, Mahboubeh Hussein-Zadeh, and Saeedeh Amin—as they collected signatures in Laleh Park in April 2007. In June, Ehteram Shadfar, a member of the Mourning Mothers Committee and a founding member of the Women's Cultural Center, was arrested and imprisoned for collecting signatures.

Yet, successes continued. The next month, women celebrated the National Day of Solidarity of Iranian Women, the first anniversary of the campaign. Women also celebrated with a general meeting of its members and supporters and the publication of a book, *The One Million Signatures Movement and Its Internal Narratives*, documenting the social injustices of clerical laws.

Three members—Mahrokht Goharshenas, Shams ol-Moluk Javaherkalam, and Shirin Ebadi—presented the One Million Signature Campaign to the Nobel Peace Prize Committee, as a candidate for the prize. Unfortunately, the Nobel Committee did not recognize the campaign and gave the prize to former U.S. Vice President Al Gore for his work on climate change. The same day, the regime arrested Amir Yaghoub-Ali, one of the male participants in the campaign, and imprisoned him for the crime of collecting signatures.

The city of Shiraz joined with a "big bang" weblog for the One Million Signature Campaign. Kurdistan women launched their One Million Signature campaign web site in late July 2007.

The next month, women activists held a seminar in the city of Kermanshah to coincide with the one-year anniversary of their campaign. A painting exhibit, "All my Mothers," opened at the same time, with proceeds going to the campaign. Late that month, women in many other cities celebrated the one-year anniversary of their joining the campaign.

Support for the campaign came from the United States, as well. In September 2007, Iranian-American women in California announced their support for their sisters in Iran and conducted a public demonstration.

Iranian-American women demonstrating in support of their sisters inside Iran

In response to these successes and wishing to teach women a lesson, the government continued its crackdowns on women activists, using even more draconian methods. In September 2007, Iranian President Mahmoud Ahmadinejad introduced legislation called the Family Protection Law, which transferred the last rights held by women to the Islamic Council. The publicity around the One Million Signatures Campaign, however, caused the leadership to decide not to present the new law to the Islamic Council.

Ten days later, twenty-five members of the Campaign were arrested in the city of Khoram-Abad in the province of Luristan. In October 2007, Ronak Safarzadeh was arrested, but despite her arrest, campaign members in the city of Zahedan established a weblog five days later.

Iranian men, too, had joined the movement at this time, creating an organization called Men for Equality and announcing their solidarity with the campaign, collecting signatures. They established their website, *Men for One Million Signatures*.

(right) A man in Iran holds a poster that reads, "Women's Rights = Human Rights" in Persian with "Freedom" below it in English, for the world to see what the struggle in Iran is about.

In November 2007, the Islamic regime began to filter the websites, online photos, and blogs of the campaign—not only within Iran but also in other countries, including Kuwait, Germany, Sweden, and the United States. In California, however, tech-savvy women re-established their campaign website. The members of the campaign in the city of Hamadan reestablished their website in the spring.

The Islamic Revolutionary Court transferred Maryam Husseini-Khah to the dreaded Evin Prison. Jelveh Javaheri, one of the Ladies of 54, was arrested and imprisoned in December 2007.

The next two Ladies of 54, Nasim Sarabandi and Fatemeh Dehdashti, were arrested for collecting signatures in the subway and were taken to prison.

In February 2008, a group in Germany called Iranian Activists of the

Diaspora established a website for the campaign. Two weeks later, two campaign volunteers were arrested in Tehran for collecting signatures. The next month, the government banned two of the founding members, attorney Nasrin Sotoudeh and Mansoureh Shojaee, from traveling outside the country.

Victories and setbacks continued to alternate. In April 2008, one of the members of the campaign, Khadijeh Moghadam, was arrested for collecting signatures, but women launched a website for the campaign in Isfahan the next day. Later in the month, two activist Ladies, Azam Sepehr Khadem and Afzal Vaziri, started working on the One Million Signature Campaign in Cyprus, and Lady organizers decided to move the campaign's headquarters from Iran to Kuwait.

By May 2008, women in most towns and cities of Iran joined the movement and amassed over one million volunteers and workshops for their underground signature collection. The clerical regime became more concerned about the potential power of the women's movement and began to filter websites and weblogs of organizations that supported the One Million Signature Campaign, including the Feminist School, Iranian Women Focus, Men for Equality, *Zanestan* (*Womanhood*), and many others.

In Tehran, in late May 2007, the AKI press reported, "Ayatollah Ahmad Elmalhoda, a highly influential prayer leader said, 'These whores, clutching a piece of paper in their hands to gather signatures, are working for foreign powers and want to destabilize the Islamic Republic.' He then called on the government to 'intervene decisively against these whores, because it is improper to leave them to act with impunity.'"

Ayatollah Elm Al-Hoda, another ruling member of the clergy regime, said, "Women who do not wear the Islamic veil as instructed turn men into animals."

The regime accompanied the verbal attacks against women activists with a powerful judicial offensive. Paramilitary forces began raiding their homes, kicking in doors at five in the morning, beating and arresting women in front of their husbands and children. One of the women arrested and imprisoned had a six-week-old baby that she was breast-feeding. Security forces did not allow her to take her baby with her.

Eight members of the feminist school involved in the signature campaign were arrested and given jail terms of various lengths and sentenced to public floggings. By the order of the Islamic Revolutionary Court, the government shut down twelve of the movement's websites.

In the first week of June 2008, Ladies of the Founding 54 were arrested. Two weeks later, just before they began a peaceful march to commemorate the National Day of Solidarity of Iranian Women, nine more activists were arrested by the paramilitary Revolutionary Guard forces. On June 13, 2008, another activist, Mahbobeh Karimi, was arrested in Tehran and the next month, Zeynab Bayazidi, a member of the campaign in Kurdistan, was also arrested.

Women activists marked the second anniversary of the Campaign for One Million Signatures on August 28, 2008. Determined to commemorate the movement, they gathered in the park, despite the threats by the Islamic Revolutionary Court and its paramilitary forces.

In October 2008, Revolutionary Guard forces ransacked the home of campaign member Parastoo Allahyari, searching for her collected signatures. The Islamic judiciary along with intelligence forces carried out mass arrests in many cities and towns in Iran. They also revoked the passport of an Iranian-American student, Esha Momeni, who was writing her thesis on the Iranian women's movement, to prevent her from leaving the country, before the Islamic Revolutionary Court ordered her arrest. The passport of Nasrin Sotoudeh, one of the Ladies of 54, was revoked to prevent her from traveling to Italy to receive the International Human Rights Award.

Many members of the campaign were prohibited from leaving the country, a practice that continued for several years:

- Talat Taghinia on January 27, 2007
- Mansoureh Shojaee on March 5, 2007
- Parvin Ardalan on March 3, 2008

- Sussan Tahmasebi on October 26, 2008
- Esha Momeni in October 2008
- Nasrin Sotoudeh on November 10, 2008
- Simin Behbahani on March 8, 2010

But organizers continued to establish new websites. In December 2008, they established a website campaign in the city of Arak, followed by a second website campaign in the city of Saary. In Italy, the Iranian diaspora established a website for the campaign, as well.

As the women activists persisted and the number of signatures grew, the clergy in power became more and more apprehensive about the consequences of the campaign. They feared that its empowerment might end in the removal of the clergy from power. The millions of signatures raised questions about the legitimacy of the rule of the clergy. The clerics were aware the campaign had attracted the attention of the international human rights community and they knew that eventually the governments of other nations would see the signatures of millions of Iranian women and men, as a clear referendum on their existence.

Regime leaders decided they should not allow the women to recall their rule though an action of civil disobedience. The Islamic Revolutionary Court and its paramilitary forces again cracked down, this time more harshly on the women activists, arresting large numbers of people and seizing the signatures that had been collected from men and women eager to sign over the course of two years, at the risk of imprisonment and torture.

The ruling clergy are the only people to this day who know how many millions of signatures were collected.

The Islamic regime's brutal crackdown on women in Iran did not affect the international community's political and economic relationship with the clerical regime and thus, unfortunately, the regime paid no price for their inhumane treatment of half of the citizens of Iran. The United Nations did not release any statement on the protests. Norway refused to recognize the struggles of Iranian women for basic human rights.

In fear of women rising again, the Islamic Council decided to make small concessions. On August 31, 2008, President Ahmadinedjad withdrew the draconian Family Protection legislation that would have made it impossible for poor women to have any human dignity. In addition, the Women Lawyers Organization continued to work actively to reduce discrimination against women through creative legal interpretations of *sharia*.

In November 2008, a working group of women lawyers established a weblog demanding equal inheritance. The Islamic Council opposed the demand of women activists for equal inheritance; however, they agreed to pass a law which prescribed equal blood money for men and women, though only in the case of car accidents.

The next month, paramilitary forces raided the office of attorney Shirin Ebadi without a warrant, accusing her of illegal political activities. They did not arrest or imprison her, because her Nobel Peace Prize gave her some protection.

The 54 Lady warriors had grown up under clergy rule. However, their elders had told them about the good old times, sharing videos and photos that documented their right to respect, equality, and freedom. The return of the clergy establishment to power forced the younger generation of Iranian women to raise the flag of the Ladies' Secret Society and fight again for their human dignity.

Parvin Ardalan

Parvin Ardalan, one of 54, is an activist, writer, and journalist who was awarded the Olaf Palm Prize in 2007 for her human rights activism. Parvin and five other women activists of the One Million Signature Campaign were arrested and charged with the crime of "threatening national security" and sentenced to four years in the dreaded Evin Prison.

Parvin Ardalan was one of the founders of the Women's Cultural Centre working for the human rights of women of Iran. She published the first online magazine, *Zanestan* (*Womanhood*), not an easy task, since she and her staff had to deal with constant government harassment and censorship.

Parvin was one of the activists who participated in protest rallies and marches that ended with paramilitary forces beating and arresting women. She was one of the founding women of the One Million Signatures Campaign who used her organization and the online magazine to further the cause.

Nasrin Sotoudeh

In September 2008, Italy gave its first international human rights award to Nasrin Sotoudeh, "1 of the 54," and a lawyer and activist with the campaign. In November of that year, Parvin Dolatabadi and Tahereh Tayere received the Reporters without Borders Jury Prize for their website, *Change for Equality*. Student members of Amnesty International produced a video supporting the Iranian women's movement. The One World's People Award nominated the One Million Signatures Campaign for its 2008 award.

In January 2009, the campaign won the prestigious Simone De Beauvoir Prize, which recognizes groups that work for gender equality. The Nobel committee, however, once more overlooked the women of Iran and gave their prize to the newly-elected president of the United States, Barack Obama.

Nasrin Sotoudeh received the 2011 PEN/Barbara Goldsmith Freedom to Write Award, and the European Parliament awarded her co-winner of the 2012 Sakharov Prize. York University gave her an honorary doctorate in law. She is now in prison in Iran.

Meanwhile, women campaigners in Iran continued to face harsh punishments. In a press release, Pen America highlighted the case of one activist, Nasrin Sotoudeh:

> An internationally recognized champion of human rights in Iran, Nasrin Sotoudeh, was sentenced to 11 years in prison, reduced to six

years on appeal last year, for giving interviews in defense of her clients following the disputed 2009 presidential elections, including Arash Rahmanipour who was executed after a trial that did not conform to international standard of fairness.

She began a hunger strike in Tehran's Evin Prison on October 17, 2012, to protest prison conditions and the government placed a travel ban on her twelve-year-old daughter, Mehraveh—a move that she and her husband, Reza Khandan, believed could be the first step toward filing charges against the children. Sotoudeh was subsisting on sugar water and salt water, and her weight dropped to under ninety-five pounds. Her blood pressure also fell dangerously.

Ms. Stotoudeh was rearrested in 2018 and in March of 2019 she was sentenced to 30 years in prison and 75 lashes.

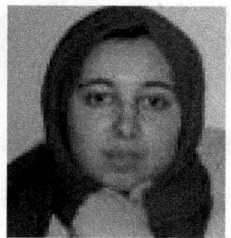

Maryam Hosseinkhani

Maryam Hosseinkhani, another "1 of 54," was born in 1980, one year after the Islamic clergy revolution. Educated in Islamic studies, she became a journalist, working for a decade as an activist, writing on women's issues in Iran.

The activist bloggers reported that Maryam was summoned to the security branch of the Islamic Revolutionary Courts on Saturday, November 17, 2007. After hours of interrogation, she was charged with "disruption of public opinion, propaganda against the state, and publication of lies through the untrue news items" on the site of the Women's Cultural Center and the One Million Signatures Campaign. The Islamic Revolutionary Court sentenced her to four years in prison. In response, Change for Equality wrote:

> Maryam, a journalist member of the Women's Cultural Center, and an active member of the One Million Signatures Campaign was arrested earlier today. A few days after the site of the Women's Cultural Center, a leading women's NGO, was shut down on order of the Min-

istry of Culture and Islamic Guidance and the Judiciary, Maryam Hosseinkhah, was the editor of the site of this organization as well as one of the editors of the One Million Signatures Campaign site.

Over the next days, bloggers continued to express their dismay, reporting, "To date, over 40 women have been arrested and two other members of the Campaign besides Maryam remain in prison. Ronak Safarzadeh and Hana Abdi were both arrested in Kurdistan after collecting signatures. They remain in prison and have not had access to their families or lawyers."

Bahareh Hedayat

Bahareh Hedayat, 1 of the Ladies of 54, was born in 1981, two years after the revolution transformed her country. She became a student activist, women's activist, and spokeswoman for the Student Unity Central Council. She was one of the members of the One Million Signature Campaign arrested many times for collecting signatures. She was last arrested in 2010 and sentenced to nine-and-a-half years in prison.

Separately, the publisher of a women's magazine, *Shahla Sherkat*, was arrested, accused of showing unpleasant images of the Islamic Republic, and disseminating "morally and questionable information." She was sentenced to six years in prison.

The following are the names of dozens of women and four men arrested, sentenced, and imprisoned among the 54 women leaders of the One Million Signature Campaign:

The women:
1. Zeynab Peyghambarzadeh
2. Nasim Sarabandi
3. Fatemeh Dehdashti
4. Nahid Keshavarz

5. Mahboubeh Hoseinzadeh
6. Ehteram Shadfar
7. Raheleh Asgarizadeh
8. Raha Khosravi
9. Zhila Bani Yaghoub
10. Farideh Ghaeb
11. Aida Saadat
12. Nafise Azad
13. Sara Loghmani
14. Aliyeh Motalebzadeh
15. Nasrin Sotoudeh
16. Jelveh Javaheri
17. Nahid Mirhaj
18. Hajar Tarbiat
19. Maryam Amid
20. Zeynab Bayazidi
21. Somayeh Farid
22. Nahid Keshavarz
23. Mahboubeh Hossein
24. Noushin Ahmadi Khorasani
25. Zahra Amjadiyan
26. Sara Loghmani
27. Parvin Ardalan
28. Jelveh Javaheri
29. Maryam Hossein Khah
30. Rezvan Moghadam
31. Niloufar Golkar
32. Sara Imanian
33. Nahid Jafari
34. Maryam Yaghoub
35. Sussan Tahmasebi
36. Nasrin Afzali
37. Minoo Mortazi Langeroudi
38. Shadi Sadr
39. Mahboubeh Abbas
40. Gholi Zadeh
41. Azadeh Forghani
42. Asiyeh Amini
43. Parastoo Dokoohaki
44. Parastoo Sarmadi

45. Fatemeh Govarayi
46. Sara Laghaee
47. Saghar Laghaee
48. Mahnaz Mohamadi
49. Ronak Safar Zadeh
50. Hana Abdi
51. Khadijeh Moghadam
52. Nahid Keshavarz
53. Parastoo Allahyari
54. Mahboubeh Karami
55. Mansoureh Shojaee
56. Talat Taghi-Nia
57. Farnaz Seifi
58. Noushin Ahmadi Khorasani
59. Shahla Entesari
60. Sussan Tahmasebi
61. Fariba Davoodi Mohajer
62. Delaram Ali
63. Taraneh Bani Yaghoub
64. Bahareh Hedayat
65. Masoumeh Zia
66. Maryam Zia
67. Aliyeh Eghdam Doost
68. Khoeeni
69. Azadeh Forghani
70. Nasim Soltan Beygi.

The men:
1. Seyed Ali Akbar Mousavi
2. Bahman Ahmadi Amouee
3. Amir Yaghoub-Ali.

The court denied the women legal representation, due process, and the right to speak in their own defense.

The Committee of 54 Ladies had begun by hoping to collect one million signatures against the gender apartheid regime of Iran, but it ended with millions of volunteers joining them to collect tens of millions of signatures in every city, town, and village of Iran.

Although the government and paramilitary crackdown resulted in the eventual disbanding of the One Million Signatures Campaign, it taught the women and men of Iran that regime change could be possible if they worked together against injustice.

This led to the next chapter of resistance: an uprising in 2009 when Iranians asked the simple, but profound question, "Where is my vote?"

CHAPTER TWENTY

Uprising: Where Is My Vote? (2009)

IN THE FACE OF INCESSANT government harassment, the organizers of the One Million Signature Campaign eventually dismantled their noble effort.

In February 2009, the Islamic Revolutionary Court ordered the arrest of thirty-three more women activists, ultimately imprisoned without any charges. After lawyers protested, forcing an inquiry, the court released the women, as long as they promised not to hold any demonstrations on March 8, International Women's Day.

On the afternoon of March 8, 2009, hundreds of women gathered in front of the Islamic Council, demanding their equal rights. The regime's paramilitary forces did what they always do: they attacked the crowd, beating many protesters and arresting eight women activists.

The protests were just a sign of things to come. The country was holding elections for president that year, and women were about to lead an uprising. Incumbent President Mahmoud Ahmadinejad was running for reelection, and women were determined to vote him out of office, despite the desires of Supreme Leader Ayatollah Ali Khamenei.

During the campaign, the country's two candidates—handpicked by the absolute leader—went out of their way to make promises to women, trying to secure their votes. Zahra Rahnavardi, the wife of candidate Mir-Hossein Mousavi, broke conventional rules and joined her husband's campaign in trying to appeal to women and young university students. She talked about restoring the human rights of Iranian women and even promised that her husband would ratify the U.N. Convention on the Elimination of All Forms of Discrimination Against Women.

Women activists did not like any of the handpicked candidates for supreme leader, because they knew no leader represented real change. Still, they decided to support the campaign of Mousavi, because his wife had promised them change.

On the night of the election, June 12, 2009, government officials announced that the incumbent Ahmadinejad won nearly 63 percent of the vote. Protests began that night, and, tapping Mousavi's campaign theme, the protesters gave their movement a name: the Green Revolution.

Frustrated Iranians asked a simple question, "Where is my vote?"

They took to the streets.

During weeks of uprising, the Revolutionary Guard continually attacked the demonstrators. With sharpshooters on the rooftops and in high-rise windows, they killed many protesters, including 26-year-old Neda Agha-Sultan. A cell phone video of Neda, bloodied and dying, went viral across the world, and she became a symbol of the courage of Iranian women in their war against the clergy's rule.

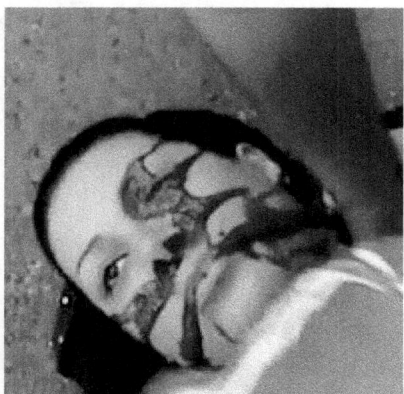

The women continued demonstrating their opposition to the regime, chanting, "Where is my vote?"

The international community, the democratic, progressive governments of the West, and Western women, largely remained silent.

Iranians chanted, "Obama! Obama! Are you with them or with us?" but U.S. President Barack Obama gave carte blanche permission to the tyrant clergy regime to continue its massacre of the Iranian people when he said, "We will not interfere in the internal affairs of Iran."

They received no support from the United States, nor the international community. No sanctions. No punishments. Not even warnings to the clergy in Iran. The Revolutionary Guard went on a killing spree over the next two years. They arrested, kidnapped, tortured, and killed anyone they wanted to eliminate, without being questioned.

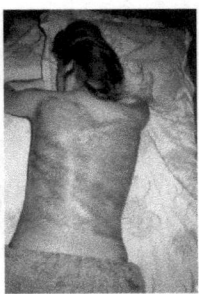

A 19-year-old university student was arrested, raped twenty-two times by seven people and flogged, but her assailants did not kill her.

For months after the uprising, the bodies of Iranians were dumped in the back alleys of Iran's cities, as a warning to potential protesters.

Taraneh Mousavi, a 19-year-old woman, was one of those bodies. One day, she was kidnapped on the street. She was brutally raped. Someone dropped her at a hospital, on the verge of death, but as soon as they learned that she might survive, they kidnapped her from the hospital and killed her. Her charred body was found in a back alley.[1]

Her news filled the hearts of Iranians with dread, but the fierce women of Iran were not going to give up.

For decades, women journalists in Iran have been at the forefront of the struggle for human dignity. Many activists, artists, journalists, lawyers and brilliant minds have been forced to leave their homeland and chose a life in exile, while many more are still in prison, with long sentences in the dreaded Evin Prison of Iran.

Shiva Nazar Ahari

Shiva Nazar Ahari was born after the clergy takeover in 1979. She is a journalist and activist member of the Committee of Human Rights of Reporters. When the Iranian government barred her from graduate studies because of her activism, Shiva joined the Council of Defense Against Education Discrimination, while working to defend the rights of child laborers and homeless children in Iran.

After the election uprising of 2009, Shiva was arrested on June 14, spending thirty-three days in solitary confinement. Prison authorities released her four months later on October 13, 2009, just to re-arrest her on December 20, and hold her without charges in solitary confinement in Ward #209 of the Intelligence Ministry.

---

1 "The Rape of Taraneh: Prison Abuse of Iran's Protesters," Shirin Sadeghi, https://www.huffingtonpost.com/shirin-sadeghi/the-rape-of-taraneh-priso_b_233063.html.

The next year, on September 4, 2010, government prosecutors finally filed charges against her for attempts to deface the Islamic government assembly, with intention to conspire against the Islamic government, disrupting the public order and *moharebeh*, an Arabic word, meaning, "waging war against God." PEN International reported:

> In a lower court hearing on 4 September 2010, Shiva was sentenced to 74 lashes and six years in prison, later reduced to four years on appeal, and was sent to Rajaee Shahr Prison. Since 2002, when she was just eighteen years old, Shiva Nazar Ahari has been jailed several times by the Iranian government for her peaceful activism and reporting on human rights violations.

In a letter to a fellow prisoner of conscience, Shiva wrote,

> When your heart trembles for the rights of another human, that is when you begin to slip, that is when the interrogations begin. When your heart trembles for another prisoner, a woman, a child laborer, that is when you become the accused. When you find faith in people and believe in humanity and nothing else, that is when you commit your first crime.

Two years later, the Theodor Haecker Prize gave Shiva an award for her courageous Internet reporting on human rights violations. Shiva was nominated for the prestigious Netizen Prize as well from Reporters Without Borders.

* * *

After the so-called elections, Mahmoud Ahmadinejad announced the inclusion of one woman in his cabinet. Obviously, this was the supreme leader's reaction to the One Million Signature campaign and the overwhelming participation of women in the post-election uprising.

As with past resistance efforts, the clergy could see the power of women in the uprising and decided to give women a token concession, by appointing a couple of women, one to the office of Family and Women's Affairs, to deflect the charges of women that they were anti-women. But these women appointees were allied with the theological rulers who limited the number of female university students, enforced an Islamic dress code for women, and pushed for nationwide gender segregation.

Ahmadinejad appointed Zohreh Tabibzadeh Nouri, a dentist, to be director of the Center for Women and Family Affairs, an agency that Khomeini had opposed when it was first established in 1975. Now, the main duty of the center was to enforce gender apartheid laws, not empower women.

The Western media rushed to celebrate the appointment and called the Ahmadinejad government a "new, female-friendly Islamic regime." The media was either explicitly covering up the regime's crimes against humanity or exhibited the outmost naïveté in understanding the nature of the Shi'a clergy after some thirty years of its dictatorial rule.

Not long after the announcement, a clergy member of the judicial committee, Mohammad Taghi Rahbar, declared, "There are religious doubts over the abilities of women when it comes to management."

Rahbar said "...the issue must be taken to the supreme leader, Ayatollah Ali Khamenei, for guidance."

Upon her appointment, Ms. Nouri declared, "I do not deny that there are gaps in the Iranian law when it comes to protection of women's rights. However, as long as I live and remain in charge of this center, I will not let anyone sign any international charter, including the Committee on the Elimination of Discrimination Against Women, as long as we can fix the gaps and existing problems through the Islamic faith. I see no reason to follow the unsuccessful western [sic] model."

In an article in the November 2009 issue of *Glamour* magazine, journalist Clara Powers recognized the legacy of years of struggle in the year's uprising, writing:

> June's postelection fervor was called a women's revolt by many, but Iranian women may have first found the courage to speak out thanks to an earlier movement: the One Million Signatures Campaign. For the past three years, members of the One Million Signatures initiative have pressed for women's rights and have endured the constant threat of jailing and beating as a result.[2]

The next year, on February 11, 2010, hundreds of thousands of people gathered for a peaceful protest in Tehran's "Freedom Square."

The Revolutionary Guard's paramilitary forces dispersed the crowd with tear gas and water hoses, injuring and killing many. Unlike in 1979, when it fawned over pro-Khomeini protesters, the Western media did

---

2 "The Women of Iran's One Million Signature Campaign: The Activists," Carla Power, http://www.glamour.com/story/the-women-of-irans-one-million-signatures-campaign.

not pay much attention to the uprising.

Since the uprising of 2009, Iranian opposition to clergy rule has changed. There is not a single day that goes by without a multitude of protests, rallies, and strikes happening around the country, mostly unreported.

The women's opposition tactics became more passive-aggressive, moving into acts of civil disobedience—and the regime decided to let the women activists leave the country, rather than have them stay in Iran and fight against their dictatorial rule.

CHAPTER TWENTY-ONE

The Struggle Continues for All Iranian Women (2010 – 2017)

As the result of Iran's geographic location on the Silk Road, it was repeatedly attacked and occupied by foreigners and destroyed during the First and Second World Wars; Iranians have become weary of conflicts, hostilities, and war. We are a peace-loving people.

Over the last forty years, the mothers of Iran have suffered like no others. They have lost hundreds of thousands of their children since the Islamic clergy took control of Iran in 1979.

The clergy began their rule by having about one million young Iranian men and boys killed and disabled. In the eight-year war, mothers were afraid to let their young boys out on the streets because they could be snatched by the Revolutionary Guard. Those whose young boys were taken away still await news of their sons.

Aside from being casualties of foreign wars, mothers have lost tens of thousands of their children in the bloody internal wars of the Iranian regime's paramilitary forces against the people. These mothers are the Mothers in Black, whose young sons and daughters have been arrested, imprisoned, tortured, raped, and killed by the regime.

These mothers continue asking questions.
"Where are my children?"
"What are they doing to them?"
"How were they killed?"
And: "Will I ever see my child again?"

They are threatened and sometimes they "accidentally die," but they have nothing to lose in their persistence, even when their sit-in strikes last weeks and months behind the gates of Evin Prison. These mothers do not give up on their children, whether dead or imprisoned.

A human rights activist and journalist, Jaleh Hesabi, was a member of the Association of the Mothers for Peace. She mysteriously died.

The Western media chronicles the courage of the Mothers of the Plaza de Mayo in Argentina and the Ladies in White in Cuba, both groups mourning their sons murdered and disappeared, but they rarely mention the Mourning Mothers Committee of Iran.

Iran's policy of gender apartheid—depriving women of rights, giving them an inferior education, forcing them to dress like every day is Halloween—has not deterred women in Iran from getting their education and determining their own careers.

A friend who went to Iran to visit her family told me a story about the strong will of Iranian women. She said, "After a while, I decided not to go out of the house unless necessary. I just could not take the fear of the hijab police and headcovers. When a friend invited me out to lunch, I proposed to just stay home for lunch, but she would not have it. 'No, this is not an option,' she said. 'They want us to go back in to the house, but we refuse. We will live in their face and challenge them to deal with it, even if we have to wear that thing on our heads.'"

Nina Siahkali Moradi

In May 2013, Nina Siahkali Moradi became an architect and married a man secure in his masculinity. At the age of 27, she ran for city council in the city of Ghazvin. Her campaign slogan was simple: "New ideas for the future of the young people."

She promised more civil rights for women and she won the election, not only with the women's vote but also with a large number of votes from brave men.

However, the clergy threw away the votes that had been cast for her and made bogus excuses to take away her right to represent the people.

A report said, "Nina Siahkali Moradi epitomized the promise of more civil rights for the country's women when she won her bid for the city council member earlier this summer. But now her election is overturned by religious conservative clergy, who have basically barred her from office for being too hot."

Nasrin Moazami

Professor Nasrin Moazami, a medical microbiologist and biotechnologist, is a pioneer in the field of biotechnology and microalgae-based fuels in Iran. The center that she established in 1987 is now a regional reference center in biotechnology for West and Central Asia. She is also founder of the Persian Type Culture Collection, an affiliated member of the World Federation of Culture Collection WFCC. Dr. Moazami established the Persian Gulf Biotechnology Research Center in 1995 at Qeshm Island, Iran. It is a center for applied research in marine biotechnology in the country. From 1990 to 2004, she was head of the biotechnology department, and, from 2004 to 2010, she was director of the Institute of Advanced Technology. Since 2011, she has been the lead scientist, in charge of the project.

Fahimeh Rahimi

Born in 1941, Fahimeh Rahimi was a writer who wrote her first mystery novel at the age of nine and published her first book in 1989. She had written forty-six more mystery books by the time she passed away in 2012 from cancer. She was called the "Iranian Danielle Steel" and many of her books became bestsellers.

This elderly woman on a motorcycle captures the spirit of Iranian women. She is poor and elderly, living in a clergy dictatorship, but she is not giving up on life. She keeps her money in the knot in the corner of her white headscarf and, by the size of the knot, this woman does not have much money. However, she has a motorcycle to earn a living, making deliveries. She is confident, self-reliant, and happy.

An Iranian actress, in an ultraconservative Islamic dress, proudly poses in front of a bas-relief of Cyrus the Great on the wall of Persepolis, the dazzling capital of the ancient Empire of Iran.

In her village, Monavar Ramezani, a self-taught artist, was called Nana Hassan, or "Hassan's mother." Young city dwellers discovered her art and displayed her paintings in Tehran's art galleries, featuring her as an artist of the "naïve outsider painting" style. She painted what she saw in her village. She said that her paintings were for fellow villagers, never intending to sell them in city art galleries.

Women have always played a significant role in Iran's economy. They have been the rice, tea, and silk farmers in northern Iran, even with their babies swaddled to their backs.

The clergy consider music un-Islamic, but they cannot stop the women who make a living, playing for the public on city sidewalks. This woman is playing a tar, or "the mother of guitar."

Moneer Homayouni

Moneer Homayouni is a financial and banking expert, but she became a volunteer teacher, like the women in the Ladies' Secret Society. To ensure future generations of Iranians will be educated, Moneer established the Center for Promotion of Children's Education. The center raises funds and builds libraries for children and adults in villages around the country.

She told a reporter from the Iranian *Washingtonian* magazine that women in villages are motivated to learn and educate their children. "In average, our libraries provide about 4,000 books per village, and the village membership of every library is about 350 to 450," Moneer said. "We also set up racks of books in front of the stores like bakeries, for the people to read while standing in line."

In 2014, the Center of Women Citizens, together with the Organization of Women Against Environmental Pollution, protested against the deadly air pollution in Tehran, which was killing people without government officials addressing the problem.

Faezeh Rafsanjani

Faezeh Rafsanjani, the daughter of the former president of the Islamic Republic regime, was elected in February 2014 to be director of the Society for Defense of Freedom of the Press. She is one of the women members of the Islamic regime, challenging the misogynist laws and policies of the regime her father helped establish.

Iranian men are typically pro-equal rights and have fought alongside women. Iranian cartoonist Hadi Heidari criticized the clergy's "Family Protection Law" in a cartoon. Hadi was arrested in November 2014 and released the next spring.

Cartoonist Toka Neyestani has been regularly chronicling the plight of the women of Iran in his Campaign's Weekly Cartoon at a website, iranhumanrights.org.

Despite arrests and violence, women have fearlessly continued to demand their rights.

The Struggle Continues for All Iranian Women 287

A woman attacks the plain-clothed paramilitary forces, as they beat a young demonstrator. Her hijab tells that she is a "true" believer and a defender of freedom.

In the fall of 2014, a clergyman attacked women with loose hijabs from the pulpit and said that they should be taught a lesson. The next day, jobless men began throwing acid on the faces of women on the streets of the city of Isfahan. Women started wearing helmets to protect themselves.

Epilogue

A New Chapter (2018 – Future)

ON WEDNESDAY, December 27, 2017, an anonymous young Iranian woman, dressed in black pants and a long-sleeved black shirt, stood on a telephone utility box on the sidewalk of the very busy Enqelab ("Revolution") Avenue, in Tehran.

Without a word, she took off her hijab.

She then wrapped her white head scarf around the end of the pole that she carried, and she began waving the flag aloft in the breeze that was freely wafting her long silky black hair.

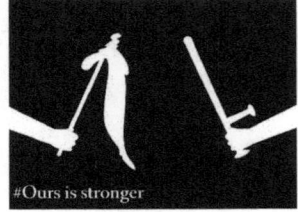

No one in the media knew her name, but the young Iranian woman waving a white scarf became a symbol of the modern-day generation of the Ladies' Secret Society. She was part of the generation of young Iranians, born and raised under the gender apartheid rule of the 1979 Islamic revolution, but who refused to be amenable and obedient. They are the newest generation, calling themselves the "millennials of Iran," seizing the mantle from the generation before that had collected millions of signatures against *sharia* and landed in the cleric's dreaded prisons. The women of the One Million Signatures movement had taken over from the generation before them, marching on the streets to demonstrate against the clergy's rule.

Now, this generation took off the scarf and waved it in the air as a symbol of a peaceful yet stanchly defiant campaign, #IAmArtamedis, harkening back to the women leaders who had fought in Iran, my motherland, for the right of women to feel the wind in their hair. However, paramilitary forces retaliated violently. They detained the young woman and killed other protesters. The clerics were afraid of the activists.

Nasrin Sotoudeh, a human rights lawyer in Iran and a member of the One Million Signatures movement, wrote a Facebook post, alerting the world to the woman's arrest. She was released shortly afterwards and then re-arrested.

We didn't know much about the woman.

Sotoudeh said, "The woman is 31-years-old and has a 19-month-old-daughter."

Family members and friends did not come forward to identify the woman publicly, to protect themselves as dissidents. They had come under added scrutiny after the unrest.

The peaceful protest of the unknown girl motivated Iranian activists online who posted memes showing the young woman's defiance of clergy power, in a campaign labeled #Where_Is_She.

In the last week of 2017, the people of Iran showed their ultimate disrespect and distrust against the clergy's rule, taking to the streets in a virtual uprising. They pulled down posters of the "sanctified" "Supreme Leader," chanting, "We don't want mullahs' rule." They tore an effigy of the "Supreme Leader" into pieces, burned posters in bonfires they set, and some even tossed the ruling party's posters into the streets, stepping on them in disrespect. The millennials of Iran marched in the streets, peacefully defiant against the occupiers of their motherland.

This new generation of Iranian millennials are tech-savvy and informed. Looking back at their history, they are unhappy with the imperialistic attitudes of the Western democracies towards them. They are finding themselves not only fighting the clergy occupiers, but they are telling the leaders of the world that they are the only legitimate citizen-leaders of Iran and, after the clergy rule falls, they will look for real friends.

Ode to Cyrus the Great

The young people of this generation are fighting for their national identity, their pre-Islamic civilization and their human dignity as a peaceful, civilized nation. Their method of opposition against the occupiers of their homeland is to choose a historical symbol of their country's strength: Cyrus the Great, the king who presented the world with the first proclamation on human rights, equality, and justice.

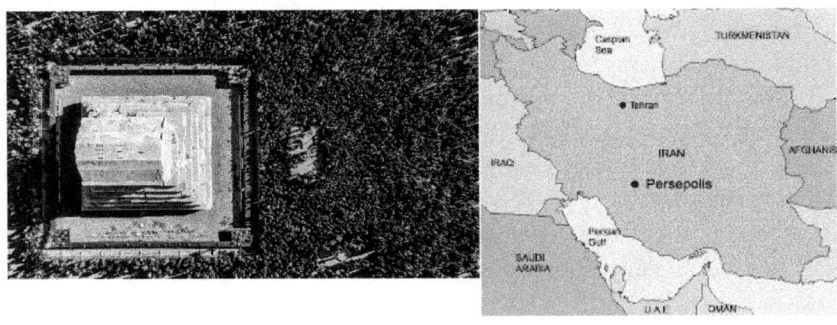

Since 2010, young people have traveled from all over the country—often times many hours and, sometimes, days—to stand at the foot of the modest tomb of Cyrus on October 29, marking Cyrus Day. Despite the clerics' denial of the existence of Cyrus and any vestiges of Iranian civilization, an increasing number of millennials have driven from around the country to celebrate their motherland and her founder. It has terrified the ruling clerics.

Assemblies of tens of thousands of young people gather and chant, "Iran is our homeland. Cyrus is our father." In the Old Persian language, "father" meant "leader."

This past October 29, 2017, the regime had become so paranoid by the annual gatherings for Cyrus, they dispatched paramilitary forces to block the roads and highways going to the tomb of Cyrus the Great. The regime created a national transportation gridlock, just to prevent young Iranians from going to the tomb. It installed barbed wire around the tomb, with armed paramilitary forces standing between the people and the tomb. Revolutionary Guard helicopters hovered above the tomb day and night, to put the fear of the tyrants in the hearts of the young

Iranians. Yet, thousands of young people made it to the Cyrus tomb to be faced with the armed military that has been created only to protect the clerical regime and power.

This generation has become the avid readers and performers of Abolqasem Ferdowsi's book, *Epic of the Kings*. Many young women are now becoming professional Ferdowsi *naqqal*, a word that means "narrator," reciting the stories of Ferdowsi's *Shahnameh, Epics of the Kings*. This movement is also a declaration of patriotism and an honoring of an oral history that Iranians have used throughout their history to say, "We will not forget our history."

In defiance of the rules of gender apartheid, the millennial women of Iran use makeup to show their personal determination. They color their fingernails in bright colors and their hijabs are sheer and festive, often loosely hanging on the back of their head so as not to mess up their well-coiffed hair. Their loose tunics have been getting tighter and shorter over the years, worn now over tight, fashionable jean leggings.

This generation of Iranians gives their children Iranian names, although they get harassed for not choosing Arabic names when registering their children's birth certificates. Today, Iranians call the ideology that controls every aspect of their lives and livelihood "political Islam."

You cannot convince the millennials of Iran that the dictatorial clergy cares about them and their motherland.

Khomeini's intention reverberates in all of their hearts. He said, "Iran is only a base for us to establish the rule of Islam throughout the world."

#IranProtests

The millennials of Iran marked the start of 2018 with an uprising by the people of Iran against rampant poverty, injustice, the de facto slavery of women and children, and discrimination, among other injustices. By all definitions and terms of international law and United Nations resolutions, Iran is a gender apartheid regime, vehemently and actively opposed by the women and men of Iran. Isn't it beyond time for Western democracies and women to stop supporting them? And support instead the legacy of the Ladies' Secret Society and the brave women who are its descendants? In late January 2018, we learned the name of the activist.

Her name is Vida Movahed. She is a living symbol of the Ladies' Secret Society. We must always remember her name.

Sahar Khodayari

On September 9, 2019; nine days after she set herself on fire in front of a Tehran courtroom, Sahar Khodayari died. The 29-year-old, now internationally known as #TheBlueGirl (her favorite team's color), was arrested by the Islamic morality police, for attending a football (soccer) match dressed as a man on account of Iranian women being prohibited from attending sports events. So on September 1st, when the Mullah judge handed down the two-year prison sentence, knowing that a prison sentence would mean having to endure every unimaginable violation a woman can suffer in prison, Sahar set herself on fire, rather than facing such an ordeal.

Sahar Khodayari was merely the latest casualty of a war the regime has waged on Iranian women for over four decades. In February 1994, Dr. Homa Darabi, a distinguished American-educated child psychiatrist and professor at University of Tehran, was the first of the Iranian women to self-immolate in a Tehran plaza while shouting "Death to Oppression, Long Live Liberty!" Professor Darabi had been forced to wear the dark mandatory hijab in her classroom and when she did not comply, she was harassed and fired by the cleric chancellor of the University.

Masih Alinejad

Masih Alinejad left her motherland to speak up about gender discrimination against the women in Iran. Being in America she had thought she would be free to tell the world about compulsory hijab on the women of Iran. She began the campaign of #WhiteWednesdays #Iran. Women were encouraged to take off their white head scarves and wave them on the streets, as an act of peaceful civil disobedience movement. These women have been arrested and given long prisons terms along with floggings. Their lawyer Nasrin Sotoudeh tried to defend them but she was arrested, held for one year without charges, and convicted to 23 years of prison and 75 lashes.

Furthermore, the agents of the Intelligence Ministry of the Islamic Republic found a way to silence Masih, even in America. According to www.amnesty.otg, www.hrw.ogb, www.pen.org, and Voice of America, Iranian intelligence officials detained three members of her family on September 12th 2019.

Masih reported, "The agents of the Intelligence Ministry of the Islamic Republic raided my brothers' house and handed him out in handcuff and blindfolded, They arrested him in front of his two small children. This is what Stalin would do. This is what a dictator would do to its own citizens."

Expressing open defiance, she continued, "The goal of the Islamic Republic was keeping me silent. I'm going to get louder against these hostage-takers."

The spirit of the Ladies' Secret Society lives to this day in every woman and girl who stands up against tyranny to defend freedom.

May we never forget them.

Appendix A

Women of Courage in Exile

Over the last 40 years, Iranian women have fled their homeland to become citizens of Western democracies, and they have flourished, contributing to the societies they call home. These women, living in exile, have had to begin a new lifestyle, adjust to new social environments, learn new languages and cultures, while often struggling to raise their children and, yes, most importantly, educate their children. I am one of those women.

Women married to high-ranking men in Iran landed in America after the "revolution," and rolled up their sleeves and went to work, although many had not worked professionally before.

One woman told me, "When we arrived in America, I had to get a job as soon as possible. I had followed my husband to exile, and I had children to raise and educate. I had done jewelry and high-fashion shopping most of my previous life, and I knew how to sell to the women of means. That is how I got my first job at Cartier and reached high sales volume in two years. Of course, my friendly culture and knowledge of [the] product were important, but my English accent helped also. In time, I became store manager and now regional manager."

Many of the women are book authors and are teaching at universities throughout the Western world. Many have become successful in the arts, sciences, and business. And many are still activists, fighting to bring the voices of their sisters inside Iran to the ears of the Western world.

The Diaspora

Marjane Satrapi, a graphic novelist, illustrator, animated film director, and children's book author, was born November 22, 1969, in the city of Rasht, Iran. Raised and educated in Iran, she moved to France to work freely as an artist.

Marjane became internationally known for her critically acclaimed autobiographical graphic novel, *Persepolis*, about her childhood in Iran before the 1979 revolution and her life later in Europe.

Persepolis was adapted into an animated film of the same name and won the Special Jury Prize in the 2007 Cannes Film Festival. The English version of the *Persepolis* was nominated for an Academy Award for Best Animated Feature in January 2008, making her the first woman to be nominated for that award. She lives in Paris.

In July 1994, Iranian girls were finally allowed to participate in the International Mathematical Olympiads.

Maryam Mirzakhani, a child of the Islamic revolution, born just two years before clerical power took control of the country, was seventeen when she finally got the opportunity to take the qualifying tests for the International Mathematical Olympiads, which she passed. She joined Iran's team and received gold medals in 1994 in Hong Kong and in 1995 in Toronto, where she finished with a perfect score, earning her recognition as a brilliant teenager. An alumnus of Sharif University of Technology in Iran and Harvard University, she received over a dozen mathematics awards, including the Blumenthal Award, presented by the American Mathematical Association.

She became the first woman to win the Fields Medal, considered the "Nobel Prize of mathematics," in honor of her contributions to the understanding of the symmetry of curved surfaces. In 2008, at the age of 31, Dr. Mirzakhani received a full professorship at Stanford University. She never forgot her sisters back in Iran and remained an active member of the National Organization for Development of Exceptional Talents in Iran.

This great mind would have been kept from progressing had the women of Iran not fought against the ruling clergy, earning her the right to travel and compete in the international arena. In 2017, at the age of 40, Mirzakhani died in Stanford, California, from cancer, leaving the Iranian people mourning and the Iranian regime even allowing her photo to be published in state newspapers in her customary short hair, without a headscarf.

 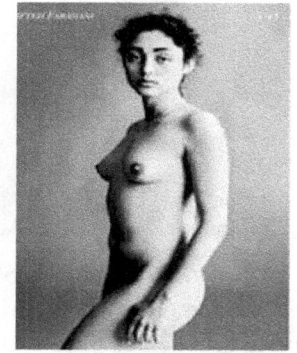

With freedom in the West, Golshifteh Farahani has become an internationally known actor. However, the clerical establishment's anti-women laws forced her to leave Iran. To prove her sovereignty from the misogynist men who had taken over her motherland, Golshifteh posed in the nude. She lives in Paris.

Shirin Neshat has flourished in the art world. Born and raised in pre-Khomeini Iran, she has tried to use her art to attract the attention of the world to the plight of Iranian women living under gender apartheid.

Through the visual effect of photography, paintings, and movies, she expresses opposition to the clerical regime governing Iran. Her art is her voice of protest against the injustices of gender apartheid. Shirin has had many solo exhibitions around the world, beginning in 1993. She has won many awards and accolades for her movies in film festivals, since 2000.

One of her photographs shows women in dark black hijab segregated from men in white shirts. She symbolizes the clergy establishment's image of men as pure and innocent and women as evil, responsible and punishable for the honor of men. She lives today in New York City and continues to support the women of Iran in their protests.

Moneer Farmonfarmanian's art is uniquely traditional Iranian architectural design. She works with bits and pieces of mirrors to create geometrical shapes. Moneer is the first Iranian whose work, capturing the geometrical art of mirrors, is exhibited at the Guggenheim Museum.

APPENDIX A: *Women of Courgae in Exile* ↛ 299

Moneer Farmonfarmanian and her artwork

On October 18, 2006, Anousheh Ansari became the first Iranian-American female in space. She is the co-founder and chair of PRODEA Systems, Inc. She participated in the Russian space program. She lives in Plano, Texas.

Anousheh Ansari

Born in 1952 and raised in a mostly secular Iran, Shohreh Aghdashloo had established her acting career on the stage and in movies when the Islamic revolution forced her into exile. She immigrated to Los Angeles to resume her career in Hollywood.

Shohreh received an Academy Award nomination for Best Supporting Actress for her performance in the movie, *The House of Sand and Fog*, in 2003. She received numerous other awards, including the Los Angeles Film Critics Association Award for Best Supporting Actress, the 2009 Emmy Award for Best Supporting Actress in a TV Movie/Miniseries, the Independent Spirit Award for Best Supporting Female, the New York Film Critics Circle Award for Best Supporting Actress, the

Online Film Critics Society Award for Best Supporting Actress, and the Satellite Award for Best Actress in a Motion Picture, Drama.

Shohre Aghdashloo

Shohreh wrote a memoir, *The Ally of Love and Yellow Jasmines*. While successful in her career in the West, Shohreh has also been an activist, speaking against the violations of human rights in Iran.

Baroness Haleh Afshar is an Iranian woman who frightens the clergy. She is a prominent Muslim feminist, a British professor, and Life Peer in the House of Lords.

Baroness Haleh Afshar

Baroness Afshar received her education in England, with a PhD degree from New Hall Cambridge. After receiving her education, she returned home to Iran, where she worked on land reform as a civil servant, ending feudalism in Iran. She also worked as a journalist and gossip columnist in Iran, and later, in England.

A member of the third generation of women in her family not to cover their hair, her maternal grandmother was a member of the Ladies' Secret Society that fought the clergy and rejected hijab. Baroness Afshar was one of the first Iranian women to be able to vote in 1962, fulfilling the wishes of her grandmother's generation. However, she had to reluctantly leave her homeland, when Ayatollah Khomeini took over Iran.

Baroness Afshar is now a professor in Politics and Women's Studies at the University of York. She is a visiting professor of Islamic law at the *Faculté Internationale de Droit Comparé* (International Faculty of Comparative Law) at Robert Schuman University in Strasbourg, France. Baroness Afshar serves on several bodies, notably the British Council and the United Nations Association, of which she is Honorary President of International Services. She was appointed to the board of the Women's National Commission in September 2008. She has served as the Chair of the British Society for Middle Eastern Studies. Baroness Afshar is a founding member of the Muslim Women's Network. She has served on the Home Office's working groups, on "engaging with women" and "preventing extremism together."

Jasmin Moghbeli (Photograph by Robert Markowitz/NASA)

Jasmin Moghbeli, born in Germany and raised in Baldwin, New York, is a new astronaut at NASA. She was picked among 18,000 applicants. Jasmin graduated from the Massachusetts Institute of Technology. She is a decorated Marine, flying Cobra gunships on one hundred and fifty combat missions in Afghanistan. Jasmin's parents fled Iran after the 1979 revolution.

Appendix B

One Woman's Story

Life of a Woman Under Gender Apartheid in Iran

In December 2013, Hajer Naili, a reporter for *We News*, interviewed Maryam Moazen-Zadeh, a former prisoner of conscience in Iran and now a political refugee. She responded with words not often heard in the United States to describe the plight of people, because her issues of human rights are often not the issues for people in the West.

While in exile, she fights to make Iran a peaceful and free homeland for all children, including her son. Her life is important to understand as a window into the plight of a population of brave women descendants of the Ladies' Secret Society, who have always considered themselves warriors, not victims. Below is her interview,[1] edited only for clarity.

Question: Can you tell me a little more about yourself? What happened to you in Iran? Why did you flee Iran? How is your life now?

---

1 This interview is reproduced with the permission of *We News*.

Answer: My name is Maryam Moazen-Zadeh. I received my bachelors of science degree in chemistry *magna cum laude* and received my masters in physical chemistry, while working. I am married and have a seven-year-old son. We are a family of political refugees without a homeland.

After I received my degree, I began looking for a job with the Ministry of Health, but when I passed the employment exam, with excellence, the positions that I was given were librarian or building labs out of the rundown rooms in a nursing college and the like. I was never given the opportunity to work as a research scientist, even though I had received my master's degree in physical chemistry and had done numerous scientific studies on different projects and had submitted written papers.

I met my husband at the Japanese embassy. We were both trying to get a grant they had announced for scientists. We got married nine months later in July of 2004.

The government refused to give me permanent employment or a position in my field. Their excuses were that I worked too hard and rushed through the halls and did not socialize enough. While they were shuffling me from one nominal job to another, I applied to work on my PhD, but I was denied.

I began teaching at the Nursing College and wrote another proposal for the expansion of a pharmacological research center that they refused to fund. Yet they did approve a grant of 40 million dollars for research on Nemaz, prayer.

When I left Iran, the government removed my name from all the projects and research that I had done.

A religious government is, in fact, a dictatorship of the worst kind. The religious dictatorship that rules Iran is insisting on a literal implementation of *sharia* law, which is unjust and belongs to millennia ago. The primitive rule that has been forced on the modern and civilized society of Iran since 1979 has had the most devastating effect on all citizens, especially on women.

I am a Muslim. I believe that my religion is a private and personal practice. I believe in the separation of religion and state, and I want to live in a democratic society. That is why in 2001, I began offering training classes for women, in order to help them understand their own human rights.

I was teaching the uneducated, naïve, religious women, who had been indoctrinated that their basic rights must be ignored based on the current interpretation of religion. The God that they had been introduced to was mean, cruel, unjust, and dictated obedience because men were their masters. They are told that Allah will not forgive them if they do not absolutely obey their men. For example, the Shi'a clerics claim that the law of ownership is only inherent in men. Hence, they owned the women and children.

What the women activists do is to teach these women that God is the source of justice and if they want to follow the true God, they must believe in justice. We taught them that God sees no difference between the basic rights of women and men. We educated them, according to this statement of Qur'an that God says, 'My religion is presented, you can accept and believe or you can refuse, there is no obligation in acceptance of my religion.' We thought if these women really believed in God, they must also believe in their own freedom and the right to choose their own lives.

On August 11, 2006, the agents of the internal security paramilitary forces kicked our door, broke into our house, and arrested me in the middle of the night. Without any explanation to me or my husband, I was taken to Evin Prison. At that time, I had a six-month-old infant son that I was breast-feeding, and they refused to allow me to take him with me, which had me seriously concerned and disturbed.

As a result of my family's and friends' efforts in spreading the word and informing the international human rights organizations and the news agencies, I was released after ten days under interrogation. I was held under house arrest and surveillance. However, I was re-arrested about a month later, in October 2006, and kept in solitary confinement in the Evin Prison.

I was kept in solitary confinement twice. The first time was about ten days in August of 2006 and the second time, I spent about five months in solitary confinement, from October 2006 until March 2007. During that time, only twice I had a visitor in my cell, acting friendly, but I knew that she was an agent trying to get some information from me.

By the time I was released from prison, I was suffering from depression, I know that they were determined to condemn me, especially when they arrested my husband and interrogated him harshly, hoping that he would give me up.

You need to know that prisoners are kept in medieval conditions in Iran and, in order to make their lives that much more of a nightmare, they are refused medical treatment, medication, and legal representation. You are basically left to die a slow death.

However, I was not going to allow them the satisfaction of my breakdown, and, after my release, I was even more determined to fight them. I could not be indifferent and let my own sweet child and other children of my country continue living in this poisonous atmosphere, this violent and unjust system.

The government blocked me out of the society. I could not get a job, work for myself, or peacefully continue my life. Therefore, I tried harder and, taking on a pseudonym, I continued to address the regime's human rights violations, to bring the government's gross violations of the people's human rights to the attention of the international community through human rights organizations and activists. Furthermore, given that we were under surveillance and constant threat, life had become dangerously hard.

During the uprising of 2009, many of my close friends and colleagues were arrested and jailed. Things became dangerous because the regime's revolutionary intelligence agents now had evidence of our activities. I was sure that this time the interrogators would get some information about my part in the campaign through torturing my colleagues, and I would be exposed.

This time, it was a more serious matter, and I knew that if I stayed in the country I would be arrested. It would be brutal, and my son would be left without his mother. Therefore, when we were summoned by the Revolutionary Court, rather than appearing in court, we had already left the country for Malaysia.

On May 13, 2010, we became political refugees and followed the rules to report to the United Nations, as such in Malaysia. Being a political refugee is truly a disgraceful experience. For the first visit to the UN office, my husband and I dressed up, but we were disappointed at what we saw and how the employees of the UN treated us. Having to stand in a long line under the hot glaring sun for many hours with a four-year-old child and nowhere to get a bottle of water or some food was denigrating. The employees of the UN are discriminatory and rude and the Malaysian police have no qualms about arresting the Iranians, at will. The Iranian currency has no value in the world, and, therefore, life becomes difficult, especially if you have a young child.

At the beginning, my son, Shahriar, was very unhappy and cried every day. He missed his life with his family and friends, his room and toys, but after a few months, he adapted and calmed down. However, despite all that we have gone through, we are still living in fear and worry, as we are constantly threatened by the paramilitary forces of the ruling clerics of Iran that are all over the world.

How do you see the rapprochement between the USA and Iran? Could the rapprochement improve the condition of women's rights in Iran?

I have no illusions, and I am not at all optimistic. Here are the obvious reasons. On the one hand, there is the lack of honesty and pathologically deceptive nature of the Iranian regime. On the other hand, there is the fact that every single bit of the Western leaders' 'dialogue' only revolves around the nuclear issue and, then, trade and their economic interests. There is never any mention of the gross violations of human rights and the vicious oppression of the people of Iran and so on.

It is on the record that while the Geneva meeting of the 5+1 was going on, tens of people were executed in Iran and hundreds of people were arrested and locked up in prison. As long as none of the leaders of the countries who are in negotiations with the clerics of Iran are discussing human rights and the format and direction of these discussions do not include the issue of human rights, nothing will change, and none of this is surprising for us anymore.

I am actually surprised at the question, regarding the way in which the relationship between the ruling clerics of Iran and the United States government can deter the human rights violations inside Iran or influence the hideous issue of gender apartheid, when the actual problem is fundamental and, quite specifically, rooted in a dogmatic religious dictatorship.

Should the relationship between the United States and Iranian people develop, it must lead to the elimination of the present constitution, a free referendum, and a change of regime to a secular democracy. Then there is hope for the Iranian people and a more peaceful world. Otherwise, there is not a chance!

The new president, [Hassan] Rouhani, has been described as a moderate. Do you agree? Could he help in changing women's conditions in Iran?

Unfortunately, the Americans are giving the title of "moderate" to Mr. Rouhani, whom they want to support against hardliners! In fact, Mr. Rouhani is far from being a new figure to us Iranians. We know him quite well, and his record shows that he is far from being a "moderate."

President Hassan Rohani has been a very ambitious hardliner and extremely active in the hierarchal levels of power. He has been a leader in both final decision-making organizations of the Expediency Council since 1991, and the Assembly of Experts since 1999.

From 1989 to 2005, he was the Secretary General of the National Security Council of the Islamic regime. Mr. Rouhani is one of the founding members of the Islamic regime's security and intelligence services, established to crush all opposition. He was the secretary-general of the High Council on National Security which orchestrated the crushing of student revolts in 1999, killing thousands, and ruthlessly suppressed the labor movement for the establishment of independent trade unions.

The campaign to assassinate over a hundred opposition leaders including [former] Prime Minister Shapour Bakhtiar and the popular TV personality Fereidoun Farrokhzad in Europe and the massacre of about 80 intellectuals, known as the "chain murders," during the reign of the former "moderate" President Khatami took place under Mr. Rouhani's charge in the National Security Council.

Given his very clear stance in the face of the 2009 post-fraudulent-election uprising against the protesters and the mass arrests, imprisonments, tortures, and killings, it is unkind of the Western elites to give him the title of "moderate."

President Hassan Rouhani's Vice President was among those who took the American diplomats hostage in 1979 and his minister of Defense was another of the hostage takers.

As President, he is now demanding that security agents be harder on the people that he calls "the enemies of the revolution." Over the last seven months that Mr. Rouhani has been president, there has been an execution spree around the country. Over 600 people, 28 of them women, have been executed so far.

Scores of people have been rounded up and arrested. In addition, the so-called moderate President Rouhani has ordered the arrests of a large number of the activists for independent trade unions. He has revoked the licenses of more than 20 publications and has arrested 14 magazine editors.

The hardline stance of President Rouhani has caused the United Nation's special envoy Christophe Haynes to warn Iran, saying, "It is deeply concerning that the government proceeds with executions for crimes that do not meet the threshold of the 'most serious crimes' as required by international law and when serious concerns remain about due-process rights."

* * *

Sadly, *We News* supported the ruling clergy's policy of gender apartheid and was not interested in supporting Iranian women as they fought to change their own lives, with political ideology trumping humanity. Their editors only included a few short, general sentences that Maryam said against the regime, while adding comments from the clergy.

On February 12, 2014, the UN Spokespersons for the High Commissioner on Human Rights in Geneva, Ravina Shamdasani and Navi Pillay reported:

> An escalation in executions, including of political prisoners and individuals belonging to ethnic minority groups, was notable in the second half of 2013. At least 500 people are known to have been executed in 2013, including 57 in public. According to some sources, the figure may be as high as 625. ...We are especially concerned about the reported execution in secret of Mr. Hadi Rashedi and Mr. Hashem Sha'bani Amouri. Their executions were reportedly carried out last month (January). The two men were reportedly sentenced to death on ill-defined charges of 'enmity against God, corruption on earth and acts against national security.' They were allegedly denied access to a lawyer and their families for the first nine months of their detention, and reportedly subjected to torture to force confessions....We regret that the new Government has not changed its approach to the death penalty and continues to impose capital punishment for a wide range of offences. We urge the Government to immediately halt executions and to institute a moratorium.

As his background makes quite clear, President Rouhani is an extreme hardline fundamentalist and radical Islamist. It is amazing that the U.S. and some European governments have decided to falsely present him as a moderate and a person who can be a stabilizing factor. This, of course, is nothing more than a mask to deceive Western voters and all those who willfully remain in denial and wish to see things through rose-colored glasses.

Appendix C

Poems

I share here a few poems relevant to life in Iran. They are written by Iranian women, many of them my friends, but I must keep their identities anonymous to protect their safety.

A Woman in The Street

The author of these words is a faithful Iranian Muslim woman with a PhD in Islamic canons and laws. Her name shall remain unknown.

A woman in the street
sells her body
for a loaf of bread
On the other side a man
grabs a loaf of bread
from the hands of a passerby.
Hungry,
we hang around
the lonely alleys of this city,
and know that some soiled hands
has have stolen our daily bread
from our tables.

It is our bread money,
that is becoming yellow cake,
in the hidden nooks,
for trimming the display of injustice

It is our bread money,
the missiles that reach Israel,
faster than the bread and water
that would never reach the towns of Arzaghon and Ahar
Look!
At those bullet casings,
the corpses of the tanks,
it is our bread money
Scattered in the streets of Hamas.

It is our bread money
that is being buried
with the pompous dreams of a gambler
in the ruins of Damascus.

It is our bread money,
spent for a loser,
in the back alleys of Aleppo,
a loser who lost the game beforehand.
It is our bread money,
The seeds of lies and corruption
that are spread for a simple farmer
to harvest his empty wishes

Our bread money is the logs of terror
that are on fire
burning everywhere

Our bread money
are the guns that are aimed
at the wrong targets

Our bread money
is in the Boushehr nuclear reactor
that is covered by the dust of the rulersrulers' lunacy

Our bread money
is the bribe
in the bulging pockets of China and Russia,

Our bread money
is the payment to the commanders
who hang the heads,
sew the lips,
so thus the hungry will not learn
who is responsible of for their hunger.

Our bread money
is the pulpit that an idiot preacher sits on,
teaching us that hunger is God's onus
and it is the good news of the upcoming of a "Savior"

And we know
that it is our fault
that an idiot is sitting on the Pulpit
It is our fault,
a bully tyrant perches on the seat of power

We know,
That the only harvest of lies and guile is
the thorns of fear and silence,
that ends in famine

Our bread money has been lost,
by gamblers,
in the casinos of politics and power

And now,
our children and us are left,
with young and green wishes,
for a home held by flimsy columns,
so frail that it will crumble if shaken,
with us alive, under its rubble
Yes!
Tomorrow, when we awake,
we, our children and our homes
will have also been gambled away.

Simin Behbahani

Simin Behbahani (1927 –2014) was a contemporary poet, lyricist, and president of The Iranian Writers' Association. She became a human rights activist, fighting the clergy through her poetry, and she suffered the consequences. She was nominated twice in 1999 and 2002 for the Nobel Peace Prize in literature, but not awarded the prize. She was unable to travel abroad, as the cleric Islamic Revolutionary Court had seized her passport to punish her.

I Will Build You Again

I will build you, again
My country, l will build you again,
If need be, with bricks from my life,
I will build columns to support your roof,
If need be, with my bones,
I will inhale again the perfume of flowers
Favored by your youth.
I will wash again the blood off your body
With torrents of my tears.
Once more the darkness will leave this house
I will paint my poems blue, color of your sky
Though gone a hundred years, I will rise on my Grave,
with fierce roar, Slit the evil's heart.
Restorer of "old bones" will grant me in his bounty
A mountain's splendor in his resting grounds
Old I may be, but given the chance I will learn.
I will begin a second youth alongside my progenies

I will recite the stories of "love and country"
With such fervor as to make each word bear life.
While still burns fire in my breast
Never diminish searing flames of love,
I feel for my people.
Forgive me again, for my poem
Is soiled by blood,
But I will build you again
Even beyond my brawn.

I Am Not a Muslim, I am Iranian

    by an anonymous Iranian woman poet

It is wine, flowing in my veins,
I am as clear as water
parasols of love is are over my head
the glows of sun is in my eyes
I am not a Muslim, I am Iranian

My words soar like butterflies
my home are taverns
in endless green fields of my lost dreams,
lights are shining
till the dawn of snowy dark nights
little birds of Hope, sleeping in my heart
I am not a Muslim, I am Iranian

through the window
I hug the nightly moonlight with my kisses
in the silence of dry yellow valleys,
I see fields of beautiful red flowers
becoming a lyric in my heart and soul
I am not a Muslim, I am Iranian

Its light that glows in my veins
the moon light, in the dark of night

it is the sound of singing birds
the scent of love dripping softly
my soul is a shining mirror of springs
I am clear, I am clear in my heart
As the light of endless suns,
I am not a Muslim, I am Iranian

happy drums of lovers are sounding
wine sellers with full barrels are behind the doors
on the streets are the songs of drink, drink
I love you, are all the words
endless love in the eyes of my people
I am not a Muslim, I am Iranian

Young women, their hair flying in the air, or
Resting freely on their shoulders
warm light of kindness glowing in their gaze
my wishes are as many as rainbow colors
living in my homeland in the garden of freedom
with one breath, and every breath
where ever I am, the height of the heaven or
the dark of this cage
My religion, is "Love" and none other
I am not a Muslim, I am Iranian

Bibliography

'Abd-al-Hosayn Nāhīd. *Zanān-e Īrān dar jonbeš-e mašrūta*, Tehran, 1360 Š./1981.

Abtahi, Hirad. "Cyrus the Great's Proclamation as a Challenge to the Athenian Democracy's Perceived Monopoly on Human Rights." *Denver Journal of International Law and Policy*. Accessed January 30, 2018. http://www.arsehsevom.net/site/wp-content/uploads/2013/06/Hirad-Abtahi_English_with-ISBN-small.pdf.

Ādamiyat, Ferydun. *Amir Kabir wa Irān*, 4th ed., Tehran, 1354 Š./1975.

Afary, Janet and Kevin B. Anderson. *Foucault and Iranian Revolution: Gender and the Seduction of Islamism*. Chicago: University of Chicago Press, 2006.

Afary, Janet. *The Iranian Constitutional Revolution, 1906-1911: Grassroots Democracy, Social Democracy, and the Origins of Feminism*. New York: Columbia University Press, 1996.

Afkhami, Mahnaz. Erika Friedl, eds., *In the Eye of the Storm: Women in Post-Revolutionary Iran*. Syracuse University Press, 1994.

Afkhami, Mahnaz. *Iran's National Plan of Action: Ideology, Structure, Implementation* (Tehran: Manuscript prepared for publication for the Center for Research, WOI, 1978).

Afkhami, Mahnaz ed., *Women and the Law in Iran 1967-1978* (Bethesda, Maryland: Women's Center of the Foundation for Iranian Studies, 1994). In Persian.

Adjudani, Mashah-allah. *Iranian Constitution*. Akhtaran Publisher, 2004 (in Persian).

Al-Mamālek. *Yāddāsthā-i az zen-dagāni-e kosusi-e Nāser-al-Din Šāh*. Tehran, 1361 Š./1982

Anonymous Syriac Chronicle. Chronicle of Seert.

Al-Saltana, Taj. Edited by Abbas Amanant. *Crowning Anguish: Memoirs of a Persian Princess from the Harem to Modernity 1884-1914*. Washington, D.C.: Mage Publishers, 1993.

Al-Saltana, Taj. *Kāterāt-e Tāj-al-Saltana*, ed. Mansura Ettehādiya and Sirus Saʾdvandiān, Tehran, 1361 Š./1982, tr. Anna Vanzan and Amin Neshati as *Crowning Anguish: Memoirs of A Persian Princess from the harem to Modernity*, ed. Abbas Amanat, Washington, D.C., 1993.

Amanat, Abbas. *Pivot of the Universe: Nasir al-Din Shah Qajar and the Iranian Monarchy, 1831-1896*, Berkeley and Los Angeles: University of California Press, 1997.

Andrew, Christopher. *For the President's Eyes Only: Secret Intelligence and the American Presidency from Washington to Bush*. Harper Perennial, 1996.

Attar, Farid ud-Din. *The Conference of the Birds*. tr. Sholeh Wolpé. W.W. Norton & Company, 2017.

Āzādi, Hamid. *Pošt-e pardahā-ye haram-sarā*, Urmia, 1364 Š./1985.

Baktīāri-asl, Fariborz. *Zanān-e nāmdār-e tārik-e Irān (Mahd-e ʿOlyā, mādar-e Nāser-al-Din Šāh)*, Tehran, 1375 Š./1996.

Bamdad, Badr ol-Moluk. *From Darkness into Light: Women's Emancipation in Iran*, edited and translated by F.R.C. Bagley. New York: Exposition Press, 1977.

Bāmdād, Badr ol-Moluk. *Zan-e Īrānī az enqēlāb-e mašrūtīyat tā enqelāb-e safīd*, 2 vols., Tehran 1347-48 Š./1968-69.

Bayat-Philipp, Mangol. "Women and Revolution in Iran, 1905-1911," in Lois Beck and Nikki Keddie, eds., *Women in the Muslim World*. Cambridge: Harvard University Press, 1978.

Edward G. Browne. *A Traveller's Narrative Written to Illustrate the Episode of the Báb*. Cambridge University Press; reissue edition, originally published 1891.

Butera, Ismail. "The Jews of Persia" (essay).

CAIS. "The First and Most Comprehensive, Informative and Scholarly Website Dedicated to Ancient Iran and Iranian Civilization." Accessed January 30, 2018. www.Cais-soas.com.

Cave, A.J., *Persianology: The Road to Persiana*. San Mateo, California: Book of Persians.

Center for Human Rights in Iran. Accessed January 30, 2018. https://www.iranhumanrights.org.

Change for Equality. Accessed January 30, 2018. http://we-change.org.

Colliver Rice, Clara. *Persian Women and Their Ways*, London, 1923. tr. Asad-Allāh Āzād as *Zanān-e irāni wa rāh o rasm-e zendagi-e ānān*, Mašhad, 1987. (The Qajar harems stimulated the fantasy of Western observers, whose accounts were often burdened with the stereotypes of the orientalist approach. However, the works of some of them contain useful information.)

Culture of Islam. "Welcome to Culture of Iran." Accessed January 30, 2018. www.cultureofiran.com.

Daftary, Farhad and I.B. Tauris. *Fifty Years in the East: The Memoirs of Wladimir Ivanow*. London: I.B. Tauris, 2015.

Dawlatabadi, Sadiqah. "Sadiqa Dawlatabadi Collection." Harvard Library. Accessed January 30, 2018. http://pds.lib.harvard.edu/pds/view/40198121?n=1&imagesize=1200&jp2Res=.25&print Thumbnails=true.

Economic Report of the Central Bank of Iran (Tehran: Government Printing Office, 1978).

Eduljee, K.E. "Scriptures Avesta." Heritage Institute. Accessed January 30, 2018. http://www.heritageinstitute.com/zoroastrianism/scriptures/.

Elahi, Cyrus. *A Comparative Study of the Socioeconomic Situation of Working Women in Tehran, Qazwin-and Kashan*. Tehran: WOI, 1977.
Elm, Mostafa. *Oil, Power, and Principal, Iran's Oil Nationalization and Its Aftermath*. New York: Syracuse University Press, 1994.

The Family Protection Act (1975).

Farrokh, Kaveh. "The Women of Persia." Accessed January 30, 2018. http://www.kavehfarrokh.com/iranica/the-women-of-persia/.

Feiler, Bruce. *Where God Was Born: A Journey by Land to the Roots of Religion*. William Morrow publisher, 2005.

Fouman. Accessed January 30, 2018. *Fouman.com* (some photos accessed through this source).

Foundation for Iranian Studies. "Legal Documents." Accessed January 30, 2018. http://www.fis-iran.org/en/resources/legaldoc.

Richard Frye. "The Zands in Iran," http://richardfrye.org/files/The_Zands_in_Iran.pdf.

Hasanli, Elaheh, Masudeh Khalifi, and Fereshteh Qaem-maqami, *Tarikhcheh va Fa'aliathayi Sazeman-i Zanan-i Iran* ("History and Activities of the Women's Organization of Iran"). Tehran: Daneshkadeh ulum va irtebatat-i ijtima'i, n.d.

Homayounpour, Parviz. *The Experimental Functional Literacy Program of the Women's Organization of Iran*. Tehran: WOI, 1975.

Iran Chamber Society. "History of Iran: Sassanid Empire." Accessed January 30, 2018. http://www.iranchamber.com/history/sassanids/sassanids.php#sthash.5GGQq9wn.dpuf.

Iran Chamber Society. Accessed January 30, 2018. http://iranchamber.com/.

Iranian Studies Foundation. "Women's Section." Accessed January 30, 2018. http://fis-iran.org/en/women.
Irangulistan website. http://www.irangulistan.com/cartes-iran.html.

Kasravi, Ahmad. *The History of Iran's Constitutional Movement.* Amir Kabir publisher, Tehran, Iran 1994.

Khorasani, Noushin Ahmadi. "Iranian Women's Calendar." Accessed January 30, 2018." http://www.feministschool.com/english/IMG/pdf/Iranian_Women_s_equality_calendar 2.pdf.

Lahiji, Shahla and Mehranguiz Kar. *Iranian Women's Quest for Identity,* Roshangar, Tehran, Iran, 1992.

Lahiji, Shahla and Mehranguiz Kar. *The Quest for Identity, the Image of Iranian Women in Prehistory and History.* Rawshangarān, Tehran, Iran 1993.

Madjd, Mohammad Gholi. *The Great Famine and Genocide in Persia.* University Press of America, 2003.

Mahdavi, Abdol-reza Hooshang. *The History of Iran's Foreign Relations; from the beginning of Safavids to the end of WWII,* Amir Kabir, Tehran, Iran 1980 (in Persian).

_____, "Les Archives Aminozzarb: source pour l'histoire économique et sociale de l'Iran, fin XIXe-debut XXe siècle," *Le monde iranien et l'islam* 4, 1976-77.

Mathers, E. Powys (translator). *Eastern Love.* London, 1904.

McGhee, George. *Envoy to the Middle World: Adventures in Diplomacy.* Joanna Cotler Books, 1984.

Milani, Farzaneh. *Words Not Swords, Iranian Women Writers and the Freedom of Movement.* New York: Syracuse University Press, 2011.

_____ *Veils and Words; The Emerging Voices of Iranian Women Writers.* Syracuse University Press, 1992.

Miller, Walter. "Cyropaedia: Life of Cyrus by Xenophon." Heritage Institute. Accessed January 30, 2018. http://heritageinstitute.com/zoroastrianism/reference/xenophon/cyropaedia/cyropaedia1.htm.

Mirzā, Soltān-Ahmad. *Life at the Court of the Early Qajar Shahs*. Mage Publishers, 2014.

Moser-Khalili, Moira. Urban Design and Women's Lives (Tehran: WOI, 1976).

Nabarz, Payam. *Anahita*. Avalonia, 2013.

_____ "New Book: Anahita." Iranian.com. Accessed January 30, 2018. http://www.kavehfarrokh.com/news/new-book-anahita-ancient-persian-goddess-zoroastrian-yazata/.

Naghibi, Nima. *Rethinking Global Sisterhood, Western Feminism and Iran*. University of Minnesota Press, 2007.

Najmabadi, Afsaneh. "Hazards of Modernity and Morality: Women, State and Ideology in Contemporary Iran," in Denise Kandiyoti, ed., *Women, Islam, and State*. London: Macmillan Press, 1991.

Nashat, Guity. "Women in Pre-Revolutionary Iran: A Historical Overview," in Guity Nashat, ed., *Women and Revolution in Iran*. Boulder, Colorado: Westview Press, 1983.

Noshiravani, Reyhaneh. "Pre-Revolution." Foundation for Iranian Studies. Accessed January 30, 2018. http://fis-iran.org/en/women/milestones/pre-revolution.

Omar, Debra. *Tehran's Underground Activities, rescuing Jewish children from the Nazis*, translated to Persian by Simon, Hooshing Zareh, Self-Published, 2019.

Oral History: Memoirs of Maryam Chamlou in the Oral History Archives of the Foundation for Iranian Studies, Washington, D.C.

The Other Half: Iranian Woman After the Revolution, Published by Iranian Women's Studies Foundation, Midland Press, 1991.

Pars Times. "Historical and Period Costumes of Iran." Accessed January 30, 2018. http://www.parstimes.com/women/traditional_costume/period/.

Pars Times. "Iran's Beauty Queens Past and Present." Accessed January 30, 2018. http://www.parstimes.com/women/miss_iran/.

Parsay, Roya. *Women and Rules of Society: A Comparative Study of the Status of Women in Different Religions*. BVT Press, 1997.

Paydar, Parvin. *Women and the Political Process in Twentieth-Century Iran* Cambridge University Press, 1995.

Paymai, Nader. *Iranian Plateau, land of Ancient Culture*, Self-published, 2009.

Persepolis. "Historical Women: Powerful Women of Persia." Accessed January 30, 2018. http://www.persepolis.nu/.

Pirnia, Mansureh. *Pioneering Women of Iran*. Maryland: Mehriran Publishing, 1995.

_____. *Madam Minister, Daughter of Freedom*. Mehriran Publishing, 2007.

Price, Massoume. *Iran: 5,000 Years of Clothing, Jewellery and Cosmetics*. Foreward by Zohreh Waibel. Anahita Prod Ltd., 2012.

_____. "Historically Significant Women of Iran and the Neighbouring Countries." Iran Heritage Foundation. Accessed January 30, 2018. http://www.cultureofiran.com/significant_women_05.html.

Project Gutenberg. "Cyropaedia: The Education of Cyrus by Xenophon." Accessed January 30, 2018. http://www.gutenberg.org/files/2085/2085-h/2085-h.htm.

Qawīmī, F. *Kār-nāma-ye zanān-e mašhūr-e Īrān*, Tehran, 1352 Š./1973.

Raeeka. "Harpist." Accessed January 30, 2018 http://raeeka.files.wordpress.com/2010/02/harpist_susa_parthian.jpg.

Rajabi, Hosay. *Mašāhir-e zanān-e irāni wa pārsiguy az āgāz tā mašruta*. Tehran, 1374 Š./1995.

Riencourt, Amaury. *Woman and Power in History.* London: Honeyglen Publishing, 1990.

Sanasarian, Eliz. *The Women's Rights Movement in Iran: Mutiny, Appeasement, and Repression from 1900 to Khomeini,* New York: Praeger, 1982.

Šayk-al-Eslāmī, P. *Zanān-e rūz-nāmanegār o andīšmand-e Īrān.* Tehran, 1351 Š./1972.

Serena, Clara. *Hommes et choses en Perse.* Paris, 1883, tr. Golām-Reżā Sami'i as *Mardom wa didanihā- ye Irān.* Tehran, 1984.

Shafa, Shodjedin. *Another Reissuance: Ancient Iran, in a New Millennia,* Farzad, 1999 (in Persian).

Shahidian, Hammed. "Feminism- i islami' va junbish-I zanan-I iran," in *Iran Nameh,* vol. 16, no. 4 (Fall 1998), pp. 611-639. (For a critique of Islamic feminism.)

_____. "The Iranian Left and the 'Woman Question' in the Revolution of 1978-79," in *International Journal of Middle East Studies,* vol. 26, no. 2 (1994). See also Haideh Moghissi, "Feminism-I populisti va 'feminism- I islami': naqdi bar girayeshha-yi muhafizikar dar mian i feministha-yi danishgahi," *Kankash,* no. 13 (1997). (For a critique of the "left" on women and the 1979 revolution.)

Shariati, Ali. *Fatemeh Is Fatemeh.* Tehran: n.p., n.d.

Sheil, Mary Leonora. *Glimpses of Life and Manners in Persia,* London, 1856.

Shuster, Morgan W. *The Strangling of Persia.* University of Michigan Library, 1912.

Soltān-Ahmad Mirzā 'Ażod-al-Dawla. *Tārik-e 'ażodi,* ed. 'Abd-al-Hosayn Navā'i, Tehran, 1376 Š./1997.

Taheri, Amir. *The Spirit of Allah: Khomeini and the Islamic Revolution.* Maryland: Adler & Adler Pub, 1986.

Time-Life Books. *Persians: Masters of Empire*. Time-Life Education.

WWQI. "Women's Worlds in Qajar Iran." Harvard University. Accessed January 30, 2018. http://www.qajarwomen.org/fa/collections/905-906-1017.html.

X, Ahreeman. "Persian Mythology, Gods and Goddesses: Part 1 & 2." *IPC*. Accessed January 30, 2018. http://iranpoliticsclub.net/culture-language/mythology1/.

Xenophon. *Cyropaedia: The Education of Cyrus*. Translated and annotated by Wayne Ambler. New York: Cornell University Press, 2001.

Xenophon. *Cyrus the Great: The Art of Leadership and War*. Xenophon. Translated by Peter F. Drucker. Edited by Larry Hedrick. New York: St. Martin's Griffin, 2007.

Yelda, Rami. *A Persian Odyssey, Iran Revisited*. A. Pankovich Publishers, 2005.

Zoroastrian Scripture: *Denkard*. digital edition copyright 1998 by Joseph H. Peterson.

INDEX

Symbols

300: Rise of an Empire 14

A

Riza Abbasi 61
Hana Abdi 268, 270
Hirad Abtahi 34
Abu Bakr 51
Academy Award 296, 299
Sabir Afaqi 91
Mahnaz Afkhami 192, 203, 212
Mastureh Afsar 125
Baroness Haleh Afshar 300
Mahin Afshar 188
Neda Agha-Sultan 273
Shohreh Aghdashloo 299
Shiva Nazar Ahari 275, 276
Jalal Al-e Ahmad 215, 216, 217, 218
Mahmoud Ahmadinejad 260, 264, 272, 273, 276, 277
Aida Ahmadzadeh 202
Nejad Ahmadzadeh 202
Ahura Mazda 30
Clara Akbar 239
Asdollah Alam 197
Alexander the Great 14
Ayatollah Elm Al-Hoda 262
Ali Ibn Abdullah 51, 52
Masih Alinejad 293
Parastoo Allahyari 263, 270
Abbass Amanat 81
American Art Award 189
American College of Tehran 141, 158
American Memorial School 96
American Society of International Law 184

Maryam Amid 97, 98, 124
Fakhri Amin 209
Saeedeh Amin 259
Mah-Soltan Amirsahi 107
Mah Sultan Amir-Sehei 119
Amnesty International 253, 256, 266
Anahita 27, 28, 30
Anatolia 24
andaruni 76, 81
Andjomaneh Serieh Banovan (see also Ladies' Secret Society) 9, 116
Anglo-Iranian Oil Company 95, 170, 171, 172, 173, 175, 207
Anglo-Persian Agreement of 1919 146
Anjoman (Association) 156
Anjomaneh Nesvan Vatan-khah 101
Anjoman Horriyyat Nsevan 82
Anousheh Ansari 299
anti-American propaganda 206
Queen Anzazewas 39
Apranik 45
Arabization 45
Parvin Ardalan 184, 185, 263, 265
Ayatollah Mousavi Ardebili 220
Artemisia 37
Arthur M. Sackler Gallery 36
Artoonis 38
Aseer (The Captive) 193
Taniya Ashut 188
Raha Askarizadeh 258
Aspas 38
Association for the Recognition of Women's Rights 102
Association of Patriotic Women 125, 128, 129
Association of Progressive Women 125

Association of the Ladies of the Homeland 119, 129
Association of the Messengers for Women's Prosperity 148
Association of the Patriotic Women of Iran, 101 126, 131
Association of Women Lawyers 182, 186, 197
Association of Women Writers and Journalists 219
Astarte 25
Astyages 32
Mansureh Atabaki 175
Atoussa H. 225
Lord Avebury, 236
Avesta 31, 37
Awlam'eh Zanan (*Women's Universe*) 129
axis of evil 16
Mirza-Abolghassem Azad 158
Azadestan 124
Foroogh Azarakhshi 120
Soghra Azarmi 188
Azarmidokht 41
Tooba Azmoodeh 101, 116
Elaheh Azodi 205

B

Báb (ism) 86, 87, 89, 90
Babak Khorramdin 38
Babylon 34
Evlyn Baghcheban 175
Bahá'í 87, 90, 98
Baha'u'llah 87
Laleh Bakhtiar 234
Shokooh Bakhtiar, 49
Shapour Bakhtiar 173, 227, 308
Bibi Maryam Bakhtiari 109, 110
Bani Abbasids 52
Bani Umayya 51
Bani Umayyads 52
Banu 38, 187
Mahin Banu 61

Shahr Banu 62
Bar Kochba revolt 34
Howard Baskerville 140, 141
Alessandro Bausani 65
Baya magazine 107
Zeynab Bayazidi 263, 269
Zaynab Begum 61
Zinat Begum 62
Simin Behbahani 240, 252
Vida Behnam 209
Golbadeh Beigom 61
Jahan Beigom 63
Maryam Beigum 62
Sahib Sultan Beigum 62
Tuti Beik 69
Bernardo Bertolucci 193
Beyond Darkness 193
bicycles 122
biruni 75, 76
The Blackboard 244
Black Marxist jihadist cults 12
Blumenthal Award 297
Bolshevik revolution of 1917 142
Ayatollah Kazemeini Boroujerdi 182, 242
Kolsum Borqani 99
Mary Boyce 65
boy-soldiers 238
Great Britain 142, 143, 145-147
British 134-136, 140-148, 151
British Museum 33, 36
Edward G. Browne 87
Reader William Bullard 168
Burnt City 26, 27, 38
Ismail Butera 33, 57
Parvin Buzari 209
James Byrnes 167

C

John Lawrence Caldwell 147, 148
caliph 51
Cambyses 31, 32
Cancer Research Institute 188, 189

caravan-saras 47, 60, 61
Jimmy Carter 10, 11, 13
Carter Library 220
Caspian Sea 92
Center for the Guidance of Children 185
Center for the World Peace 185
Center for Women and Family Affairs 277
Center of Women Citizens 285
Change for Equality 258, 266, 267
Yousef Salim Chashti 91
Christianity 45
Meimanat Chubak 176
Winston Churchill 95, 167, 172, 207
CIA 199, 207
Catherine Clement 225
Hillary Clinton 239
David Cochran 19
John and Katelin Cochran 19
Joseph Plum Cochran 141
Rev. John Cochran 96
Code Pink 19, 225-6
Cold War 167, 169, 170, 175, 219, 210
Committee on the Elimination of Discrimination Against Women 277
Communist Revolution 142
Conference of the Birds 28
Congress for Peace and Women 176
Congress of Oriental Women 159
Congress of the Free Men and Free Women 199
Constitutionalist Women's Association 104, 107
constitutional monarchy 134
Constitutional Revolution of 1906 10, 11
Convention on the Elimination of all Forms of Discrimination Against Women 245
Cossacks 109

Council of Defense Against Education Discrimination 275
Council of Iranian Women 176, 177, 207
Council of Women of the Center 148
Edward Byles Cowell 48
Crowning Anguish 81, 83
Marie Curie 177
John Curtis 36
Lord Curzon 92, 143, 146, 147
Cyropedia 32, 33, 36
Cyrus cylinder 33, 36
Cyrus the Great 9, 14
Cyrus the Great: Arts of Leadership and War 35
Cyrus tomb 291

D

Danesh-Saraay'eh Aali (The Teacher Education College) 161
Simin Daneshvar 217
Dante 48
Homa Darabi 293
Parvin Darabi 209
Darius the Great 38
Badieh Davari 123
Dick Davis 48
Sadigeh Dawlatabadi 117, 129, 130, 131
Fatemeh Dehdashti 261, 268
Marguerite Del Giudice 253
Demetrius II 38
Denmark 191
Farah Diba 214
Disaster 119
Divine Comedy 48
Dokhtar'eh Lur (The Lur Girl) 160
Parvin Dolatabadi 266
Sadigheh Dolatabadi 131, 179, 251
William O. Douglas 69
Mehrangeez Dowlatshahi 181, 191
Anis ol-Dowleh 78, 94
Fakhr-Al'Dowleh 96

Dushizegan (Young Ladies) School 101, 181

E

Eastern Women's Magazine 149
Shirin Ebadi 240, 249, 250
Edalat 116
Effatiyeh School 119
Egypt 17
Sheikh Ahmad Ehsaie 86
Einoddoleh 114
Elamite 25, 39, 42, 43
Mostafa Elm 94
Elm (Knowledge) school, 158
Emancipation Society 158
Encyclopedia Iranica 74, 77
Epic of Kings 46, 49, 291
Edwin William Ervin 13
Muhtaram Eskandari 117
Parvaneh Majd Eskandari 241, 242
Mohtaram Eskandary 125, 128
Bibi Khanum Estarabadi 159
Etelaa'aat'eh Banovon (*Women's News*) 195
Parvin Etesami 160, 161
Mansoureh Ettehadieh 123
Etteleat Banovan (*Ladies' News*) 233
eunuchs 59, 60
Evin Prison 245, 216, 265, 267, 275, 281, 305

F

Ayatollah Falsafi 182
Family Protection Act of 1967 184, 185, 205
famine of 1917 to 1918 143
Golshifteh Farahani 297
Farangeez 110, 111
Farda, Radio Liberty 15
Moneer Farmonfarmanian 298
Fereidoun Farrokhzad 227, 308
Forough Farrokhzad 193
Maliheh Farshid 213

Fatima is Fatima 205
fatwa 112, 113
Fedayeen E Khalq 219
Mozafar Fee 191
Ma'sumeh Feili 130
Feminist School 258, 262
Abolqasem Ferdowsi 46, 52, 291
Fertile Crescent 8, 24
feudalism 198, 200
feudal system 92
Fields Medal 297
Fifty Years in the East 109
Maryam Firouz 189, 190
Safieh Firuz 176
Daryoush Forouhar 242
Michel Foucault 224
Foundation for Iranian Studies 114
Foundation of Mostazafeen (the Foundation for the Disadvantaged) 232
Founding Ladies of 54 256, 257, 262
Freedom Square 277
Freedom to Publish Award 258
Freer Gallery of Art 36
Richard N. Frye 67

G

Moammar Gaddafi 17, 211
Mahasti Ganjavi 54, 257
gender apartheid 12, 13, 16, 18, 20-22, 226, 229, 232, 233, 240, 242
Genghis Khan 53
Germany 190, 191
Gharb-zadeh'gee (*Westoxification*) 217
Ghaznavids 52
girl scouts of Iran 164
Girls' Industrial Arts School 176
Glamour magazine 277
Gnosticism 69
Derakhshandeh Gohar-Naraghi 158
Mahrokh Goharshenas 102

Mahrokht Goharshenas 259
Good Housekeeping 151
The Great Famine and Genocide in Persia 1917-1919 143
Green Revolution 273
The Guardian 224, 226
Guardians of Orthodox Islamic Culture 237
Guggenheim Museum 298
Gunda Werner Institute of Heinrich-Böll-Stiftung 244

H

Habl ol'Matin 106, 117
Mr. Hambarson 165
Hanafi school of jurisprudence 57
harem 59, 60, 61
Harvard University 297
Fa'ezeh Hashemi 240
Nana Hassan 283
Christophe Haynes 308
Bahareh Hedayat 268, 270
Ghodsieh Hedjazi 201
Hadi Heidari 286
Sara Heidari 158
Heil ol'Matin 110
Shamsi Hekmat 209
Emperor Heraclius 40
Herat 73
Jaleh Hesabi 280
Hezb'eh Zanan (The Women's Party) 176
Hezbollah 12, 215
Hidden Imam 86
High Council of Iranian Women 207
High Council of the Organization of Iranian Women 196, 197
High Council on National Security 308
hijab 123, 129, 130, 131, 132
The History of Zand-ieh 65
Alireza Hojabri-Nobari 37
Moneer Homayouni 284, 285

Homayoun Nameh, The Important Letters 61
Homer 48, 49
Soltan Hosein 211
Maryam Hosseinkhani 267
The House of Sand and Fog 299
Huma Houshmandar 170
Amir-Abbas Hoveida 212
Hulagu Khan 53
Saddam Hussein 234
Maryam Husseini-Khah 261
Mahboubeh Hussein-Zadeh 259
Robert E. Huyser 221

I

Ibrahim the governor of Shiraz 67
Ikhwan ol'Muslimin 199
Sara Imanian 259, 269
International Alliance of the Women Lawyers 184
International Communication Committee of National Organization of American Women 184
The International Court of Justice 174
International Human Rights Award 263
International Islamic Social Justice 217
International Mathematical Olympiads 296
International Research and Training Institute for the Advancement of Women 211, 212
International Women's Conference 132
International Women's Congress 131
International Women's Day 130, 228, 244, 245, 246, 251, 252
Inter-Parliamentary Union 184
Malake-ye Iran 105
Iran Bethel 160
Queen Irandokht 39

Iranian Activists of the Diaspora 261
Iranian Girls magazine 129
Iranian National Ballet Company 202
Iranian National Bank 155
Iranian National Handicrafts Center 208
Iranian Women Focus 262
Iranian Women from the Constitutional Revolution to the White Revolution 151
Iranian Writers' Union 176
Iran Post Journal 219
Iron Curtain 169
Isfahan 109, 110
Ishtar 28
Isis 28
Islam 44, 45
Islamic Council 233, 235, 239, 245, 260, 264, 265
Islamic Revolutionary Court 246, 261-264, 267
Wladimir Ivanow 108, 109

J

Peter Jacks 133
Malakeh Jahan 97, 151
Huma and Shams ol'Muluk Jahanbani 158
Jahaneh Zanan (*Women's World*) 126
jahazi 118
Jame ol-Koliat (*Opus of Principals*) 69
Hasan Javadi 100
Jelveh Javaheri 261, 269
Shams ol-Moluk Javaherkalam 259
Jeanne d'Arc girls' school 123
Thomas Jefferson 35, 36
'The Jews of Persia" 57, 58
jihad 203
Johns Hopkins Hospital's Cancer Research Institute 188
Samuel Martin Jordan 141

Judaism 45
Judea 34

K

Mirzā Taqi Khan Amir Kabir 78, 79, 80
kafir 202
kalian 94
Kamnaskares III 39
Kanoon Banovaan (The Lady's Center) 151
Kanoun'eh Banuvan (The Ladies Association) 160
Mehrangiz Kar 25
Karbala 88, 89
Mahbobeh Karimi 263
Nosrat ol'Moluk Kashanchi 176
Ayatollah Kashani 173, 180
Kashf al-Qeta 98
Shams Kasmaii 123
Nilofar Kasra 77
Ahmad Kasravi 110
Ziba (Zahra) Kazemi 245, 246
John F. Kennedy 220
Mirza Reza Kermani 78
Laleh Keshavarz 251
Nahid Keshavarz 259, 268-270
Keyhan 210
KGB 162, 169, 206, 211
Khaaneh Siaah Ast (*The House is Black*) 193
Azam Sepehr Khadem 262
Efat ol'Moluk Khajenuri 176
Khajenuri School of Fine Arts 176
wife of Mirza Khalil 63
Ayatollah Sadeq Khalkhali 224
Ayatollah Ali Khamenei 272, 277
Fath-Ali Khan 72
Mirza Malkom Khan 107
Reza Khandan 267
Akhtar ("Sunshine") Khanom 9
Baji Khanoom 117
Bibi Khanoum 99, 100, 101

Khadijeh Khanoum 99
Bahar Khanum 156
Dilaram Khanum 62
Ezzat ol-Nesa Khanum 62
Haji Alaviyeh Khanum 116
Malekzadeh Khanum 79
Pari Khanum 182
Kharazmians 53
Ayatollah Mohammad Khatami 240
khaterat 80
Khaterateh Taj Saltaneh 81
Jahan Malek Khatun 54
Turkan Khatun 53, 54
Sahar Khodayari 292, 293
Ayatollah Ruhollah Khomeini 10-13, 20, 22, 182, 187-190, 193, 197-209, 212, 215-217, 220-234, 237, 238, 241, 242
Nooshin Ahmadi Khorasani 107
Khosrow Anoshirvan 41
Khosrow Parviz 41
khums 200, 206
khutba 54
Nooreddin Kianoori 189
Morasa Kohrugi 201
Marc Kravetz 224

L

lace 41
The Ladies Association 160
The Ladies Finger 248
Lady Sun 75
Shahla Lahiji 25, 257
Eghbal Lahouri 158
Laleh ("Tulip") Park 245, 259
George Lansing 145, 146
law of *Qesas* 235
League of Nations 167
John Lee 14
Library of Ancient Iranian Culture 208
U.S. Library of Congress 221
Lurestan 8, 9

Lur(s) 26

M

Ma'ayib al-Rijal 100
Neil MacGregor 36
Ayatollah Mohammad Baqer Madjlesi 112
Mohammad Baghir Madjlesi 56-59
Mullah-Bashi Mohammad Taghee Madjlesi 211
Madresseh'yeh Doushizegan 116
Mahd'eh Olya 74, 78, 79, 80
Homa Mahmoudi 130
Mohammad Gholi Majd 143
Zia'uddin Majd 130
Majlis (Parliament) 112-116, 196
Samira Makhmalbof 240, 244
Makr'eh Zanaan (*Women's Trickery*) 99
Badr ol'Moluk Malekzadeh 130
Mandana 9
Mandane 31, 32
Noor Al Hoda Mangeneh 150
Hassan Ali Mansour 199
Mehrangiz Manuchehrian 182-185, 199, 203
Fasih ol'Moluk Maram 152
Robabeh Mar'ashi 118
Clements R. Markham 65
Marriage Act 165
Marshall Plan 168, 170
Masoodieh Park 119
Amuni Mastan 132, 133
Le Matin de Paris 225
Mausolus 37
Mawali 51, 52
Median Empire 8
Meds 8, 9
Monir Mehran (Asfia) 176
The Memoirs of Taj Saltaneh 81
Men for Equality 258, 261, 262
Men's Shortcomings 100
Mesopotamia 44

MI6 207
millennials of Iran 289, 292
William G. Miller 200, 220
Tabibeh Mirdamadi 130
Maryam Mirzakhani 296
Miss Teen Iran 210
Mithra 27, 30
Dor'rat ol-Mo'ali 107
Heshmat Moayyad 161
Nasrin Moazami 281, 282
Maryam Moazen-Zadeh 303, 304
Khadijeh Moghadam 262, 270
Ma'sumeh Moghadam 180
Fariba Davoudi Mohajer 250
moharebeh 276
Nikchehreh Mohseni 209
Mojahedeen E Kalq (MEK) (*Jihadists of Masses*) 211, 218, 219, 224
Molla Badji 99
Esha Momeni 263, 264
monajameh 54
Bibi Monajameh 54
Bidjeh Monajameh 63
Le Monde 225
Akram Monfared 204
Mongols 53
Charles de Secondat, Baron de Montesquieu 59
Nina Siahkali Moradi 281
Shams ol'Moluk Mosahab 176, 181, 199
Mirzā Hosayn Khan Mošhir-al-Dawla 80
Mohammed Mossadegh Ol'Saltaneh Qajar 95, 151, 154
Mothers in Black 280
Mourning Mothers Committee 258, 259, 280
Mir-Hossein Mousavi 272
Taraneh Mousavi 275
Vida Movahed 292
mullah bashi 56, 81
Muslim Brotherhood 181, 199

N

Payam Nabarz 28
Ashraf Nabavi 130
Saeed Nafisi 65
Hajer Naili 303
Robabeh Najafizadeh 210
najis 94
Najmieh Hospital 95
Homayoun Nami 259
Banu Namus 132
Nana 28, 30
Napir Asu 39
naqqal 47, 291
Naser-al-Din Shah 74, 76, 78, 80
National Day of Solidarity 241
National Front Party 171, 173, 222
National Geographic 253, 254
National Iranian Council of Resistance 12
National Iranian Oil Company 197
National Iranian Resistance Council 211
National Union of the Iranian Women Lawyers 184
National Women School 149
National Women's Society 124, 176, 179
Joseph M. Naus 134
Nawmoos (Chastity) School 116
Neda'yeh Vatan 106
Negan 38
Attar Neishaburi 28
Jinous Mahmoudi Nemat 194, 195
Neolithic 8, 17, 23
Shams ol'Zoha Neshat 189
Shirin Neshat 297
Netizen Award 276
New Gift, Monthly Journal 152
New Iran Party 191
New York City 208
Toka Neyestani 286
Shohreh Nikpour 212
Nobel Peace Prize 249, 250

Sheikh Fazlollah Noori 112, 113
Reyhaneh Noshiravani 226
Zohreh Tabibzadeh Nouri 276
Zahra Sadr-Azam Nuri 240

O

Barack Obama 266, 274
Off-side 247
Ohrmuzd 30
Olaf Palm Prize 265
Malek-Jahan Mahd'eh Olya 78
One Million Signature Campaign 255, 257-260, 262, 265, 268
One Thousand Families 92, 97
One Worlds People Award 266
Organization for the Cooperation of Women's Associations 182
Organization for the Defense of the Human Rights of Iranian Women 157
Organization of Democratic Women 170
Organization of Iranian Women 196, 197, 203, 204, 205, 209, 211, 212, 214
Organization of Progressive Women 170
Organization of Women Against Environmental Pollution 285
Oseeyaan (*Rebellion*) 193
Mahin Oskouei 176
Ottomans 58
Our Awakening 170

P

Mohammad Reza Shah Pahlavi 56, 67, 95, 120, 129, 159, 171-173, 180, 183, 189
Princess Ashraf Pahlavi 196
Queen Farah Pahlavi 208, 209, 213
Reza Khan Pahlavi 128, 151, 152, 153, 154
Pahlavi Dynasty 154

Amineh Pakravan 162
Amine Pakravon 66
Palace of the Shah 196
Jafar Panahi 247
Pantea 38
Pari Satis 38
Paris Match 236
Paris Peace Conference, 1919 144
Parliament (see also Majlis) 196
Fakhrafagh Parsa 126, 127, 129, 186
Farrokhrou Parsa 186, 187
Anthony Parsons 221
Parthian era 39, 41, 43
Abbas Parviz 66, 67
Patriotic Women of Iran 126, 128, 129, 131
Patriotic Women of the Homeland 111
Pen America 266
PEN/Barbara Goldsmith Freedom to Write Award 266
Persepolis (graphic novel) 296
Persepolis 33, 38, 39
Persia 28, 31, 33, 34, 36, 39, 40
The Persian Book of Kings 48
Persian Gulf 72, 81, 142, 169, 170, 282
Persian Gulf Biotechnology Research Center 282
The Persian Letters 59
petroleum 167
Zeynab Peyghambar-zadeh 257
Peyk'eh Sa'adat'eh Nesvan (Women's Prosperity Courier) 130
Navi Pillay 309
Jacob Eduard Polak 89
Politics and Harem 77
Pourandokht 40
Clara Powers 277
Princess Taj 71, 81, 82
Prophet Muhammad 51, 52
The Protesters 116
Purandokht 45

Q

Alamtaj 'Jaleh' Qa'em-Maghami 101
Agha Mohamad Khan Qajar 72
Fakhr-Al-Dowleh Qajar 156
Maleka Jahan Khanum Qajar 78
Mohammad Ali Shah Qajar 113
Vosough Al-Doleh Qajar 146
Qajars 67
Qanoon 106, 107
Badro' Zaman Qarib 241
Qom 128, 244
Qorrat al-Ayn 90
Qur'an 46

R

Rabehe 49
Julian Raby 36
Radio Liberty 15
Fereshteh Rafsandjani 233
Faezeh Rafsanjani 285
Hashemi Rafsanjani 233
Mohammad Taghi Rahbar 277
Mina Rahbari 241
Rah'eh No (The New Path) 181
Fahimeh Rahimi 282
Zahra Rahnavard 233
Zahra Rahnavardi 272
Rajaee Shahr Prison 276
Mohammad-Ali Rajai 233
Monavar Ramezani 283
Mehri Rasekh 209
Red Shi'ism 12, 205, 215-218, 224
Reporters Without Borders 276
Reporters without Borders Jury Prize 266
The Response to Supporters of Emancipation 132
Revolutionary Guard 226, 243, 244, 252, 253
Princess Rhodogune 38
Amaury De Riencourt 24, 28
Roghieh Chehr Azad 257
Roman Empire 34

Eleanor Roosevelt 21, 172
Franklin D. Roosevelt 167, 168, 172
Roshangaran (*The Intellectuals*) 257
Tuba Roshdieh 102
Jamileh Roshdiyeh 181
Rostam 28
Zeinab Rostamali 91
Vakil ol'Rowaya 119
Roxanna 38
Royal Bank of Iran 92
Royal Belgian Art Award 189
Rudabeh 28
Mowlana Jalaluddin Rumi 55
Salman Rushdie 112
Dean Rusk 200
Russian Embassy 219

S

Sa'adi 7, 21
Saam 28
Shirin Sadeghi 275
Zabihollah Safa, 49
Safar'eh ashk (*Journey of a Tear*) 161
Ronak Safarzadeh 261, 268
Navabeh Safavi 130
Navob Safavi 181
Safavid(s) 53, 55, 59, 60, 61
Ismail Safavie 55, 56, 58
Shah Sultan Hossein Safavie 56, 62
Nayereh Saidi 187
Saïd Mohsen Saïdzadeh 243
Sakharov Prize 266
Shoja'-ul Saltaneh 80
Taj Al-Saltaneh 71, 80-82
Farkhondeh Samii 130
Mokhtar Saqafie 52
Nasim Sarabandi 261, 268
Sāsān-dokht Sāsāni 204
Sasanian dynasty 40, 41, 115
Satanic Verses 112
Marjane Satrapi 296
Saudi Arabia 44, 51
Fatimah Sayyah 162, 176

Sazmaneh Zanoneh Iran 203
The Seas of Light 56
The Secret Alliance of Women 116
seegheh 218
Seemorq 28
Sein(a) 25
Sepandarmaz-gon 29
Azam Sepehr-Khadem 219
Seven Sisters Brigade 108, 109
Raziyeh Shabani 177
Ehteram Shadfar 259, 269
Shah-Beygom Khanom 77
Shahla Sherkat 268
The Shah-Nameh (*The Book of Kings*) 28, 46, 47, 49
Shahr-e Sukhteh 26
Ravina Shamdasani 309
Shapur I 34
Shapur II 34
Farzaneh Sharafbafi 241
sharia 12, 22, 178, 196, 197, 200, 206
Ali Shariati 215, 216, 218, 222
Ayatollah Shariatmadari 199
Sharif University of Technology 297
Sheikhieh Order 86
Sheikhiyeh movement 89
Shi'a 55, 57, 58, 59, 61
Shi'ism 12, 51, 52
Shining Faces 190
Shiraz 129, 132
Salmeh-beigom Shirazi 69
Seyyed Ali-Mohammad Shirazi 104
Queen Shirin 41
Bagher Khan Shirkesh 99
Mansoureh Shojaee 258, 262, 263, 270
William Morgan Shuster 19, 120, 135
Silk Road 42, 279
Simone De Beauvoir Prize 266
siqeh 59, 238, 239
Sister Brigade 108
Society for Defense of Freedom of the Press 285
Society for the Freedom of Women 116
Society for the Welfare of Iranian Women 148
Society, Government, and the Movement of the Iranian Women 192
Society of Christian Women Graduates of Iran 124
Society of Patriotic Ladies of the Motherland 147, 148
Society of the Ladies of the Homeland 136
Society of the Patriotic Ladies of the Homeland 152
Society of Women's Liberation 82
Society of Women Teachers 186
Masomeh Soltan 209
Soraya 106
Sorush 30
Nasrin Sotoudeh 262-264, 266, 269, 289, 293
Sovashon (*A Persian Requiem*) 217
Soviet Union 169, 174, 190
Sowgoly 61
Joseph Stalin 169. 172, 206
State Department Bureau of Intelligence and Research 200, 220
Stateira 38
Philip H. Stoddard 11, 220
The Strangling of Persia 135, 136, 139
Student Unity Central Council 268
Parvin Sufi 187
Sufi 57
William Sullivan 220
Sunni 55, 57, 58
Sura 28, 38
Sur-Israfil Magazine 106
Nisha Susan 247, 248
Queen Susan 41

T

Shahin Tabatabai 234

Tabriz 96, 106, 107, 108
Tadjlu Khanum 61
taffeta 41
William H. Taft 135
Talat Taghinia 258, 263
tahereh 88
Tahereh Ghorrat Ol Ein 87, 88
Amir Taheri 21
Tahir Square 17
Malik Taj 95
Talbot RJY Company 94
Azam Taleghani 232
Talimeh Zanon 107
Tamerlane 53
tar 153
Hadjar Tarbiat 201
Hajar Tarbiat 160, 176, 269
Alenush Tarian 177
Tahereh Tayere 266
Teacher Education College 161, 162
Tehran 113, 114, 117-124, 127, 128
Tehran Music Conservatory 175, 192
Tehran National University 186
Tehran Rudaki Opera House 175
Atefeh Tejaratchee 149
Effat Tejaratchi 161
temporary marriage 218
Badri Teymourtash 176
Theodor Haecker Award 276
The Third Force 217
The Threatened Faith 97
Tobacco Boycott 93, 107
Aboul-Hassan Tonekaboni 130
Treaty of Gulistan 73
Treaty of Turkmenchay 73
Harry S. Truman 169, 172, 174, 206
Tudeh Party 162, 169, 171, 175
Tudeh Party's Women's League 169
Tunisia 17
Turkan Khatun 53, 54

U

ulama 57, 200, 201

UNESCO prize 187
UN General Assembly 211
UNIFEM 20
Union of Women 139, 148
United Nations 20, 21, 33, 174, 176, 185, 239, 240, 251, 211, 230, 232, 234
United Nations Commission on the Status of Women (UNCSW) 20
United Nations Convention on Elimination of all Forms of Discrimination Against Women (CEDAW) 240
United Nation's Peace Award 185
University of Neuchâtel 173
University of Tehran 155, 166

V

Sheikh Mohammad Vaez 114
Vakil 65, 66
Monir Vakili 196
Vatan 106, 116
Vatican of Shi'ism 128
Afzal Vaziri 262
Badri Vaziri , 158
Qamar-Moluk Vaziri 152, 153
Bibi Vazirof 116
Velayate Fagheeh 234
Velayat E Fagheeh 56
Venus 28

W

waqf 62, 200
Washingtonian magazine 285
We News 303, 308
Western Struck 205
West of the Indus 69
White Revolution 198, 200
Sir Henry Drummond Wolf 93
Woman and Power in History 24, 28
Women-Gods 23

Women's Association for a New Path (WANP) 191
Women's Cultural Centre 246
Women's Efforts 148

Women's Party of Iran (*Hezb'eh Zanan'eh Iran*) 177
Women's Police Academy 241
Women's Society of Shokoofeh 124
women's swim team 178
Women's Trickery 99
World Cup 246, 247
World War I 142-144, 151, 152
World War II 14, 31, 135, 142, 168, 170, 173, 189, 191, 206, 210

Marzieh Zarrabi 148
Bibi Shah Zeinab 108
Zendegi'eh Roosta'i (Village Life) 181
Zia-Ol-Saltaneh 77
Zohr'eh Zan (Women's Mid-day) 175
Zoroaster 29, 30
Zoroastrian Cinema 156
Zoroastrianism 9, 13, 27, 29-31, 45

X

Xenophon 32, 35, 36
Xerxes I 39
Xerxes II 39

Y

Yazata 27, 29, 30
Yazdgerd III 41
Mohammed Yazdi 119
Safieh Yazdi 119
Farangees Yeganegi 207, 209

Z

Zaal 28
Zabaneh Zanan (Women's Language) 129
Zagros Mountains 8, 17, 160
zakat 200, 206
Jafar Khan Zand 67
Karim Khan Zand 64-66, 68, 69
Zand era 64-71, 206
Zanestan (Womanhood) 262, 265
Pari Zangeneh 192
Zan-Khodayan 23
Zanon'eh Iran (Woman of Iran) 129, 148
Fatimah Zarin-Tadj 87, 88